The Complete Guide to

Surfcasting

Joe Cermele

BURFORD BOOKS

Printed in the United States of America.

10   9   8   7   6

Library of Congress Cataloging-in-Publication Data is on file with the Library of Congress.

The Complete Guide to

Surfcasting

Contents

Introduction

Obsessed with Sand and Waves

I can see my breath inside the truck. Though it's only mid-November, the predawn hours bring temperatures hovering just above freezing. The wind is light, but out of the northeast. Perfect. It hums gently outside, jostling the radio antenna and making the taut lines of the rods up on my roof whine just a little. The only part of me that's warm is the one hand clutching my coffee. Far down the beach, two little white headlights sweep the sand and quickly flicker off—a sure sign of a good surfcaster. He doesn't want to cast the beams on the water and scare any fish potentially cruising tight to the shoreline.

I'm waiting for the first shred of daylight to see if the birds are forming into tight flocks low to the water. So far I can only hear the waves breaking. There's nothing but black. Within the next hour it will be false dawn—that hazy-gray period in the morning when the sun isn't really up, but you can begin to see shapes forming around you. I've already been fishing much of the night, and the weariness is creeping in. There's one striped bass in my cooler, and though I don't plan to keep another, the tide and wind suggest that the stripers will push the baitfish—large bunker in this case—over the sandbar this morning within easy reach of my casts. Tired as I may be, I can't go home. I can't drive away.

Not knowing when to give up is a problem among dedicated surfcasters. That's because, as in all fishing, there is always that possibility that the monster you've been waiting for is swimming in on the next wave. Just ten more minutes, just ten more casts, and you could have a dream catch tied on.

Though this book is designed as an introduction to the sport of surf fishing, let this be a warning: Once you feel the pulse of a fish in the breakers, there is always the chance you will become obsessed. I enjoy tremendously every fish I catch from a boat, but to say that catching one with my feet planted on the sand isn't more gratifying in many ways would be an utter lie. It infects you and cuts deep into the guttural drive of man versus animal—you on solid ground, the fish in his sea.

And it goes far beyond simply catching a fish. It's the sunrises and sunsets, your hair matted with salt spray, the smell of wet sand and fresh seaweed, warm summer breezes and cold fall gales. No matter what beach you choose to cast from, I can promise every one of your senses will awaken.

I was both blessed and cursed being born and raised in New Jersey. On the one hand, this tiny state is a rat race of highways, shopping malls, and industrial buildings with a habit of putting one of the above on any undeveloped piece of land remaining. On the other, I am within easy reach of some of the finest surf fishing the Northeast has to offer. My home state continues to be one of the top producers in the surf.

But it's only fair to say that my first few years seriously pursuing gamefish from the beach were often frustrating to say the least. Call it youthful impatience, but I had no interest in learning

Noted Northeast surfcaster Alberto Knie holds a surf-caught striped bass that weighs over 50 pounds. Knie's drive and dedication to the sport give him an edge in finding trophy fish of this size. Photo: Alberto Knie

live in the shadows, change trucks regularly so as not to be followed, and rarely divulge where they're catching their fish. They don't fish on weekends. They don't start fishing until after sundown and they'll be gone shortly after sunup. However, an addiction of this magnitude goes far beyond the need to put a fish on the sand.

"Surf fishing is primitive. It's about the hunt," says Knie. "Fishing from shore forces you to explore. It forces you to get in tune with the science of the fish on a deeper level than I ever experienced in a boat. Following the fish on the beach for a season is an incredible learning experience."

Funny thing is, Knie's reasons for finding the surf so appealing are what can also make it intimidating to newcomers. With the challenge and the hunt comes certain vulnerability. Fishing from a boat gives you the power to cover more water, which can naturally help you find more fish. There is a given sense of control on a boat that does not need to be earned in the same way as it does on the surf. To stand on the sand and look out on a horizon can make you feel small. Therein lies the reward of catching fish in the waves. Facing an ocean on your own two feet and having the ability to use limited tools and your intuition to pull a fish from the breakers can make you feel like you've just beaten Goliath. But there are plenty of other reasons to begin surf fishing. Victory is sweet, but the dollar value of catching fish on the beach is sweeter.

The Economics of Surf Fishing

When you boil it down, a rod, reel, line, hook, and bait are all you need to catch fish in the surf. Of course there are thousands of lures, specific weights, leaders, rigs, and other intricate pieces of tackle that will maximize productivity, but in essence surfcasting is fishing in its simplest form. As with any sport, the amount of gear you buy is limited only by the thickness of your wallet and how intense a surfcaster you plan to become. But I can tell you from experience, even if you were to purchase every piece of high-end surf gear on the market—plus four-wheel-drive beach permits and fishing licenses—the cost wouldn't come close to that of boat ownership.

Fuel cost alone makes surfcasting a budget-friendly pastime. With the price of marine fuel today, you think long and hard about running your boat those extra ten miles when a friend calls on the cell phone to say the bite is going off. There are no slip fees or launch fees, no engines to winterize, and no expensive electronics to buy. You'll learn in the pages ahead how your eyes become your sonar and how birds become fishfinders.

I once had the pleasure of fishing for tuna on a new 65-foot Viking sportfishing boat. It was quite an experience, as the interior was more spacious and comfortable than that of my house. On deck there was a mezzanine bench—you can read that as "couch"—and from the overhang above it, freshwater mist would spray down at the push of a button to cool you off. This is where you sat as the mates worked the deck. You waited in utter comfort until a fish struck. This boat had a $7 million price tag, and while I love offshore fishing, in a way something didn't feel right. I wasn't dirty enough. I didn't have to do any work. Many people feel that the only way to catch truly large fish is to have access to a luxury craft such as this, or at least a boat big enough to get well offshore. In truth, a cheap hunk of frozen fish and the right spot on the surf is all it takes to land true monsters. You'd be shocked at what cruises in the waves.

Unexpected Monsters

Bluefin tuna are undoubtedly one of the most prized gamefish in the ocean. They have been known to sell for thousands of dollars apiece at fish markets where Japanese buyers show up on behalf of famous sushi restaurants. They can weigh upward of 600 pounds, and even when only small fish are in any given area, fishermen work themselves into frenzies. Rumors of bluefin hanging out over a wreck will draw 300 boats there on a Saturday. Everyone wants a piece of the action whether the fish are 20 miles offshore or 60. Any offshore fisherman who has a boat capable of reaching them will pray for a weather window and call out sick from work, because bluefin can move so fast that a spot where hundreds are caught one day may go dead overnight for the rest of the season. Bluefin are a coveted fish, yet they were the last things on Mike Cragin's mind back in September 2002, when he cast a chunk of mackerel into the surf at Humarock, Massachusetts.

It was early morning and still dark when the fish hit. Cragin was sitting in a chair holding his rod. "The strike was explosive," he wrote on his website, StriperMike.com. "The fish never even flinched. Never even turned . . . never even faltered. It just went out at breathtaking speed. If it had been light I think that watching the line disperse [off the reel] so quickly would have caused me to overreact. It was better that this chaos be given to me in the dark."

Throughout much of the fight, which lasted over an hour, Cragin believed he was battling a 50-plus-pound striped bass. What he ended up landing was a bluefin that weighed 75 pounds. Considering that bluefin are typically open-water wanderers, this feat became big news in the Northeast surf fishing community. Have other bluefin been caught from the beach? Yes, but it is an incredibly rare occurrence with actual landings often being more rumor than hard fact.

At Padre Island National Seashore on Texas's Gulf coast, large sharks are very common surf catches. Many anglers target them specifically using rods and reels usually reserved for offshore ad-

Albert McReynolds stands next to his world-record 78.8-pound striped bass, caught from the New Jersey surf in 1982. The record still stands today. Photo: Courtesy of Rick Bach

If McReynolds's theory holds true, it means an 80-pounder could easily be caught from the beach by anyone with a line in the right place at the right time. Realize that it could even be you who gets that handshake. With every cast into the waves there is the chance for angling greatness, and not just with striped bass. Many gamefish, such as red drum, tarpon, and black drum, offer the chance to connect with a specimen weighing from 40 pounds to more than 100.

A Family Affair

"There is just always something to see on the beach, even if the fishing is not hot at that precise moment," says outdoor writer and San Diego surfcaster Paul Sharman. "I'm a wildlife nut and having the chance to watch dolphins surfing the breakers and the occasional gray whale calf cruise right into to shore is captivating, not to mention the squadrons of pelicans cruising the waves."

No matter what beach you're fishing, Sharman's statement remains true: There is more to focus on than the tip of your rod. I must admit that I've been put in a deep trance watching tiny shorebirds called piping plovers feed near the waterline, scampering up and down the beach in perfect synchronicity, deftly avoiding being swallowed by lapping waves. I'm not above stopping to kick through a pile of shells looking for a treasure on my way to the next fishing spot. I once nearly lost a fishing rod when a bluefish struck because I was too busy feeding doughnuts to a bright red fox that appeared from behind the dunes. The beach is alive.

Surf fishing is a sport that can be enjoyed by anglers of all ages, and the serene setting, with wildlife to view and miles to explore in between bites, make a beach outing enjoyable for non-anglers as well. Photo: Darren Dorris

I'm not suggesting that there aren't wonderful and amazing things to see 80 miles offshore. Whales, giant turtles, and free-jumping sharks are just a few creatures that make appearances. The difference is that getting there is more involved—and more costly—than spending a day fishing the beach. Surf fishing is a sport that can be enjoyed by nonfishermen just by the nature of the location. My wife will gladly spend a day on the beach while I fish even though angling is not one her favorite pastimes. Getting her to come offshore with me is not so likely. Aside from wildlife, there is water and sand—two of my favorite things growing up, and I know I wasn't the only kid to feel this way.

Whereas taking youngsters out on a boat can require tailoring a trip's length to their attention spans, there is always something to keep them occupied on the beach between bites. There is no seasickness. There is no confinement. And I believe there is no better place to introduce children to saltwater fishing than on the beach. Species like croakers and pompano provide scrappy fights for fish of a smaller size. There is no intimidation in catching them or fear of not being able to handle the fight, yet that little croaker was still taken from a vast ocean. It's something any kid would be proud of, and hopefully sets the tone for a lifelong angling passion that leads to monster catches down the road. Veteran Delaware and Maryland surf guide Floyd Morton is quick to admit that what makes him happiest on the beach is seeing his daughter or the child of a client holding a bowed rod.

"I'll never forget the expression on my little girl's face when she caught her first fish," says Morton. "It took me back to my first fish and I thought right away that this is what surf fishing is all

experience. Betty & Nick's has been a staple of the Island Beach surf fishing scene for over 50 years. Attached to the bait shop is a luncheonette that serves the finest breakfast in Seaside. Bacon sizzles on the grill and waitresses shove to-go coffee orders in brown bags for guys heading out to the beach. At five in the morning, the counter is lined with anglers already suited up in their chest waders. Outside, surf rods shoot skyward from bumper-mounted rod racks on the trucks. In a way, especially this early in the morning, it feels as though you've stepped into an exclusive clubhouse. The truth is, even if you know no one in the room, you are a surf fisherman, so you belong.

As I wait for my order to come up, I'll take a look at some of the ancient photos of fish weighed at the shop hanging by the booths and bluefish mounts that are falling apart from age on the wall by the door. I've looked at them hundreds of times, but they never get old. Overhead, right in the middle of the restaurant, surf rods line the ceiling. On the counter are the most recent photos of fish brought in. I can still remember my excitement the first time I had my photo taken out front with the shop's old Polaroid camera. Even though the photo had to remain in the store, I had to have it and asked owner John Bushell to mail it to me later. It's still tacked to my wall.

Places like Betty & Nick's are not unique. Most coastal areas with noted surf fishing hot spots have bars, bait shops, and restaurants where the local surf crowd hangs out to shoot the breeze. In Montauk, New York, Paulie's Tackle is like the Elks Lodge for local "sharpies," or the elite that gather at this surf Mecca. Johnny's Bait and Tackle is just up the street, but when I first started fishing in Montauk, several reputable surfcasters told me that only tourists go to Johnny's. Does it make sense? Not really, but surfcasters are fiercely loyal and adopt establishments like Paulie's that become part of the lore. When a day on the surf is over, you'll find the many of the same crowd from Paulie's at the Shagwong Pub or Liar's Saloon, even though there are plenty of other bars in town. Across the country in California, the atmosphere may be different, but the culture is the same.

"The chance to stalk species like corbina and spotfin croakers at close range is something I could never get tired of," says Paul Sharman. "Mix this in with the local surf culture and watching the guys do their thing out on the water, then going to enjoy a breakfast burrito with them afterward at the local hangout is pretty cool."

This culture was once strictly found in the tackle shops and local hangouts, but as the Internet grew, it began to spill online and can now be called up with the click of the mouse. Online communities and Internet message boards dedicated to surfcasting are innumerable. For every state on every coast, you can find a website where anglers congregate to post fishing reports, talk tackle, brag, and most important, share their wisdom with newcomers.

In the Northeast, StripersOnline.com, TheBassBarn.com, and StriperSurf.com are just a few popular online communities where surfcasters from New Jersey to Massachusetts gather. In Southern California, SCSurfFishing.com is a well-known online meeting place. On the Texas coast, Eric Ozolins's ExtremeCoast.com and TexasFishingForum.com are a few notable message boards. For the Outer Banks in North Carolina, surf guru Rob Alderman's FishMilitia.com is a premier online surfcasting hot spot. But the sites mentioned here are drops in the bucket compared with the number out there. As you become more involved in the surf, you'll find one or two that you frequent most often because they relate best to your area. These sites are a great resource for any beginner, as asking questions from the comfort of home can be much less intimidating than approaching anglers in tackle shops or on the water when you're first starting out.

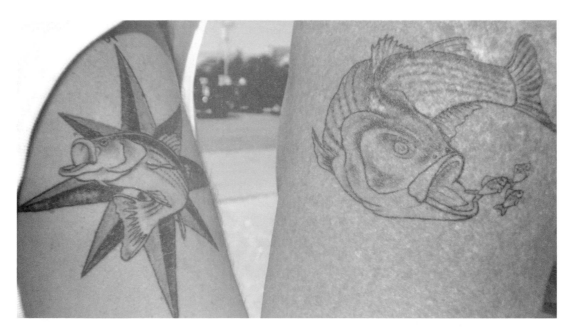

Two surfcasters proudly show off their love for striped bass with tattoos that will forever remind them why they live for fishing the beach.

Surf fishermen flood the annual tackle expo at Asbury Park, New Jersey. This is a popular show throughout the Northeast where anglers come to see the latest lure designs and gear for the beach.

In most coastal states it's also possible to find local surfcasting clubs, many of which hold clinics and seminars, plus annual tournaments. Through the years, I've dealt with many surfcasting clubs, and most tell me that they are always interested in new members, regardless of skill level. Part of this is because anglers take pride in showing someone the ropes and passing on their skills, but even more so, angler numbers are down in general. Clubs need new blood to carry on long-standing traditions and help pass the torch to the next generation of fishermen.

Reasons for surf fishing are yours and yours alone. Big fish, the chance to bring the whole family, and the opportunity to become part of a group of the some most dedicated anglers on the planet are a few good incentives. I'm sure many people will pick up this book for no other reason than to learn to catch a fish or two. I promise it will help achieve that, but it would be a shame not to insist that when you're out on the beach you should take time to admire your surroundings. There is nothing quite like fishing where the ocean meets land, whether you're with a bunch of friends, family, or all alone.

For Pop.
I hope the catfish are huge
in heaven.

Chapter 2

Getting Ready for the Beach

Preparing for Beach Battle

In surfcasting, as in any sport, the amount of equipment you'll need to play the game depends largely on how involved you plan to get. This chapter will present the basic tools for successful surf fishing, as well as introduce a few items that come in handy for specific surfcasting scenarios. Where applicable, you'll also find examples of gear in different price ranges to better help you choose your weapons based on budget as well as necessity. But the end result regardless of what you select in the tackle shop will be the same so long as you understand what each piece of equipment does, and how it fits into the puzzle for productive surf outings.

Walking into a tackle shop can be daunting for a surfcasting newcomer. But selecting the right gear for success is not as difficult as you might think.

Why the Long Rod?

I have found that there is a common misconception among those just getting started in surf fishing. Many anglers assume that long, stout rods are used on the beach to muscle large fish effectively. In some instances, that's absolutely true, but for the most part a long rod is necessary only for effective delivery of specific lures and rigs. A long rod will also keep your line higher off the water. This is particularly important for anglers fishing with bait, as the less line there is in the waves, the less your offering will get pulled around. Less line in the water also means less grass collection.

Though surf rod lengths vary greatly, the middle-of-the-road, all-around best length for the vast majority of surf applications is 10 feet. Though you'll come to understand where fish are most often located along a shoreline in chapter 6, know now that reaching them often requires a cast that places a bait or lure past the breaking waves where the water is deeper. On top of having to cover that distance, doing so means casting sinkers that can weigh up to 12 ounces in some cases.

Even though the fish you are chasing may be more fun to fight on a light, 6-foot rod more suited to freshwater fishing, that outfit may not allow you to place your offering in the fish's feeding zone. This is not always the rule, however, as certain species, areas, and situations may call for a lighter outfit. As an example, anglers fishing the Texas Gulf coast opt for 6- or 7-foot light baitcasting outfits because the surf line is often calm, the sea trout and redfish they're chasing feed very close to the beach, and the lures that most effectively catch them are better suited to be cast on a lighter rod. As you become more involved in surfcasting, you may find the need to tailor your outfit to your area, but for starters a 10-foot rod could effectively catch those same fish.

On the flip side, I've seen anglers attempt to bomb heavy weights—coupled with heavy chunks of bait—on light rods, only to end up snapping their stick in mid-cast due to lack of backbone needed to support such a rig. But thanks to modern rod technology and materials, many 10-foot surf rods are designed to provide support for delivering heavy rigs and lures, as well as maximizing the feel of the fight, even with smaller fish.

Understanding Rod Materials

One of the most common materials used in rods today is graphite, but the price depends on the "strain" of the graphite use to build a particular rod. To simplify the process, graphite is created in two parts under extreme heat. The hotter the temperature in the furnace, the stronger the graphite. The stronger the graphite used in a blank, the more sensitive and expensive the rod.

The result with graphite is a "fast" rod, meaning the butt section—the end near the reel—doesn't flex very much, but the tip has more give, thus allowing you to cast heavy offerings but still enjoy the fight of the fish. Graphite rods are great for any surf scenario, but I'd particularly recommend

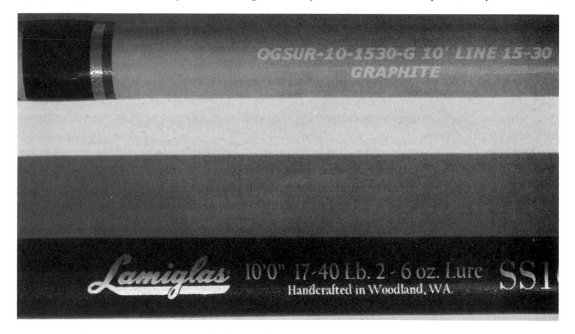

Important information about a rod's length, line weight, and construction material is often stamped right on the blank near the butt.

A reel's line capacity is often stamped directly on the spool.

Most spinning reels will tell you how many yards of line it takes to fill the spool based on the line's diameter or pound test. For example, a Penn 750 Spinfisher SSm spinning reel, which is a good-sized reel for a 10-foot rod, holds 320 yards of 15-pound-test monofilament line. Step up to 25-pound-test monofilament line and the spool only holds 185 yards. The difference in the diameter of those two lines may be measured in fractions of a millimeter, yet the amounts that will fit on the spool vary significantly. Just as a 10-foot rod is a good all-around length, a reel that can hold roughly 200 yards of 20-pound-test monofilament is a great start.

Another important factor in selecting the proper reel is figuring out how well it balances with your rod. I always recommend that when purchasing a reel, you bring along the rod you intend to use so you can put the two together and see how they feel. If you can get outside for a test cast, that's even better, but it's not always possible. What you want is an outfit that does not feel too heavy in the butt once the reel is attached. The combo should not feel cumbersome or awkward. Remember that you might be casting it hundreds of time in a day; you won't want your arms to tire.

Finally, it's worth considering the drag capabilities of a reel, especially if you intend to target large fish like striped bass, snook, or red drum. The drag mechanism can be loosened or tightened to set how hard a fish must pull in order to peel line off the reel. In other words, larger fish will need something to run against. If a drag were tightened to the max and a fish tried to bolt away, however, your line would probably snap. Since you want a smooth, dependable drag, I would avoid super-inexpensive reels and step up a bit.

Realize that the surf is a harsh environment for reels, as constant wave splashing and drops in the sand can rust parts and ruin internal drag gears. Certain reels are just better designed to handle the beach. On the more affordable end of the spectrum, Penn's Spinfisher SSm series (www.pennreels .com) are very tough and dependable. If you want to start at the top of the food chain, Van Staal (www .vanstaal.com) produces anodized surf reels with fully sealed drags that will not let in any water or sand. Of course, the price difference is more than minor.

The Right Line for the Surf

In the early years of surf fishing, anglers used line made of linen that had to be stripped off the reel, washed, and properly dried after each use. We've come a long way since then, with many significant advances happening fairly recently. Just about 15 years ago, anglers relied primarily on monofilament fishing line made of nylon. "Mono" is still widely used today and remains a fishing staple. But thanks to technological advances, braided line has quickly gained mass popularity in the angling world. To understand the difference between the two, let's first look at how fishing line is rated for breaking strength and why that's important for success.

Line is rated in pound test, meaning how many pounds of pull pressure it can withstand before parting. But don't take that to mean line rated for less than the weight of a fish you have hooked

Monofilament lines like these are still the choice of many surfcasters because of their abrasion resistance and stretch, which can really help land big fish.

simply by paying attention as you spool up. Always be sure to not to fill until the line is even with the spool's edge. Leave a slight overhanging lip on the spool.

Perhaps the easiest way to make sure a reel is packed tight enough is to have someone else hold the spool of line, keeping tension on it as you wind. But if no help is available, try placing the line spool on the ground and winding the line onto the reel through a closed phone book. It's an old trick but it works for me. Over time, both braid and mono will weaken from extended use, exposure to salt water, and even exposure to sunlight. It's always wise to put fresh line on all your reels before the beginning of each new season. All the right knots and connections for spooling your reel are covered in chapter 5.

Making the Cast

Okay. Your weapon of choice has been selected. The rod is right for you and the reel is spooled up with fresh line. Now what do you do with it? Casting a surf rod is not a complex process, and furthermore, it has nothing to do with arm strength. The trick is letting the rod do all the work and shifting your weight and body properly to achieve a nice, long cast. This is why it's important to choose a rod based on what you plan to cast most often. Naturally, a 12-ounce weight is going to go farther than a 2-ounce plastic lure. Physical strength won't make that lure get any more distance, but the right rod matched with proper casting technique will. Here are the basic steps of proper casting, with both a spinning rod and a casting rod. Note that these instructions are for right-handed casters. All hand and foot positions would be opposite for southpaws.

Remember that the weight of what you are casting, be it a lure or bait rig, will determine how much line to let out prior to making a cast. As a rule of thumb, the more weight, the more line you'll want to let out. For lures weighing up to a few ounces, I'll generally have them dangle halfway between the rod tip and sand before casting. With heavier lures or sinkers used in bait rigs, I'll let them dangle just off the sand, or actually let them sit on the sand. The longer leader combined with the heavy weight will give the rig more "pop"—like a slingshot—when the rod comes forward.

Step 1: Stand facing down the beach with your feet spread slightly apart. Your left foot should be pointing at the water, while your right foot points down the beach. This creates a 45-degree angle with your feet.

Step 2:

Spinning: Wrap your right hand around the reel seat, placing the reel stem (the shaft connecting the reel seat with the body) behind your

fingers. If it's more comfortable, you can also place the reel stem between your fingers. Flip the bail open and let the line catch on your index finger. This finger will keep tension on the line, stopping it from spilling off the spool, until you release the cast.

Casting: Grip the reel seat with your right hand from the underside, placing your index finger in front of the reel, and your middle, ring, and pinkie fingers behind it (you can vary this grip for comfort based on your own outfit). Place your thumb tightly on the spool and switch the reel into free-spool so the line will release. Keep pressure on the spool with your thumb until you're ready to release the cast.

Step 3: With your left hand, get a good overhand hold on the rear grip of the rod anywhere from just above the butt to 12

SPINNING ROD

CASTING ROD

inches up depending on the length of the grip and overall comfort. Rotate your hips around and bring the rod back behind you, keeping it level with your waist. Note that your feet should not move.

CASTING ROD   SPINNING ROD

Step 4: Quickly swivel your hips back around to the front while simultaneously raising the rod and bringing it forward over your shoulder. It's at this point you should feel the rod "load," meaning the tension created by whatever lure or rig you have tied on will cause the line to come taut.

Step 5: Continue the swing of the rod, bringing it straight over your head. Your right leg should pivot forward during this swing. Release your thumb on a conventional outfit (your index finger if you're using a spinning reel), thus letting the lure or rig fly, just before the rod is in front of your body. If you wait too long to release, the lure or rig will lose

its forward momentum. With a baitcasting rod, remember that you cannot completely release your thumb. Your thumb's grip should only loosen enough to allow the line to come off, but maintain enough tension to keep the spool from spinning out of control and causing a bird's nest.

Step 6: As with a golf swing, it's important to follow through after releasing a cast. Keep the rod pointed straight out, following your rig or lure as it flies through the air. Don't move the rod or begin reeling until the offering splashes down.

Sand Spikes

Sand is the enemy. There are very few reels on the market today that are designed to withstand being covered in sand with no ill effect, and those are pretty pricey. Sand in a bail spring, rotor, or any reel gears might mean having to replace the reel altogether, or at best require some disassembly and cleaning. All it takes to avoid this is a sand spike.

Sand spikes are simply rod holders made for use on the beach that have multiple functions. One of these is giving your rod a resting place for baiting up or changing lures. The other, of course, is serving as a place for your rod to sit while you wait for a fish to pick up your bait. Though sand spikes are one of the simpler pieces of surf fishing tackle, there are few different designs that offer different advantages.

A basic, inexpensive spike is usually cut from PVC, with one end sheared off to create a point that gets driven into the sand. A metal or plastic pin runs through the center of the spike to serve a rest for the butt of the rod, keeping it from resting directly in the sand. These spikes generally cost anywhere from $5 to $10. One plus of a shorter PVC spike is that it's light, thus making it easy to carry if you're taking a long walk to your spot. I usually carry a PVC spike if I intend to fish one particular spot all day, even if I only plan to cast lures. The spike gives me a safe place to rest my rod and makes lure changes easier. But one disadvantage of this style is that once it's driven into the sand, the amount of tube protruding is often short. That means when baitfishing, your rod tip is not as high as it could

Sand spikes are essential tools for keeping your rod and reel out of the sand. Though short PVC spikes are the least expensive, taller metal spikes (left) are stronger and can be driven deeper into the sand for added protection against hard-striking fish. Photo: Melissa Pulicare

be. And the higher the tip, the easier it is to see strikes and the more line you can keep out of the closer waves that will push and pull your rig up or down the beach.

Many serious baitfishermen employ metal spikes that can measure up to 6 feet in length. The actual rod holder is welded to one end of the long blade-like shaft, which gets driven into the sand. Not only will this style of spike keep your line high off the surf, but the long, thin shaft can be driven very deep into the sand, making it very difficult for a large fish to pull the spike—and subsequently the rod—down into the sand when it strikes and runs. PVC sand spikes are not known for staying as firmly in place, so if you use them, keep a sharp eye on your lines at all times. I know from firsthand experience the heartache of watching a surf outfit get ripped down the beach and into the water.

There are a few other styles of sand spike on the market, but the basic design principles of the two described hold true. No matter which you choose, bang in your spike with a rubber mallet if possible. Though not always a convenient tool to carry, the mallet helps ensure the spike is driven deep enough to handle a hard strike.

Storing and Carrying Your Tackle

How you carry your lures, rigs, and terminal tackle onto the beach, like almost everything else covered thus far, boils down to the type of surf fishing you do most often. A simple plastic tackle box is all

Surf carts make it easier to carry rods, coolers, bait, and tackle when a long walk is in order and you don't have four-wheel-drive access to a beach.

that is required if you fish only on the occasion, have a short walk to your spot, or don't plan to move around too much. Bait anglers may opt for a regular molded tackle box for storing lures, weights, pre-tied bait rigs, and other tools. If the beach you fish allows four-wheel-drive access, carrying your bait bucket, cooler, sand spikes, and other tackle is a snap.

But if you plan to walk on and need to cover some ground to reach your desired spot, surf carts are an option. These carts have welded frames that hold coolers of various sizes, as well as tackle boxes and buckets. They also feature rod holders welded to the sides. Oversized wheels make pulling these carts easier on soft sand, and they range in price from $125 to $300. The Fish-N-Mate line from Angler's (www.rodrack.com) includes surf carts to fit any needs.

For the lure angler on the move, there is no shortage of surf bags in many shapes and sizes designed specifically to increase mobility while keeping your lures close at hand, and protect those lures from rust and corrosion. A few of the more popular brands of surf bag include AquaSkinz (www.aquakskinz.com), BW Sports (www.bwsports.com), and Van Staal (www.vanstaal.com). These bags feature cylindrical or square tubes for the storage of long lures. The rear hook hangs on the lip of the tube, allowing easy access when you need to change it up. Many of these bags also feature pouches made to hold small lures or jigs. But all of them have strong shoulder straps that allow you to sling

Lure bags that sling over your shoulder, like this one made by AquaSkinz, offer a convenient way to carry tackle comfortably on long treks down the beach and keep your arsenal within easy reach.

Princeton Tec is just one company that produces compact, lightweight LED headlamps used by surfcasters from coast to coast.

quality and affordable headlamps. It's just a matter of choosing the one that suits your needs and is the most comfortable.

Suiting Up from the Waist Down

In many areas throughout New England, there are surfcasters who take to the beach in full wet suits. These are perhaps the most extreme anglers on any beach, as they'll actually swim out to offshore rocks and stand on them to fish. Luckily, you can skip the wet suit, as I couldn't rightfully recommend this style of fishing to a beginner surfcaster, especially when it's a version of the sport in which I don't even partake. But you will want to consider whether or not you need chest waders. That decision can be based on a number of variables.

The first and probably most important is your location. Many of the best surf seasons coincide with colder water periods, and that holds true for almost every coastline. That considered, don't think of chest waders as a means to get yourself farther out off the beach; consider them a way to fish comfortably and effectively while staying dry and warm. Trust me, you will get plenty wet just standing on the water's edge casting a lure. Even if you plan to primarily baitfish, waders will let you walk in far enough, or protect you from waves crashing right on the beach, so you can achieve a longer, more accurate cast. Of course, during summer months, or in southern states, a bathing suit may be all you need. Likewise, calmer beaches, or those where productive holes can be reached without wading, may only require hip waders or a knee-high pair of rubber fishing boots.

Wader materials vary greatly, from rubberized canvas, to neoprene, to light, breathable fabric sometimes referred to as "fly light." When the water and air are both cold, neoprene waders are the way to go. This material is thicker and tight fitting; it's the same fabric used to make wet suits. It's also relatively inexpensive. But on warmer days, even if the water is still cold, neoprene can get uncomfortable. I usually wear neoprene waders in the Northeast only during the early winter through very early spring. Otherwise, I prefer breathable waders, as they're less constrictive and easier to walk in should you need to cover long distances. They won't keep you very warm, but that's nothing a pair of thermal underwear won't fix. Breathable waders range in price, but Hodgman (www.hodgman.com) and Simms (www.simmsfishing.com) make some of the very best. Be sure to pick up a wading belt if one doesn't come with your waders, as they're a necessary safety precaution. These tight belts are worn at or just above the waist, and help keep water out should you fall.

Waders with attached boots are a better option for the surf angler, because they keep sand out and clean up much easier than waders with separate boots.

One recommendation I can offer regardless of the wader style you choose is to buy a pair with boots attached, known as "bootfoot waders." Stockingfoot waders that require separate wading boots often come with gravel guards, which are thick bands that wrap around the top of the boot at your ankle to keep silt and rocks out. However, I promise no matter how tight you make them, sand will get into your wading boots, and over time it will wear away the soles of the stocking feet. On top of ruining them, this makes for added cleaning time, as you'll have to dump and spray the sand out the boots. With boots attached, no sand can get inside to degrade the waders, and all you have to do at the end of a trip is spray your waders down with a hose.

Bootfoot waders are offered with felt soles or "lug" soles. I always opt for felt soles, which are designed to give you a better grip on slick rocks in trout streams. The flat felt has no tread, so on the

Flats boots can guard your feet against sharp shells or stingrays when wading in warm-water areas or during the summer months when chest waders aren't necessary.

beach your feet tend to stick less in the sand. That makes walking long distances easier on the legs. It also may save you from getting soaked. Lug soles feature aggressive treads that will dig into the sand. As waves push and pull at your feet, lug soles won't have as much give once they're planted and buried. Should you have to turn quickly to avoid a large incoming wave, felt may help you unglue your feet a little faster.

During warmer times of the year, or in regions with warmer water temperatures, flats boots are an accessory to consider even if waders are not necessary. These wading shoes, often made of neoprene, are designed to protect your feet from sharp shells and stingrays on the flats. Though oyster beds and sharp shell piles are not nearly as much a concern on the ocean or Gulf beaches, stingrays still pose a threat. Flats boots have a thick rubber heel and toe, which are often the spots on the foot a stingray's tail will contact if you accidentally step on one. A simple pair of old sneakers might work, but flats boots ride high on the ankle, making it nearly impossible for strong wave action to pull them off your feet. If you've ever tried to wade into the ocean wearing flip-flops, there is a good chance you lost one or both in the process. You can find flats boots for $25 at Bass Pro Shops (www.basspro.com), or pick up a pair of classic canvas Converse Chuck Taylor All Star high-top sneakers. That's a secret of the old flats fishing pros.

Dry Tops and Slickers

In rough surf conditions, chest waders do have one drawback. While they'll keep your legs and upper body dry, they can't stop waves from crashing against your chest and spilling down into the waders. Though waders that fit properly won't fill like a bucket due to splashing, on chilly days with cold water, being even a little wet under your waders is rather uncomfortable. That's why most serious surfcasters, in the Northeast and Southeast especially, will wear either a rain slicker or a dry top over their waders.

As far as slickers are concerned, there really isn't one that's better for surf fishing than another. Those made by Grundéns (www.grundens.com) and Helly Hansen (www.hellyhan sengear.com) are designed for commercial fishermen, and range from $30 to $80. While the PVC material used to make them might be a bit more rugged than that old yellow rain slicker you have in the garage, the fact is, they won't keep you any more dry on the beach. Even waterproof windbreaker-style jackets will do the trick. But if you're looking for the most protection from the surf you can possibly get, you may want to invest in a dry top.

Dry tops are made from many different materials, though they all share a few key elements. The cuffs of the sleeve, collar, and waist are very tight fitting to create seals that will not let in any water. If you're wearing a quality dry top and good pair of waders, you are essentially in a wet suit, though I wouldn't go for any intentional swims. Dry tops are particularly favored by anglers who fish from rock jetties or cast artificial lures, as they need to be right in the path of incoming waves to fish effectively. Bait anglers who cast and return rods to sand spikes farther up the beach can skip dry tops.

By far the most notable name in tops for the surf angler is Long Island, New York–based AquaSkinz (www.aquaskinz .com). This company produces several dry tops to accommodate various surf and weather conditions. I am a particular fan of their Hurricane Top, which is made from heavy neoprene and provides warmth on top of wave protection. AquaSkinz's Raptor Top is designed to keep water out, but is also lighter and breathable.

The AquaSkinz Hurricane Dry Top features watertight seals at the cuffs and neck, plus a tight-fitting waist to keep cold surf water out. A dry top can really increase comfort during rough or chilly conditions.

Just be sure the style of surf fishing you plan to pursue—and more important, the conditions you'll be fishing in—warrant a dry top, as they are expensive. Still, a quality dry top can be your best friend on a December night when the waves are pounding.

Polarized Sunglasses

On a windy day when the waves are churning, polarized glasses aren't going to do too much to aid your success. But when conditions are calm and the water clear, a good pair of fishing shades can really boost your hookup rates. Polarized glasses are designed to eliminate glare, helping you see into and under the water. Anglers in Florida, the Gulf States, and Southern California rely heavily on polarized glasses, as calmer surf conditions in these areas lend themselves to better sight-fishing conditions for a variety of species that feed close to shore in the shallow wash.

Though conditions are often rougher in the Northeast, Southeast, and Northwest, polarized glasses are still a useful tool for picking out certain species in the curls of the waves or as they feed in troughs between waves. Most tackle shops sell inexpensive polarized glasses, though if you're interested in a sturdier pair with top-notch lenses, Costa (www.costadelmar.com) and Maui Jim (www.mauijim.com) both produce excellent glasses starting around $150. Aside from improving your underwater vision, glasses are never a bad thing to have when fishing crowded beaches, as they can potentially save you from a stray hook, lure, or sinker in the eye.

Cast Nets

A cast net is no doubt an important piece of gear for the surfcaster, though one only necessary for special situations. These circular nets are designed for collecting live bait on the beach. As they're thrown, they spread open and land on a school of baitfish. Weights around the net's perimeter cause it to sink quickly to the bottom, trapping the baitfish inside the mesh. As you retract the cast net via a rope around your wrist, it draws closed around the bait.

Cast nets are specialized tool used by anglers to collect live baitfish from the surf. Mastering the art of throwing one takes practice. Photo: Courtesy of Cabela's

Though a cast net may not be a tool you'll use every day on the beach, they can come in handy during migrations of baitfish like mullet or peanut bunker, especially when large gamefish are on their heels. Learning to throw a cast net properly is a matter of trial and error, and I'll be the first to admit that my skill at deploying one is far from top-notch. Websites like CastNetWorld.com provide detailed instructions with photos for throwing a net of any size.

That said, know that cast nets come in a wide variety of diameters, but those with a small radius (6 to 8 feet) are best for the beach. This is because they are lighter and more manageable, making them easier to launch quickly and accurately at a fast-moving school of bait in the waves. You should also check local regulations for bait collection before tossing a net, as some states limit what species can be collected, and how many you can legally keep.

Basic Gear Maintenance

Salt water is an incredibly corrosive liquid. Just a small spot of rust on the line roller of a reel can cause your line to abrade. Waders left with salt on them can quickly dry out and rot, thus causing leaks. Lures not washed properly will rust and tarnish, making hooks dull and finishes fade. Cleaning your gear thoroughly after a surf trip is of the utmost importance, both to ensure that it functions on the next outing, and to avoid shelling out money on new equipment more frequently.

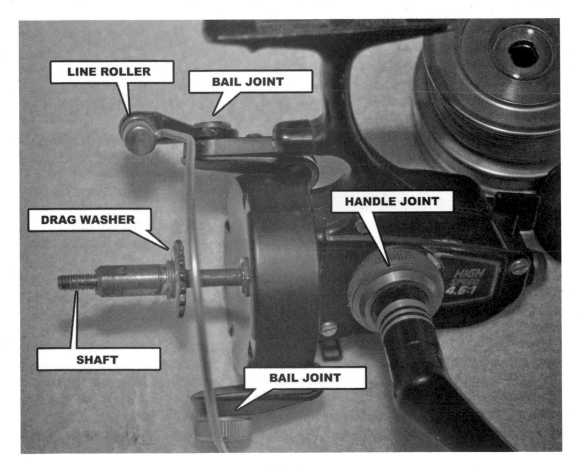

Shown here are the parts of a spinning reel that need oiling for preventive maintenance against saltwater corrosion.

Many beaches offer anglers four-wheel-drive access, but knowing how to drive on sand safely is as important as knowing how to cast. Photo: Melissa Pulicare

to switch into four-wheel drive high or low to combat soft sand. Most current SUVs and pickup trucks have these features.

Every beach has a different sand consistency, from hard-packed to loose, or what can be called "sugar sand." Until you get to know the consistency of the beach you'll be fishing, it's wise to deflate your tires to about 16 pounds to create more surface area under the vehicle. And remember, aggressive-tread off-road tires are designed to dig, which can actually be a hindrance on the sand. Smoother-tread tires are preferred. Here are some things you should pick up before cruising the beach:

Tire Gauge: Use a tire gauge to deflate to the proper pressure when airing down and refilling your tires later.

20 × 20 Plywood Board: If you get a flat tire or run into any situation where you need to raise your truck, a jack won't work too well on sand. You'll need a hard surface to place and support the jack.

Tow Strap: Whether you get stuck and need help getting pulled out, or you need to help a fellow fisherman with a buried truck, a tow strap is a must.

Traction Mats: Foldable, hard-rubber traction mats slide under your tires to give them something to grip when you're trying to get out of a rut in the sand.

Shovel: The first step to getting unstuck might be to dig out your tires. Don't hit the beach without a shovel. A foldable army-style spade is good, but a full-sized garden shovel is better.

Always park your truck above the high-water mark, beyond the tide's reach.

Once you're ready to drive out, follow in tracks already created by other vehicles, as they'll be the most hard-packed. Be sure to park above the high-tide line, and when you're ready to leave your spot, step on the gas slowly. Trucks most often get stuck as the wheels spin too quickly and dig upon takeoff. Be sure to check regulations and requirements at the specific area you'll be fishing before driving onto the beach, and don't forget to spray your vehicle's undercarriage with fresh water to ward off rust when the trip is over.

Fishing Licenses

While all states require a license to fish in fresh water, most now require licenses for saltwater angling. Exceptions can occur when you're fishing with a professional beach guide; you are generally clear to fish under his or her guide's license, though this varies state by state. Many state fish and wildlife agencies have established online web stores that allow anglers to purchase licenses on the Internet. The vast majority of tackle shops, or retailers such as Walmart, are authorized to sell state fishing licenses should you prefer to pay cash. Getting caught fishing without a license carries a hefty fine, and in some states means an automatic ban from being able to legally purchase a license in the future. No matter where you're fishing, check state license regulations ahead of time, and check with hired guides to find out whether or not you need to be licensed when fishing with them.

Chapter 3

Baiting Up

Choosing Your Bait

As I was talking to surf fishing guide Floyd Morton, we got on the subject of catching weakfish along the Delaware coast. Weakfish are a species I grew up chasing, and they're one of my all-time favorite targets. They are ambush predators that strike with ferocity. In my experience, catching them often required live bait, such as a mud minnow, grass shrimp, or peanut bunker.

"Chicken," said Morton with a laugh. "Boneless, skinless chicken is a big bait for weakfish in Delaware. I didn't believe it when I first heard it. I thought the guy who was telling me this had to be kidding. Then I watched him reel in a 5-pound fish on a piece of chicken."

The point here is that the right bait for the surf is often tailored to niche areas. What's best for a certain species in one region can be totally wrong for another. Like using boneless chicken for weakfish in Delaware, I've heard of using chicken livers for striped bass in New Jersey. These are examples of unconventional baits, though you may find that something obscure like this is the top producer in your area and a "secret bait" of the locals. But there are a plethora of baits that are more universal and produce well throughout much of the United States. Those are the baits covered in this chapter.

Any tackle shop worth its salt will always carry the top-producing baits based on its location. Depending on the season and migration patterns of baitfish, they will offer fresh or live bait whenever it's available, but most shops stock a wide variety of frozen baits year-round. As you'll come to learn, there can be advantages and disadvantages to using frozen bait.

Some of the bait species mentioned ahead are better secured by catching them yourself, and where that's the case, you'll learn the best way to go about collecting them. Believe it or not, catching bait can be as much fun as catching gamefish with it, if not more, and it's a great way to get kids involved in the outdoors. I'll never forget one September watching a father throwing a cast net to catch mullet on the beach. His young son dug a depression in the sand near the water and kept tossing a few mullet in the little pool. Later, Dad connected with a nice bluefish, but the boy was more interested in watching his pet mullet swim than reeling it in.

Thanks to recent technological advances, some of the bait covered in this chapter is completely synthetic. No, I'm not talking about lures, but actual scented soft-plastic bait molded to look and smell like the real thing. Surprisingly, these baits have proven effective on myriad species, and in some cases will save you money on expensive live bait.

Finally, you'll learn about all the terminal tackle needed to fish the baits covered, as well popular bait rig styles that are universal in effectiveness across the country, but can easily be modified to suit the bait you're casting and the species of fish you're trying to entice.

Squid

From Washington State, to Louisiana, to Maine, squid is one of the most versatile and universal baits. Almost every species will eat it. Few and far between are the tackle shops catering to saltwater anglers that do not stock squid. What makes this bait so popular is that it can be presented to fish many ways and tailored to almost any situation, plus the frozen variety still maintains its bright white color and

Squid are among the most universal baits in saltwater fishing. Their firm texture helps keep strips on the hook for a long time, and the color of their flesh serves as a visual attractant. Photo: Dave Skok/dwskok.com

potent smell. Although it is possible to find fresh squid, frozen squid is inexpensive and can last you a while if you store it properly.

A squid's flesh is firm and rubbery, allowing it to stay on the hook a long time and making it difficult for fish to tear it away. Its white color stands out in the water, making it a visual attractor as well as a scent attractor. Squid is packaged in a variety of ways, and sizes ranges from a few inches to more than a foot long. These days, you can also find frozen containers of precut squid. Sometimes these strips are dyed to add more color, or the liquid in which they've been frozen is spiked with scent attractant to boost the smell. Although precut strips are convenient to carry, I prefer to buy a frozen bag of large-bodied squid and cut the strips myself to be sure they're exactly the size I want based on what I'm chasing.

One of the most commonly used cuts of squid is a long triangle shape that resembles a sports pennant. The strip is hooked at the wide end, allowing the narrow end to flutter and undulate in the water. This is perhaps the most common cut for flounder, which will inhale the whole strip. Strips cut in this fashion can also be used to tip jig lures to add more action and smell. But since squid is a tough bait, it's important to cut the strips to the proper size for your target species. As an example, a small croaker would simply peck at the end of long strip intended for flounder and may not get the hook. For small-mouthed species like croakers and kingfish in the Gulf and Atlantic, and redtail surf perch in the Northwest, squid should be cut into tiny ¼-inch-by-¼-inch squares and fished on a small hook.

When cut into pennant-shaped strips, a squid flutters and undulates in the water. This cut is popular with anglers chasing flounder in the surf, and can also be used to tip artificial lures. Photo: Darren Dorris

Small- to medium-sized squid can also be fished whole, though this is not a common practice. In the Northeast, squid will often migrate close to the beach with striped bass and bluefish on their heels. In this case, a fresh-caught whole squid is a good bait choice, though securing a live squid to fish whole is not an easy task. Sharp anglers use special squid jigs at night around lighted docks and piers to secure fresh bait.

Squid also stores very well, as it can be refrozen without significant degradation of the flesh. But you can also salt squid strips that have been cut to your desired size for use all season. After slicing up your squid strips, roll them in kosher salt until they are thoroughly coated. Divide the strips into piles equal to the amount you use on an average outing and vacuum-seal each pile separately. The salt will dry out the squid, and if done properly the bait does not need to be stored in the refrigerator. The night before a trip to the beach, open one package and soak the contents in water to rehydrate the strips.

Clams

Much like squid, clams are a favorite food of a long list of gamefish across the country. One of the most popular species is the surf clam, which can be found fresh in many Northeast tackle shops, and frozen in strips almost everywhere else on the Gulf coast and eastern seaboard. Because many clam varieties have tough exterior shells and live buried in the sand and mud, they can be a difficult food for gamefish to obtain naturally. That said, sending a clam into the waves is like presenting a rare morsel.

"Hundreds of people can swarm the beach to dig razor clams in Washington and Oregon," says Northwest surf expert Kelly Corcoran. "While doing so, they expose them and break shells. The redtail surf perch will go crazy. The first high tide after a dig is the best time to catch them."

Shown here are seafood fanatics digging razor clams on the beach in Washington. The dig will release clam scent and broken shells into the surf—both calling cards for redtail surf perch. Photo: Kelly Corcoran

The problem with fresh clams is that they're very soft, and wave action alone is enough to tear them away from the hook. They also have a tendency to fly off when you cast. You can avoid losing your clams by threading them on the hook instead of just running the hook through once. I like to puncture the tough foot first and draw the hook all the way through. Next, I pass the hook through the soft belly and back through the foot again. I'll finish by threading the lip membrane onto the hook, because it's tougher and can help stop the clam from sliding down. Finally, I'll wrap the entire clam with nylon bait thread. Start by tying the end of the thread to the hook below the barb. Make several wraps around the clam, break off the thread, and tie that end under the barb as well. Important to note is that clams also wash out quickly and lose their scent. I like to change clams at least every half hour.

Menhaden: The Fish with Three Names

In the South they're called "pogies." By the book, they are menhaden. But as I'm a Northeast native, I'll stick to my local surfcaster-speak and refer to this large oil-rich fish as "bunker"—a prime bait for enticing some of the biggest gamefish species that roam close to shore.

Bunker is sold frozen in most tackle shops, and though it will catch fish, the fresh variety is always preferable, as the freezing process greatly reduces their pungent odor and ability to release oil. Most commonly, bunker is fished in chunks. They are a very popular bait throughout the range of the striped bass, as well as the mid-Atlantic and southern states that experience a run of large "bull" red drum. However, black drum, cobia, sharks, and bluefish are other hefty species that commonly fall to bunker chunks.

Preparation is simple. With your bait knife, cut the fish into four parts. You should end up with the head severed right behind the gills, two "steaks" from the middle of the body, and the rear section with the tail removed. You can also cut bunker into smaller chunks, though big pieces tend to catch bigger fish. Tail and center chunks should be hooked once through the back, or thickest part of the bait. To help reduce spinning, a bunker head should be hooked through both lips. The point

Menhaden—aka bunker or pogies—are large baits that entice some of the biggest fish in the surf. When cut properly, as shown here, you will end up with four chunks of bait. Photo: Dave Skok/dwskok.com

Weighted treble hooks like this one are commonly used to snag bunker for bait. The trick is finding bunker in casting range to snag.

should enter under the chin and exit through the tip of the nose. Because bunker chunks are large and the rigs used to fish them feature heavy sinkers, it is important to use a stout rod to cast the combination. Fresh bunker will catch fish any time of year, but when this baitfish is migrating in the spring and fall along the Atlantic coast, it's often more productive than any other offering. Good bait shops will carry fresh bunker in season, but when buying it there are a few things to remember.

Bunker spoils quickly, and as with any other bait, you want maximum freshness. Take notice of whether the fish's eyes are yellow or pink and sunken in. Look for a pink twinge on the sides of the fish. All of these signs point to old bunker that's been sitting around. The eyes should be clear and the body vibrant silver and gold. You can also give the bait a poke with your finger. If an indentation remains, it means the flesh has softened from age. Fresh bunker are firm.

Of course, the best way to ensure fresh bunker is to catch your own, but that can be a challenge from the beach. When bunker are running thick in massive schools, they often come into range of a snag hook. These large weighted treble hooks are cast into a pod of bunker, and if you whip the rod during your retrieve, they snag fish one at a time. If you find bunker close enough to snag, you now also have the option of fishing them live. Instead of reeling the fish in and cutting it up, simply open the bail on a spinning reel or flip a conventional reel into free-spool. The snagged bunker will attempt to keep up with the school, but lag behind because of the weighted hook. Gamefish trailing the school will often recognize your snagged fish as being distressed—aka "an easy meal"—and attack it. You'll know when this happens, as line will start sizzling off the reel.

Since bunker are so large, you need to give fish time to swallow. Always let a fish run with a bunker for a long 10-second count before locking the reel and setting the hook. I promise it will be the most eternal 10 seconds of your life, but if you set too early, you risk ripping the bunker right out of the fish's mouth.

Peanut Bunker

Peanuts are simply juvenile bunker that measure approximately 3 to 5 inches. You'll most often find them in large schools along the beach as they migrate out of back bays in the fall months, though it is possible to see them cruising in the ocean at other times of year. Unlike adult bunker, which are hearty baits, peanuts are very fragile. This limits opportunities to fish them live in the surf.

For one thing, obtaining live peanuts requires catching them with a cast net, as they are too small to effectively secure with a snag hook. Though they can be found cruising along the beach within

The skin of a mackerel is highly reflective, making it a great choice for a strip bait. Photo: Darren Dorris

The flesh of a frozen mackerel can be very mushy upon thawing, causing it to easily come off the hook. Anglers who frequently fish with mackerel strips will often cut them to size and sprinkle them with kosher salt the night before a trip. The salt will draw out some of the moisture, thereby toughening up the strips so they last longer.

Sandworms and Bloodworms

Sandworms and bloodworms easily get the vote for most hideous surf baits. These mud-dwelling writhing ribbons are dug by hand at low tide, with a large portion of the supply industry based in Maine. Sandworms are typically longer and fatter than bloodworms, with the former having brown to green coloration, and the latter being deep brown or red. But what makes them monstrous is their business ends.

Sandworms have two large black pincers similar to those of a beetle, while bloodworms sport four black retractable teeth. Make no mistake about it, both species will try to latch onto your skin, but dealing with these nasty morsels is worth it, as they are top producers on the beach. In fact, during the early spring throughout much of the Northeast and into Delaware, sea worms are one of the most effective baits for catching the first striped bass of the year. They can be in such high demand, tackle shops struggle to keep them in stock as anglers cooped up all winter begin the first bass hunts of the season.

As the water slowly begins to warm, worms are often the first baits to reappear before baitfish begin moving. Worms are also meals that require little effort for bass to obtain, considering they are not as apt to chase forage in the colder water. In this situation, smaller worms should be fished whole with the hook threaded through the head several times, allowing the tail to wriggle and flutter. Larger

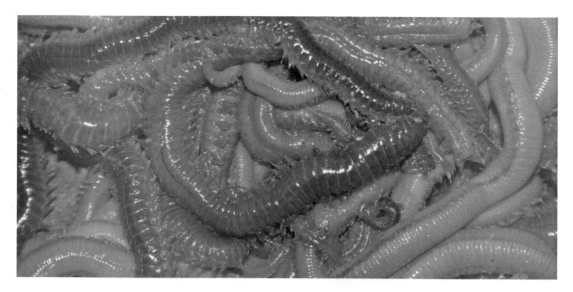

Sandworms and bloodworms may not be much to look at, but these wriggling ribbons are one of the best baits for early-season striped bass and myriad other popular surf species. Photo: Darren Dorris

worms can be rigged the same way after being cut in half. But early-season stripers are not the only species that go crazy for worms.

Whereas smaller species like kingfish, croakers, sea trout, and flounder are quick to strike a small clam or squid strip, a tiny piece of fresh bloodworm or sandworm is like offering filet mignon. Worms release an odor unlike any other bait, that's so potent, companies like BioEdge (www. bioedgefishing.com) have created liquid attractants and wands similar to lip balm, that match worm scent, allowing you to smear it on other baits or artificial lures.

Live worms often come packed in damp grass or seaweed, and so long as you keep this packing moist with salt water and store the worms in a cooler or the refrigerator, a box can last longer than a week. That's important to remember because sand- and bloodworms also rank high on the list of most expensive baits. Because worms are dug by hand, labor costs, packing costs, and shipping costs add up quickly. Considering that bait shop owners also want to make a profit, a dozen live sea worms can cost $20 or more. Another option for buying sea worms, should your local shop be out, is ordering directly from MaineBait.com, which ships live sand- and bloodworms to the New England states, Pennsylvania, New Jersey, Delaware, Maryland, Virginia, and North Carolina.

So potent is the scent given off by bloodworms and sandworms, companies like BioEdge are producing liquid attractant with the same odors for use on other baits.

eel, this style of fishing requires being in the right place at the right time, plus having live eels handy, which is not always easy in the southern states.

Most tackle shops from New England to North Carolina will carry live eels for at least part of the season. Like sea worms, this bait can be costly. With that said, eels are not the bait to purchase if you're sending two rods out and sitting on the beach with the kids. Should the area you're fishing fit the profile of prime eeling territory, they can be the key to connecting with true surf trophies.

Mullet

Mullet are one of the most prevalent species of live bait found in the surf from Texas to New England.
Photo: Chad Love

Ask any surfcaster from Texas, to Florida, all the way to Cape Cod in Massachusetts, what's the most important baitfish, and a large percentage will answer "mullet." Though there are more than 100 mullet species found worldwide, the most common in the United States are striped mullet and white mullet, sometimes referred to as silver mullet. One reason mullet are so significant is simply because every large gamefish species in the Gulf and Atlantic eats them. But their real appeal comes from their migration patterns.

Generally starting in the late summer or early fall, mullet school together and move en masse out of bays and estuaries into the Gulf and ocean. But whereas finding bait like bunker right on the beach is a matter of chance and proper conditions, mullet prefer to hug tightly to the shoreline, by nature. When mullet begin to move, it prompts every gamefish in the area to start eating. Simply stated, mullet bring monsters into the surf.

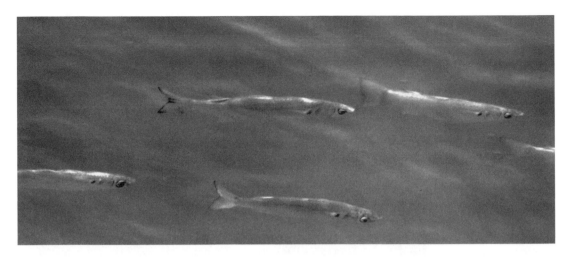

You can often spot mullet in the shallow wash right where the water meets the sand. This pod was swimming just outside Corsons Inlet in New Jersey during the beginning of the September run. Photo: Chad Love

In Florida, the mullet migration coincides with prime snook fishing from the beach. In Texas, they bring behemoth tarpon and sharks right into the breakers. In the Northeast, the mullet run is considered the kickoff to the fall striped bass season, as bass that have been lazily hanging around all summer will suddenly perk up and go into attack mode. And finally, on North Carolina's Outer Banks, the first sign of mullet means it's time to bust out the big sticks and start targeting bull red drum.

An angler throws a cast net into the wash trying to bring in a passing mullet school. Cast netting is probably the most common way surfcasters acquire live or fresh dead mullet. Photo: Darren Dorris

Another huge advantage of mullet is that unlike fragile peanut bunker, this bait is hearty, so it offers great opportunity to live-baitfish, and also works very well as dead bait. Tackle shops often carry fresh dead mullet in season, and bags of frozen mullet are staple of almost every bait freezer. Every once in a while you may find live mullet, but transporting it to the beach is a chore. Most often, live mullet is obtained by throwing a cast net on schools as they cruise along the beach. When they are running particularly thick on beaches popular with anglers, it's not rare to find netters selling live and dead mullet on site. Since mullet are tougher baits, a few will live for a while in a bucket so long as you don't overcrowd the container, allowing them more room and oxygen.

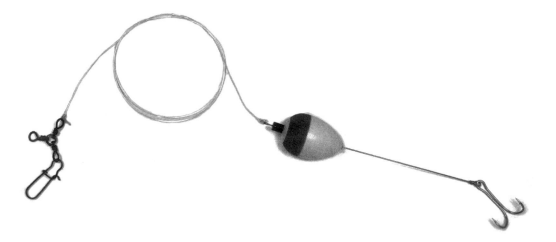

This rig is specifically designed for fishing whole dead mullet, and is particularly popular with anglers chasing bluefish. The wire is run through the body of the bait and out the mouth, leaving the double hooks seated near the tail.

I prefer to hook a live mullet through the lips or in the back near the tail. If gamefish are pushing schools around close to the beach, you can sometimes cast a mullet with no weight and get it to the target. But these fish will also produce well if slung far out on a weighted bait rig and left to sit on the bottom.

Dead mullet can be cut into smaller pieces for use on croakers, small red drum, small striped bass, and small bluefish. Mullet average 3 to 6 inches, but larger ones can be netted and used for bigger chunk baits that give off a ton of scent. There are also special rigs popular in the Northeast for fishing a whole dead mullet on a piece of wire leader behind a colored float to specifically entice bluefish.

Spot

What makes spot so interesting is that they go just as well on a hook as they do dredged in cornmeal and dropped in the frying pan. They are both exceptionally productive baits for very large species, but also gamefish in their own right, which makes collecting them that much more fun.

This smallest members of the croaker family is thickest in the surf in the late summer and into the fall, usually around the same time as mullet begin running the beach throughout most of the North and mid-Atlantic states. Most spot will average 6 to 10 inches, though bigger specimens do exist. You can actually get your hands on live spot in well-stocked tackle shops, but given that they can cost more than $3 apiece and you have the hassle of getting them to the beach, you'll save money and have a blast catching your own.

Though spot—the smallest member of the croaker family—are both terrific baits live or chunked for red drum and striped bass, they also make a fine addition to the frying pan. Photo: Melissa Pulicare

Spot are quick to eat squid or clams presented on the bottom. The key to avoiding frustration is using very tiny hooks and bite-sized pieces of bait. If you think your bait is too small, cut it in half again. I'll literally thread on only enough bait to cover the tip of the hook, and I frequently use hooks more suited for tying trout flies than surf fishing. Spot have very small mouths and are nibblers. When they're thick in the waves, they can strip your bait before you even flip the bail, so using multiple hooks is wise. Fishing for spot is a great way to introduce young children to surfcasting. Best of all, you can always opt to take a few home for the table.

For chunk fishing, spot should be cut in half behind the gills and fished like bunker chunks with the hook through the eyes or lips on the head, and through the back of the rear chunk. Fresh spot chunks are a favorite of the surfcasting legions from Maryland through North Carolina who target red drum migrating in the fall. In the Northeast, chunks work well for striped bass, though spot are more commonly fished live with the dorsal fin clipped off and the hook run up through both lips, or crossways through the nose.

Rain Bait

On every coast there are multitudes of small baitfish that are a huge part of the surf ecosystem. Though it is more of an East Coast term, these fish can be classified as "rain bait," as a school of them swimming near the surface can look like raindrops hitting the water. The name also stems from the way they scatter across the surface when being attacked. Almost every gamefish large and small feeds on rain bait. Much like a whale gulping plankton, bigger gamefish will cut through a school of rain bait, inhaling as many as possible on each pass. But given the fragility and size of these morsels, it is almost impossible to use them live from the beach.

Spearing are one common baitfish species that falls under the "rain bait" category. Though they are a primary forage of many larger species, they are best used dead for smaller surf dwellers. Photo: Dave Skok/dwskok.com

Truth be told, you'll have more success throwing lures that mimic these baits around schools of gamefish that are attacking, but that's not to say fresh dead and frozen varieties aren't useful or productive.

Also known as silversides or glass minnows, spearing are staple baitfish throughout much of the country. Their average length ranges from less than an inch to approximately 4 inches, and their bodies are translucent in the water.

Spearing can be found frozen in most tackle shops and are an excellent all-around choice for general beach fishing during the summer months or when not on a quest for monster fish. After thawing, spearing can be used on light rigs to hook flounder or weakfish. They are also are a good bait for small bluefish and sea trout. Whole spearing should be hooked through the eyes, but you can also cut spearing into small pieces for croakers or kingfish.

Frozen sand eels are also easy to come by on the East Coast and can be fished exactly the same as spearing. Though thin, long, and silver, sand eels aren't actually eels, but a baitfish with a pointed head and small mouth that buries in the sand. They can be found in great numbers in the Northeast surf during the fall and into the winter as the striped bass migration draws to a close. Though they are

Sand eels are found throughout much of the East Coast, and are a particularly popular meal for late-season striped bass and bluefish in the Northeast. Photo: Dave Skok/dwskok.com

prime striper forage, again a lure that matches their profile will be far more productive than trying to obtain and fish one live.

On the West Coast, Southern California beaches experience runs of grunion between March and August. These small silver fish beach themselves by the hundreds of thousands to spawn at night. Though grunion are very seasonal baits, San Diego surfcaster Paul Sharman says they can be highly productive, live or dead, for halibut that will feed on them as they stage for their late-night mating ritual.

Mud Minnows

Mud minnows are small, fat baitfish usually measuring 1 to 3 inches. In New England they are commonly referred to as mummichogs, while anglers from New York through Delaware often call them killies or fatheads. Though mud minnows are small, they don't fall into the rain bait category because finding massive schools of them right off the beach is an infrequent occurrence.

Mud minnows dwell in shallow bays and estuaries, where they are caught in traps and sold live in bait shops. What separates them from baits like spearing or sand eels is that they are sturdy little fish that if cared for properly will live a very long time. One way to do that is by using a designated minnow bucket. These buckets use a swinging door to stop bait from escaping and feature vent holes that allow water to rush in and out. On calm beaches, you can tie a bait bucket off to a sand spike and simply let it bob in the water. If this isn't possible, just walk the bucket down the surf and occasionally let water flush in.

to draw weakfish like a magnet, though they can cost a pretty penny at the cash register. Larger dead shedders should be cut into pieces and fished like any other chunk bait. But a live shedder can easily earn you a trophy weakfish from the beach. If you can't find shedder crabs, try dousing squid strips in shedder crab oil, which is bottled and sold in most tackle shops.

Sand Fleas

Whether you call them sand fleas, sand crabs, "cookies," or mole crabs, these small crustaceans are very important surf baits and some of the easiest to obtain for free. Sand fleas live in the sand where the waves meet the beach. Dig down a few inches, let the sand filter out of your hand, and you'll often find a flea or two scampering across your palm. You can also purchase a rake that allows you to scoop and sift larger amounts of sand to obtain baits fast. Toss them in a bucket of wet sand to keep their gills moist and they'll stay alive all day. Submerging them in a bucket of water will cause them to drown.

You can also freeze sand fleas, though according to Florida surf expert Mike Conner, the baits greatly benefit from blanching prior to freezing. Thawed sand fleas that were frozen fresh will be soft, and therefore not stay on the hook as well. Conner will collect fleas, put them in a mesh bag, and dip the bag in boiling water for 8 to 10 seconds. The shells turn an orange color that he believes is appealing to pompano, plus the shells stay firm. You can also refreeze blanched sand fleas with no bait degradation. Some baits shops in the pompano's range sell frozen blanched fleas.

Though largely overlooked in the Northeast, sand fleas are staple baits of pompano fishermen from North Carolina through the Gulf. They are also popular in California for surf perch and corbina. Photo: Melissa Pulicare

Aside from being a top producer for pompano from North Carolina to Texas, sand fleas are wildly popular on Southern California beaches for surf perch and corbina. According to noted SoCal angler Paul Sharman, "The premium baits are those with orange egg sacs, which many believe, myself included, help attract more bites." This bait is widely overlooked in the Northeast as it is not associated with any common species, though I can tell you from experience, I've caught some of my biggest croakers from the New Jersey surf with fleas.

Sand fleas should be hooked through the head, which is designated by two small antennae. Small wide-gap hooks are preferred to achieve a more natural presentation, and fleas can be fished effectively on almost any style of bait rig.

Scaled Sardine

Scaled sardines are popular live bait in Florida, particularly for snook. On the Gulf coast, they are sometimes referred to as "whitebait." However, much like peanut bunker, these fish are delicate and prone to longer life when stored in a livewell on a boat that is constantly cycling clean salt water. Though they can be found within range of a cast net on the beach, most anglers who use them frequently net them in back bays and estuaries over grass flats. Some bait shops do carry live sardines, though finding them may not be easy. If you do have the opportunity to buy some and plan to drag them onto the beach in a bait bucket, your best shot at keeping them alive is changing the water frequently without dumping it violently into the bucket and stirring them up rigorously.

Considering that snook feed relatively close to the shoreline, you can often present sardines with no extra weight. In fact, too much terminal tackle on the line is more likely to scare snook away.

Like peanut bunker, scaled sardines can be tricky to catch and transport live onto the beach. However, they are one of the best baits for big snook in the surf.

but according to the company it releases 400 times more scent than even the freshest natural bait. Exactly how they reached that number, I'm not entirely sure, but I do know that that Gulp! baits have caught on in a big way with certain fishing circles.

One that comes to mind first is the group of Northeast anglers who fish for early-season striped bass through March and April. As previously mentioned, sandworms and bloodworms have always been top producers this time of year. But because live worms can be very expensive, many surfcasters have switched to Gulp! sand- and bloodworms to save money. These worms look and feel like the real thing and can be fished whole or cut into smaller pieces. Best of all, they're durable, so after catching a few fish, anglers will put the worms back into their package to reabsorb more of the "secret juice." The Gulp! line also features sand fleas, clams, small baitfish, and colored strips that can be used as squid alternatives. These are not lures that need to be worked with the rod. Simply hook them as you would the real bait, and cast away.

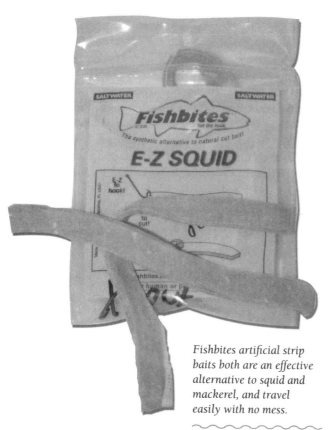

Fishbites artificial strip baits both are an effective alternative to squid and mackerel, and travel easily with no mess.

Fishbites is another company making artificial baits; unlike Gulp! products, these have no liquid component that can make them messy. Their strip baits are tough, so they stay on the hook well, and they come in a wide array of scents, including shrimp, clam, and crab.

"Fishbites make summer fishing simple," says Virginia surf expert Ric Burnley. "There's no mess and no need to buy fresh bait every time I want to just go chase some croakers. I'll toss a small knife and bag of Fishbites in my pocket and I'm all set. Just cut a little piece of the strip, hook it up, and you're fishing."

Terminal Tackle for the Baitfisherman

Regardless of the species you intend to target and the bait you plan to use, it's important to have basic knowledge of the tackle elements that make up common bait rigs, both so you understand what they do and how they work, and so you can build rigs to your own specifications. Although many companies produce pre-tied rigs for just about every species under the sun, you might be surprised by how constructing your own rigs will build confidence, as well has help you fine-tune bait presentations to your style of fishing. First, let's take a look at the key components.

LEADER MATERIAL

The first step to building a rig is choosing a leader material. Rarely will you tie the components of a rig directly to your main line, though you may find an exception here and there. Leaders can serve as bite protection and add extra strength to your rig. Sometimes all you need is a simple length of regular monofilament fishing line to get the job done, but there are other leader materials available today of which you should be aware.

Fluorocarbon leader is a relatively new creation that has majorly caught on with anglers across the globe. "Fluoro" provides far superior abrasion resistance than standard monofilament, and is significantly stronger. However, what makes fluoro so appealing for tying bait rigs is that it practically disappears underwater, giving you an edge with wary fish. On the downside, fluorocarbon can be stiff and more difficult to tie. It's also more expensive than other materials, though many anglers agree the benefits far outweigh the price. There are quite a few fluorocarbon makers around, but Seaguar (www.seaguar.com) and Gamma (www.gammafishing.com) produce some of the best.

Companies like Ande (www.andemonofilament.com) manufacture monofilament leader material that is a little stronger and more translucent than regular mono you'd buy on a large spool for your reel. It's also possible to find pink or red mono leader material, as both of these colors help reduce visibility underwater. Though it may seem pointless to buy more mono for rigs when you've got

Choosing the right leader material for your surf rigs is as important as selecting the right bait.

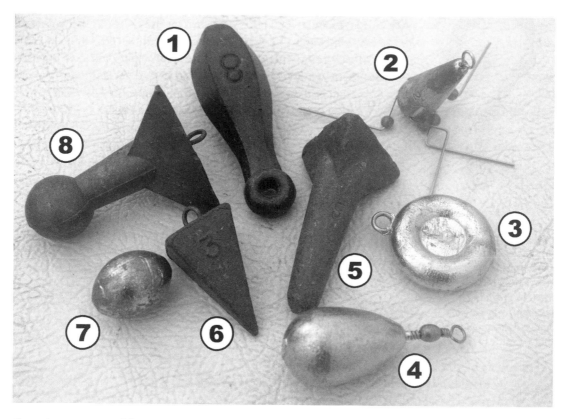

Shown here are some of the most common styles of surf sinker. 1. Bank sinker, 2. Sputnik sinker, 3. Disk sinker, 4. Teardrop sinker, 5. Hatteras sinker, 6. Pyramid sinker, 7. Egg sinker, 8. Storm sinker. Photo: Melissa Pulicare

Anchoring sinkers are also meant to be fished in conjunction with larger baits, such as bunker chunks or live spot. Since these baits are heavier and have wide profiles, they are more prone to catching the current and creating drag. This adds to the need for a weight that is more difficult to pull out of the sand.

Bank sinkers and teardrop sinkers both have rounded bodies that serve a few purposes. First, they won't snag as easily on beaches with scattered rocks or other structure. Where anchor sinkers would get lodged, the round sinkers are designed to bounce off hard surfaces. Aside from producing fewer lost rigs, these sinkers are perfect for calmer beaches where there is some merit to letting your baits get pushed around by the wave action. As an example, surf guide Floyd Morton prefers small bank sinkers when targeting croakers and kingfish simply because they let his baits move.

"These fish follow small, wavy depressions as they migrate up the beach," says Morton. "If your sinker sticks to the bottom and happens to be in the wrong depression, the fish may swim right by it. But a bank sinker will roll in and out of these depressions as the waves push it, increasing your chance of finding the fish."

Unlike bank and teardrop sinkers that will roll, disk sinkers are meant to hold on muddy or sandy bottom in areas of light to moderate wave action. Because they lie flat once they're down, disk sinkers are less affected by current, though they are best used with smaller baits that won't create much resistance. This makes them a popular choice among anglers targeting weakfish, flounder, croakers, and sea trout, which regularly pick up smaller, low-profile baits.

Egg sinkers have a hole running through their center. Instead of clipping them to a rig with a snap, these weights would be slid onto your main line before tying on your rig. The barrel swivel at the head of your leader will act as a stopper. The advantage to egg sinkers is that they make your entire rig more streamlined than those with weights that dangle off at an angle. Egg sinkers are most commonly used to add just a little weight to live baits, such as eels or mullet, though they are not meant to hold baits in place.

HOOKS

The number of hook styles available in tackle shops is staggering. Luckily for the surf angler, you can effectively catch just about every species from the beach with a few different hook models. Overall, the most important decision you'll make when buying hooks is the size. I've seen more fish missed and lost because the hooks are too small or too large for the species being targeted. Hooks that are too small might not stick in a big fish's mouth as securely as you'd want for a successful fight and landing. On the reverse side, smaller species that don't have wide mouths will peck the bait right off a large hook without ever getting the point. You need to remember that you want the bait to be matched with a hook that will both hold it effectively and fit in a fish's mouth.

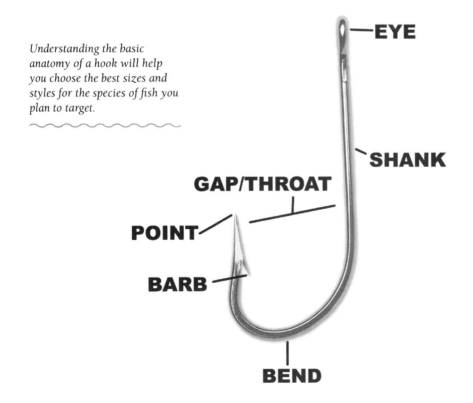

Understanding the basic anatomy of a hook will help you choose the best sizes and styles for the species of fish you plan to target.

The design of a Kahle hook places the point farther back in a fish's mouth when it strikes. This is useful for species with thin or soft lips, such as flounder or weakfish.

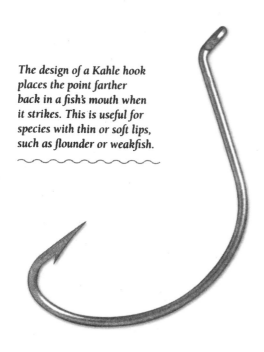

One final hook style worth mentioning is the Kahle hook, sometimes referred to as a "flounder hook" or simply "wide-gap hook." Though it looks like a circle hook at first glance, it doesn't work the same way and should be set with an upward sweep of the rod like a J-hook. Kahle hooks are particularly popular among flounder, weakfish, and croaker anglers. You'll often find them incorporated into pre-tied rigs for these species. One thing these fish have in common is thin lips that tear easily. The orientation of a Kahle hook's point places it farther back in the mouth upon the strike. This reduces the chance that the hook will pull through the lips when you set the hook or during the fight.

Another factor to consider in the tackle shop is whether you want in-line or offset hooks. Many hook styles are available in either variety, and though the difference is subtle, there are advantages to both.

Shown here is the difference between in-line and offset hooks. Notice that the point of an offset hook is positioned to the side of the shank. This slight change in orientation can help the point bury in a fish's mouth faster.

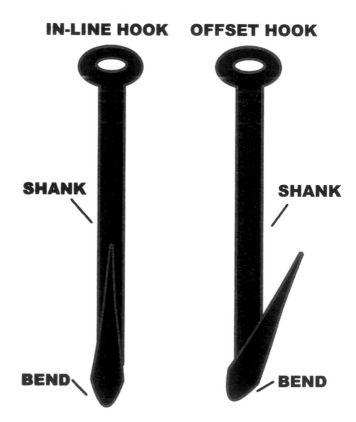

IN-LINE HOOK   OFFSET HOOK

SHANK   SHANK

BEND   BEND

"In-line" refers to hooks that have a bend perfectly lined up with the shank. If you were to drop an in-line hook on a table, it would lie flat. The bend of an offset hook is positioned slightly to one side of the shank. The advantage is that the point is now more exposed and will grab hold and set in a fish's mouth faster. This can be very important when using baits that require giving the fish time to run with the line before setting the hook, or when a fish strikes a line connected to a rod sitting in a sand spike. As the fish swims off and the line comes tight, the offset point is more likely to stick. However, this style of hook is most commonly used for larger species that have big mouths. Offset hooks can be hindrance when targeting smaller species. In-line hooks are more streamlined and compact, making them better suited to small baits. Their overall profile also makes it easier for smaller species to get the hook in their mouths.

The Standard Bait Rig

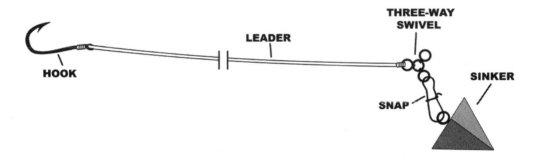

This standard bait rig is one of the easiest to tie and will effectively deliver any bait or beat any fish when made with the right components.

Detailed here is the most simplistic bait rig you can use in the surf. Tied with the right components to match the size and strength of your desired species, it will effectively land any fish and deliver just about any bait. In this configuration, a snap that will hold the sinker is first attached to one eye of a three-way swivel. Next, the leader of your desired length is tied to a second swivel eye. The hook is tied to the end of the leader, and the main line from your reel connects at the third swivel eye. If there is one flaw in the design, it's that your bait is exposed to crabs since it is sitting directly on the bottom. If your bait keeps disappearing without any sign of a strike, try adding a float.

Foam floats come in an array of shapes and sizes and provide a way to keep your bait suspended just off the bottom when using a standard rig. Not only does this make it more difficult for crabs to steal the bait, but also reduces strikes from unwanted fish like skates and stingrays that lie flat on the bottom.

In some cases, floats can actually serve as visual attractors that increase strikes. According to Delaware surf expert Floyd Morton, float colors can be as important as bait choice.

This rig had been modified with a foam float. Floats help keep baits hovering off the bottom, out of the reach of scavenging crabs.

"If I'm targeting kingfish or croakers, I'll let the amount of light dictate my float color," he says. "On bright days I'll use light colors like yellow or plain white. If it's dark or cloudy, I might go with green. It's amazing how much of a difference that can make."

But don't assume that a float always offers an advantage. Sometimes they can make a bait appear unnatural and turn fish off. If you suspect this is happening, lose the float, as sometimes a surfcaster just has to deal with some crab-stolen baits and stingrays between hooking target gamefish.

Different float designs attached to your leader in various ways, and I've always found peg floats to be the most reliable. Simply remove the central peg and run the leader through the hole in the float. Obviously you'll need to do this either before tying the hook to the leader or before tying the leader to the swivel. Once on the leader, slide the float where you want it to sit and push the peg back in place. The heavier your bait, the larger the float you'll want to use to increase buoyancy.

Floats are available in many styles that let you match them to the weight of your bait, or use them as visual attractants to increase strikes.

With a few beads, a spinner blade, and a dressed Kahle hook, this standard bait rig was modified specifically for targeting flounder.

The standard bait rig can also be modified visually to entice specific species. As an example, flounder anglers frequently used a Kahle hook dressed with bucktail, feathers, or a plastic skirt in place of a plain hook. They'll slide beads and spinner blades onto the leader to create extra flash and vibration. After tipping the hook with a strip bait, such as squid, they cast out and slowly retrieve. The sinker drags across the bottom, kicking up sand as the spinner and dressed hook trail behind. This is just one example of a standard bait rig with a little extra flare.

The High-Low Rig

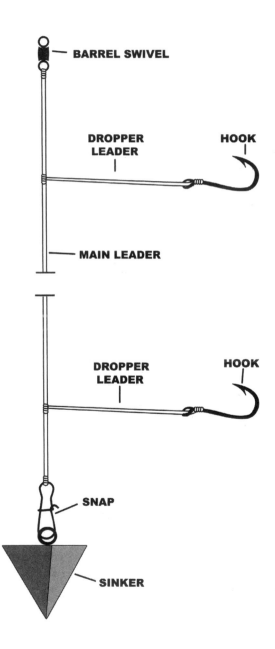

Also very popular among surf fishermen coast to coast is the high–low rig, which is designed to suspend two baits at different levels in the water column. The low hook is positioned closer to the sinker, thus presenting one bait on or just off the bottom. The second hook placed farther up the leader suspends another bait higher in the water. Though the idea is to give fish cruising at different depths options, the high–low rig provides a method of fishing multiple baits with less frustration. If you were to tie two leaders with two hooks to the same swivel eye in a standard bait rig, more likely than not, those leaders would twist together while rolling in the waves or during a cast, making your baits look unnatural.

To create a high–low rig, start by tying one end of a long leader to a barrel swivel. Now comes the part that takes practice. Tie two dropper loops (see tying instructions in chapter 5) into the leader, spacing them apart at your desired distance. At the bottom of the leader, tie on a snap to hold the sinker.

The dropper loops form the two "dropper leaders" that extend off the main leader at right angles. Try to avoid making these leaders too long, as they can spin around the main leader and cause tangles. Short dropper leaders are stiffer and better for keeping baits extended. To con-

High–low rigs allow you to present multiple baits without tangling your leader, plus keep them in place at different levels in the water column.

nect the hooks to the dropper leaders, pinch the loop near the end and feed it through the eye of the hook, pass it around the shank, and pull tight. You can also snip one side of the loops near the knots to create two longer single-strand dropper leaders as shown in the diagram. Then use your preferred knot to tie each hook to the ends. Snipping one side of a dropper loop will not compromise the knot's strength provided it was tied correctly. Note that this rig can also be very effective with only one dropper leader and one hook. This is especially true when fishing large chunk baits. Two chunks or whole clams may make the rig too heavy or cause twisting, whereas one hook will successfully suspend a large bait in place.

This light high–low rig is tied specifically for kingfish. Note the addition of two small floats on the dropper leaders; these serve as attractors.

It is possible to tie two three-way swivels on the main leader instead of using dropper loops to create a high–low rig, but this comes with potential issues. Though small and seemingly weightless, three-way swivels can cause the rig to collapse and lie flat on the bottom. They can also collect more grass or seaweed. Dropper loops add no extra weight, keeping the entire leader light and slim in profile. Light high–low rigs designed for pompano and croakers often feature small round or pill-shaped floats on the dropper leaders, which provide even better suspension and add some color for visual attraction. Other variations on the high–low rig you might come across in the tackle shop include those with stiff wire or hard-plastic arms in place of dropper leaders.

Slide Rigs

The final rig every surfcaster should be able to tie is a slide rig. These can also be referred to as "fish-finder rigs." What separates them from high–low and standard bait rigs is that the sinker is free to slide up and down the main line. It is a design that serves two purposes.

First, rigs with sliding sinkers allow live baits to swim more freely. They are a particular favorite of anglers who use live spot or live mullet when targeting red drum or striped bass. Because the main line can move through the weight, live baits don't drag the sinker, making them look more

Chapter 4

Building Your Artificial Arsenal

Don't Be Afraid of Lures

If you've never visited a Cabela's or Bass Pro Shops mega-store, you are missing out on quite an experience. What these stores have that many local shops lack is an inventory consisting of just about every lure for every species on the market today. While this can be awe inspiring for a seasoned angler, it also confirms the fear new anglers often feel in even the smallest local tackle shops. There are so many lures out there these days, picking the ones that work best can seem confusing enough to make your head spin. I promise it is not. First know this: A ridiculous percentage of fishing lures are designed and packaged to grab *your* attention, not the fish's.

I see staggering numbers of guys in tackle shops groping for the latest lure with holographic eyes, built-in LED lights, and photorealistic paint jobs. Their packaging will feature phrases like "super-sonic rattle attraction" and "laser-etched scale pattern technology." I'm not saying that such fea-

The amount of lures found in tackle shops these days can be overwhelming to a surfcaster just starting out. But by learning a few key elements about how fish view and react to lures, much of the mystery behind which ones to buy will be solved.

tures don't have a place in fishing or enhance productivity, but tackle manufacturing is a business like any other where sales and the bottom line matter most. Fish don't buy lures, you do. The fact remains that some of the oldest lures used with incredible success in the surf were made from cut pieces of broom handle painted white, with one hook attached to the rear via a screw-in eyelet. I can attest that this exact lure will still catch fish—big ones at that—in the surf today. I know because I've made my own broom handle lures.

Our discussion of lures can be broken down into three parts: size, shape, and color. Every other feature of a lure, from the action to the depth it's meant to be fished, is secondary to the big three. If you think about it, a lure at the proper depth won't do much good if it's the wrong size, shape, or color. First you need to understand the three main elements, and then the rest will fall in place. Though the most popular lure styles will be covered ahead, it is not possible to detail every conceivable lure used in the surf on these pages (it would be another book in itself!). But doing so would not be necessary anyway: Once you understand how to apply the three elements to surf lures, you'll be picking out the top producers in your area in no time.

enough to eat it to come through the area. In the meantime, all the other pompano might not be able to fit the jig in their small mouths. Considering that your original jig was catching fish, you can assume it was matching the size of the bait the fish were eating. That said, there is no reason to think that a mega-pompano wouldn't eat it, too.

I've put plenty of time in on the beach, so sometimes I will opt to head out looking specifically for larger-than-average fish. But for the most part, I am always more interested in just bending the rod than spending long days searching for a "maybe" with no action between. To that end, I'm always sure to carry lures that match a wide variety of forage sizes, as you never know which bait species you'll run into. Keep in mind that you might be on a beach where four or five species of baitfish are present at once. When that happens, it's your job to figure out which one the fish are eating most heavily by experimenting with lure sizes. This, of course, is all part of the fishing challenge.

So what happens when there is no bait visible and you have no idea what to use? Size will still save you, as on just about every beach around the world, you can rest assured there is some species of 4- to 7-inch forage fish that frequents the surf line. When in doubt, choose a lure in this size range and you'll effectively match bait you didn't even know existed.

Getting in Shape

If size is the first key to choosing the best lure, shape is a close second. It may seem obvious that you want your lures to look like the bait in the area, but it's not quite so cut-and-dried. To begin with, some lures change their appearance completely in the water, so what you see in the tackle shop may not seem like an ideal choice. One shape-shifting lure that comes to mind is the bucktail jig. When dry, bucktails are fluffy and have a wide profile. But as you move them through the water, their hair condenses and pulses. It looks very much like a baitfish, though in the store you may never see it.

Many anglers have a tendency to put more emphasis on color than shape. This is a mistake. Some lure companies' claims to fame are finishes that look incredibly realistic. Others push holographic finishes for maximum flash. A lure's paint job can be so real, it's as though the scales had been peeled off a

Lures should always match the shape and profile of the forage you're trying to mimic. Here, a thin-profile Point Jude Po-Jee metal lure bears a very striking resemblance to a live sand eel.

live baitfish and stuck on the imitation. It's all well and good, but a great finish doesn't mean much if the lure's shape doesn't match the bait.

I recently spoke with John Prochnow, the product development director at Berkley. Prochnow is in charge of an army of designers who create some of the hottest lures for the brand. When I asked him how highly he regarded color when choosing lures, his answer was that of a wise angler.

"Tell you the truth, I don't really care about color at all," Prochnow told me. "I'm all about profile. When a fish sees a lure from far away, or when the light is low, it may not be able to even see the color. But you can bet it sees the profile, and if it doesn't match what that fish wants to eat, he's not going to come after it."

With Prochnow's words of wisdom in mind, let's say you are trying to choose a lure to match live mullet. One plastic swimming lure in your bag has a painted finish that resembles a mullet perfectly. The lure is 7 inches long and has the tapered shape of a generic baitfish. But the schools you're seeing on the beach consist of mullet that are only about 4 inches long. You also have a soft-plastic shad that matches the length and girth of the bait at hand very closely. However, the lure is red. Which one do you use?

The answer would be the red shad. Even though the plastic swimmer may be specifically painted to look a mullet, in this case its profile doesn't match the bait in this school as well. Is red the ideal color? Probably not, but in a situation like this, you're likely to get more strikes on a lure that matches the baits' shape rather than color alone. Remember that just because a manufacturer says a lure is a perfect match for a certain bait species doesn't mean it will resemble it all the time in every situation.

Colors That Kill

You've picked a lure that best matches the size and shape of the bait species you're most likely to encounter on your home beach. Now it's time to select a color. On the tackle shop wall hangs a seemingly endless palette of choices. Colors have names like "Electric Hot Potato," "Metallic Pink Lightning," and "Fire Hazard Red." Browns mix with greens, pinks blend to purple, which then blends to gold. I have to admit that I am sucker for crazy color schemes with funky names and am always eager to try them out. But in a situation where you have no idea what colors to select, the answer is unfortunately pretty boring.

You can catch any species of fish with an all-white lure. It's highly unexciting, yet white is by far the most productive, versatile, and consistent color whether you're using a 3-inch soft-plastic baitfish imitation for California corbina or casting an 11-inch wooden swimbait for 50-pound striped bass off Cape Cod. As with all things lure-related, the reason comes back around to bait.

Almost all baitfish have a white belly, regardless of size or unique coloration on their sides or backs. Though nature provides baitfish with coloration to help them blend with their surroundings, their white bellies are often what gamefish recognize. White also closely resembles translucent species, so it is still a fine choice for shrimp or glass minnow imitations, both of which can appear clear when in the water. White stands out in dirty or clean water, in low light and on bright days, and at the bottom of deep holes or on the surface. If you could only ever fish with one lure color, white would be my recommendation. But since that's not the case, there are other colors you should know about.

Catching a fish on a topwater lure is easily one of the most exciting experiences in surf fishing. Here, a large blue-fish blows up on a topwater right in the crest of a wave. Photo: Darren Dorris

The scooped mouth of a popper causes it to splash, spit, and gurgle as it moves across the surface.

Poppers are perhaps the most universal style of topwater. They feature a scooped mouth that when moved through the water with aggressive jerks of the rod tip will splash and spit and throw spray from side to side. These lures can be worked at any speed, which is important to know, as another misconception is that topwaters need to be constantly moving.

Although there are times when "chugging" a popper quickly across the surface draws strikes, you'd be surprised by the amount of hits you'll get on a popper that's sitting still. This actually applies to all topwater lures. When an injured baitfish is moving across the water, it will often splash around, and then stop moving. To mimic this action, it's important to use a little finesse by making one or two chugs and then letting the lure just float in place for a few seconds. Should a fish come up and miss a popper that's sitting still, I like to immediately begin working the lure fast to make the fish think its prey is trying to escape.

One style of popper particularly favored for big striped bass and giant red drum from New England through North Carolina is the pencil popper. These lures have a tapered design that puts their weight at the rear. This weight orientation makes them cast a mile, even through a strong headwind. Pencil poppers are generally large, ranging from 8 to 12 inches long, which makes them ideal for mimicking an adult bunker splashing around the surface. But there is a little more to working one of these oversized topwaters than just jerking the rod tip.

Notice the wide trail of nervous water this large pencil popper leaves in its wake. It's this kind of surface disruption that makes these lures a wise choice for mimicking an injured adult bunker. Photo: Melissa Pulicare

Pencil poppers bob in the water at an angle unlike most other topwaters. Instead of floating horizontally, the wider rear end of the lure dangles below the surface, while the thinner head sticks almost vertically above the surface. To achieve the proper action, you need to get the lure moving like a seesaw, where the head comes farther out of the water and slaps forward, then the heavy tail of the lure dunks back below the surface. To do so, make the cast and wedge the rod butt between your knees. With your nonreeling hand, grab the rod ahead of the grip, about 6 inches below the first guide. As you reel, whip the rod back and forth aggressively. This technique works particularly well with a fiberglass rod that has a softer, more flexible tip.

Some of them are cherished more as works of art than fishing tackle, but they can be deadly when used correctly. Because surface swimmers have a lip more commonly seen on diving lures, many anglers expect them to run subsurface, and to that end, they'll reel them in too fast. Swimmers should be reeled slowly and steadily to maximize their action. These lures wobble and roll side-to-side, creating a V-wake behind them as they move across the surface. This presents the image of a very life-like baitfish snaking across the surface, and if bass are around, explosions abound.

Diving Swimmers

Diving swimmers encompass a vast range of lures that come in all shapes and sizes, and are most often referred to by surf fishermen as "plugs." These lures can be molded in plastic or carved from wood, but one thing they share is a lip that allows them to dive to a preset depth. What this lip also controls is how tightly or erratically these lures wobble and shake on the retrieve. Plugs are some of the most effective lures to for mimicking baitfish both in profile and action.

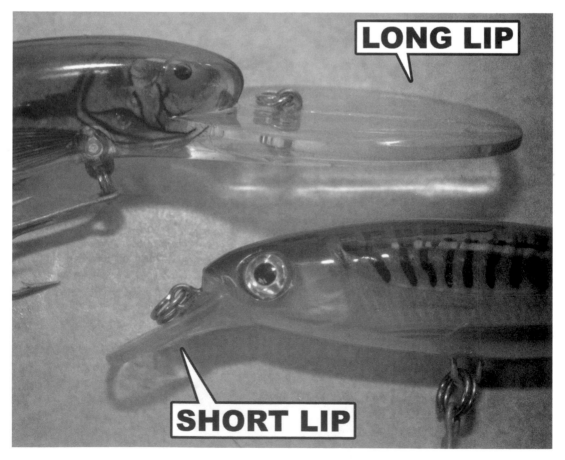

The length of a plug's lip determines how deep it runs and how tightly it wobbles on the retrieve.

The longer a plug's lip, the deeper it will dive. There are lures on the market designed to dive to 30 feet or more. There are also plugs that sink. However, even though it's possible to find deep holes in the surf, beaches are generally shallow overall, so a plug that dives much more than 8 feet or sinks quickly will rarely be of use. In fact, deep-diving or fast-sinking plugs can actually be counterproductive, as they'll dig into the sand, causing them to swim incorrectly. Understand that a deep hole in the surf may only be 20 feet wide and equally long. Although a plug that dives deep might run true in the hole, it will have such a narrow window in which to do so, you'll only get a couple seconds of proper action in the zone. Plus, as the surf is roiled and baitfish are constantly cruising through at different depths, a fish sitting at the bottom of that hole is likely to shoot up to grab a lure riding just under the surface. The same cannot be said for water 30 feet deep offshore. Here, it becomes far more critical to get your lure down to the fish, as they're not likely to rise to an offering swimming high over their heads.

The majority of the most popular surf plugs will float and have a short lip designed to keep them riding 1 to 3 feet below the surface. While there is not much mystery or skill involved in using them, they are very versatile. A simple, steady retrieve is all it takes to get a swimmer working, and quite often this happens to be the most productive retrieve. However, these lures can also be reeled quickly to mimic a fleeing baitfish. Slowed down with occasional pauses, a plug can match the action

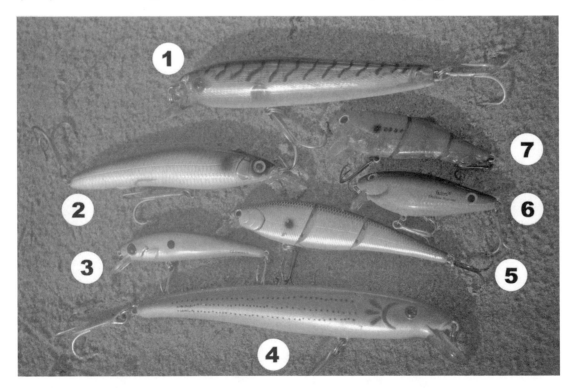

Diving swimmers—better known as plugs—are generic replicas that resemble multiple baitfish, while others are tailored to be close copies of specific species. 1. Rebel Wind Cheater, 2. Yo-Zuri Live Bait Minnow, 3. Bomber 14AF Long A, 4. Bomber Long A Magnum, 5. Lucky Craft Pointer 125, 6. Heddon Shallow Runner, 7. ABT Gladiator Shad. Photo: Melissa Pulicare

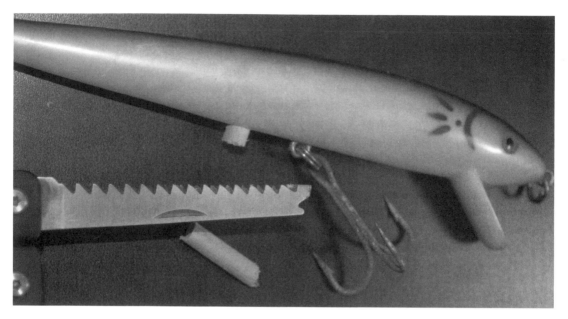

By tapering one end of a piece of wooden dowel, you create a cork for stopping the hole in a loaded plug.

tion as it floats. Though plugs are effective right out of the box, loading is something you may want to play with down the road.

Lipless Plugs

Not all plugs that are designed to run below the surface have lips. Many of these lures are classified as "suspending twitchbaits," as they sink slowly and move much like a topwater Spook, darting from side to side as you jerk the rod tip. Because of the subtle action you can create by pausing the lure, letting it fall, and changing speed, this plug style is particularly popular among southern and Gulf surfcasters chasing wary species like tarpon and snook that sometimes require real finesse to induce a strike. Sea trout and red drum frequently fall to suspending twitchbaits as well, and while their action mimics a wide variety of baitfish, the lure style doesn't share the same popularity in the Northeast. This is mostly because they work best in calm surf found more frequently from Florida to Texas. Likewise, working them with the 10-foot rods used commonly in the North can be a challenge.

Another style of lipless lure that actually qualifies more as a "crankbait" than a plug is the Rat-L-Trap. These wide-profile baitfish imitators are available in many sizes that allow you to match local forage species. Their bodies are filled with BB-like balls that add weight for casting distance, cause them to sink quickly, and produce a high-pitched rattle as they move through the water. This sound can be heard underwater from very far away, making the Rat-L-Trap an excellent choice for dirty surf conditions. Though this lure is not one of the first that comes to mind when talking about classic surf lures, it's an overlooked addition to the lure bag that many in-the-know surfcasters rely on heavily. They are especially deadly on sea trout and weakfish, though striped bass will also take a swipe.

Lipless plugs, like the MirrOlure Catch 5 (top), have a subtle darting motion favored by southern surfcasters. Rat-L-Traps (bottom) produce a high-pitched rattling that can draw in far-off fish.

Rat-L-Traps are primarily cast out and brought back with a steady retrieve. Occasional jerks will cause them to dart forward, while a pause lets them drop down. One perk of a "Trap" is that you can work it effectively at any level of the water column.

Metal Lures

Metal lures, sometimes called "tins," are time-proven surf killers that not only catch fish, but also offer an advantage few other lures can match. Commonly made from lead or nickel, metal lures are heavy and streamlined, which means on the windiest of days they'll punch through the gusts and get farther out than other lures. On a calm day, you can send a metal far beyond the breakers, making them ideal

Metal lures are a must-have for every surfcaster. While they are one of the best imitators of small baitfish, they also cast a mile through the meanest wind, allowing you to reach fish other lures can't. Photo: Melissa Pulicare

If there is one situation where metal lures fall short it is in dirty water or at night. It's not impossible to catch fish on them in these conditions by any means, but as previously discussed, shiny lures rely on light to flash. Lures like plugs and paddle-tail shads produce lots of vibration as they swim. Therefore, fish can still sense them in dark or dirty water. Metals give off vibration, too, but to a much lesser extent. They are more a visual lure that requires fish to see them in order to draw a strike. Even on bright days, the sun's rays may not penetrate murky water deeply enough for a metal's flash to be seen close to the bottom. But despite this minor shortcoming, I wouldn't recommend hitting any beach without a few metals on hand. I promise there will be times when nothing but a metal will get you into fish.

Soft-Plastic Lures

It would perhaps be fair to say that in recent years, no other style of lure has proven itself in the surf like soft plastics. That's not to say the material is anything new. The plastic worm developed for large-mouth bass anglers has been around since the 1960s, but only in the last 15 years or so have many companies started producing state-of-the-art soft plastics specifically for the saltwater angler. Surf fishermen have benefited greatly, and though plugs and metals once held the title of most widely used surf lures, soft plastics have come on full force and earned their place in every tackle bag.

No small part of their popularity stems from their price tag. For less than the cost of a metal lure or plug, you can purchase an entire bag of soft plastics. Naturally, the trade-off is that they won't last as long as hard lures, especially when toothy bluefish or sea trout abound. But losing one doesn't sting quite so bad as breaking off a $10 plug. And price is not nearly the only appeal. Soft plastics are utterly deadly in the surf. There are thousands on the market, and as with every other lure, many are simply variations on similar design concepts. Here's a look at the styles most important to surfcasters.

BAITFISH IMITATIONS

Along many coastlines, soft-plastic lures that mimic area baitfish are going to be used most heavily. Two of the most popular variations include "finesse style" (sometimes called simply "shads") and "paddle tails." These terms are used to categorize a huge number of lures from various manufacturers, though they share common characteristics.

Finesse-style soft plastics are typically long and slender. Some have a bulging belly with a slot running down its length to help hide the hook point in certain rigging techniques. Others have bellies that come together like edge of a knife. These lures can have split tails, curly tails, or sometimes no tail at all; the body just tapers into a long, wiggly point.

Finesse-style soft plastics can range from a few inches long to a foot long and colors are as vast as brands. Some of the more popular models include Zoom's Super Fluke, Bass Kandy Delights, and Hogy. But regardless of the maker, these lures match a wide range of bait, and they're versatile when it comes to rigging for different situations.

Because distance is often a factor that makes or breaks success, finesse-style soft plastics are usually rigged on a jighead for use in the surf. These leadheads are available in a ton of different weights, colors, and shapes, though the ones I find most universal are standard round and oblong,

Finesse-style soft-plastic lures, sometimes simply called "shads," match a wide variety of baitfish and are available in innumerable sizes, colors, and varying shapes. Shown here is Berkley's Power Minnow.

sometimes referred to as "lima bean" jigheads. Other jighead styles, such as wedge, "boxing glove," and arrow, are more popular along the Gulf and Southern California coasts with anglers chasing halibut, sea trout, and red drum. No matter which style you prefer, it is important to match your jighead to the size of the soft plastic you'll be using. A jighead that's too small may not provide enough weight and will also cause the hook to sit too close to the lure's head. This can greatly affect productivity, as fish that short-strike the lure won't get the hook. Jigheads that are too large will make a lure too heavy and seat the hook back too far, thus hindering the action.

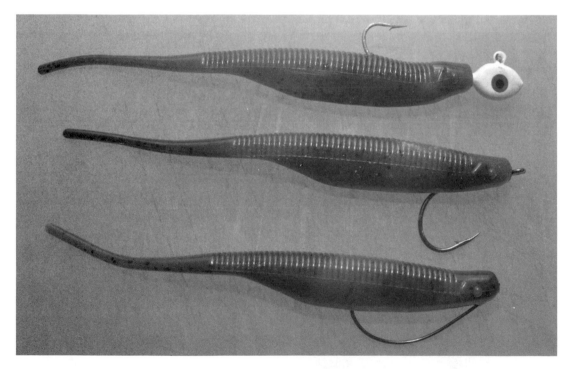

Shown here is the same finesse lure rigged three ways. At the top, the lure is threaded onto a weighted jighead. In the center, a plain J-hook is fed through the nose and out through the belly. On the bottom, a wide-gap hook is seated so the point is hidden. This rigging style is referred to as "weedless," as it reduces the amount of grass the lure collects.

As with paddle-tail soft plastics, the power of the curly tail lies in its rear end. The tail flows like a ribbon as it falls and during the retrieve, creating both vibration and strong visual attraction. To achieve the best action, curly tails should be fished on a jighead that best matches their length. You want the hook to protrude through the lure's center. Weighting the nose is key to getting maximum flutter from the tail when fishing grubs solo, although curly tails can also be incorporated into bait rigs and used in combination with natural squid strips or a live mud minnow.

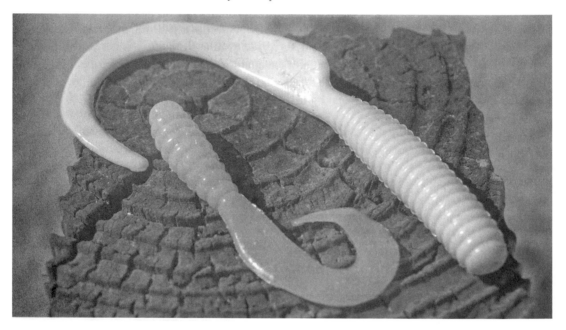

Grubs are one of the most productive soft plastics in all of fishing—not just surf fishing—as they match a wide range of forage gamefish crave. Photo: Melissa Pulicare

The D.O.A. Shrimp continues to be one of the most effective and natural-looking shrimp imitations on the market.

When fishing a grub-and-jig combo, anything goes as far as the retrieve is concerned. If sea worms or shrimp are the main forage at hand, try letting the grub sit on the bottom, imparting occasional flutter with a short hop by lifting the rod tip. Fish will actually pick up the jig as it's sitting still. You can also rip a larger grub across the surface to mimic fleeing mullet or squid. White grubs will catch just about any fish that swims, though you'll find that specific colors do come into play in certain areas. As an example, according to Southern California surfcasting expert Paul Sharman, "motor oil"—an ugly shade of brown with red glitter flakes—is a top grub color for corbina. In Delaware and Maryland, pink is prime for weakfish.

SOFT-PLASTIC SHRIMP

Before soft-plastic lures designed specifically for salt water hit the scene, surf anglers targeting species like snook and sea trout that commonly forage on shrimp didn't have much choice but to mimic this prey with bucktail jigs. That's not to say these jigs didn't work, and as you'll come to learn in this chapter, bucktails are still one of the most productive shrimp and baitfish imitations around. But when Mark Nichols, founder and owner of D.O.A. Lures, brought his soft-plastic imitator to the market, everything changed.

To this day, the D.O.A. Shrimp is considered a staple on the Gulf and southern Atlantic coasts. There may have been a few others before it, but none featured the internal weight that allows the D.O.A. to sink slowly and naturally or move with the same subtle action when you pop the rod tip.

This little flounder helped itself to a Berkley Gulp! Ghost Shrimp in the New Jersey surf. Notice that the lure was reverse-rigged to mimic the natural backward swimming of a live shrimp.

Today there are hundreds of soft-plastic shrimp available in tackle shops, with the Berkley Gulp! Shrimp and Old Bayside Shrimp being two of the most popular. While D.O.A. Shrimp come pre-rigged, many other brands require a jighead or plain hook depending on how you want to present them. When using these lures, remember that shrimp actually swim backward, and though it's not required that you rig them to move this way, some manufacturers make the tail section thicker so it can receive the hook, while the head imparts the action. Fish shrimp in short, slow hops, and don't be surprised when they get inhaled on the fall.

Bucktails can benefit greatly from a trailer. In this case, the jig has been tipped with a curly-tail grub.
Photo: Melissa Pulicare

big stripers on the beach is tipping a white bucktail with a red pork rind trailer, such as those made by Uncle Josh. Can you use a green pork rind? Of course, but red is a staple of the Montauk scene, and proof that niche surfcasting crowds formulate their own patterns and traditions.

Truth be told, there is really no wrong way to fish a bucktail. Most commonly, one of these jigs is reeled back at a moderate pace while whipping the rod tip upward, causing the lure to rise and fall. However, I know surfcasters who reel very slowly, simply dragging the bucktail across the bottom to imitate a shrimp. In some situations, working a bucktail quickly while jerking the rod produces the action that makes gamefish go on the attack. But how you retrieve a bucktail is less important than making sure you've sized your offering to your target species.

Bucktails can weigh more than 8 ounces, though rare is the occasion when you'll need one this heavy in the surf. Though smaller bucktails mean lighter bucktails, don't forget to consider hair length. Small bucktails designed for pompano have their hair trimmed back until it's about even with the bend of the hook. This stops these small-mouthed gamefish from simply nipping at the hair without getting near the hook. Should any species continually short-strike your bucktail, trimming back the hair is a solution.

Tipping bucktails with a red pork rind, like those made by Uncle Josh, is a long-standing Montauk, New York, tradition that catches lots of stripers.

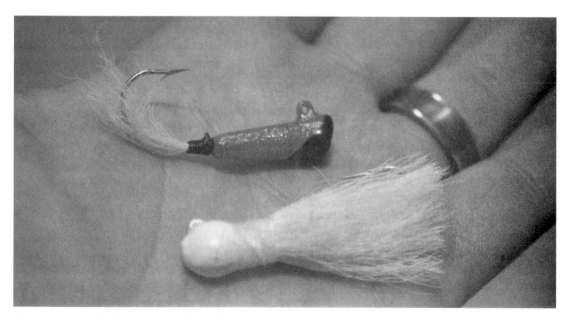

Though designed for freshwater shads, shad darts (top) can technically be considered a form of bucktail; when tipped with a small piece of bait, they work wonders on weakfish and croakers. The other bucktail shown here with a trimmed-down skirt and smaller profile works well on species like pompano.

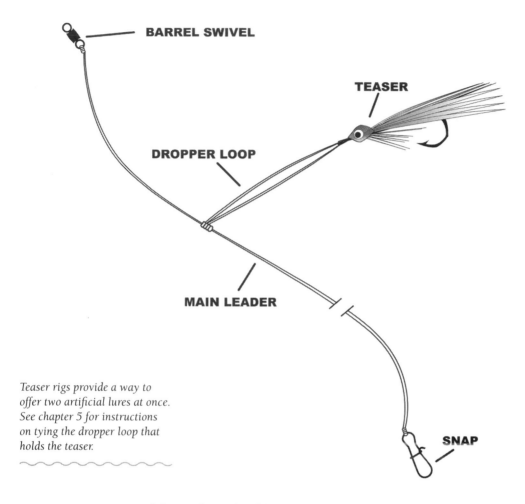

BARREL SWIVEL

TEASER

DROPPER LOOP

MAIN LEADER

Teaser rigs provide a way to offer two artificial lures at once. See chapter 5 for instructions on tying the dropper loop that holds the teaser.

SNAP

you retrieve a teaser rig, fish see a larger baitfish (the main lure) chasing a smaller baitfish (the teaser), which can trigger their natural instinct to attack.

Teaser rigs are very popular in the Northeast with striped bass anglers, though they can be used for species like snook and sea trout. This rig is simply a standard snap and barrel lure leader with a dropper loop (see instructions in chapter 5) tied in the middle to hold the teaser. Simply feed the loop through the eye of the teaser's hook, pass it around the whole teaser, and draw it tight.

When creating a teaser rig, it's important not to make the dropper loop too long or it may get tangled with your main lure. Though teasers can be used with many lures, they work particularly well with paddle-tail soft plastics, swimming plugs, and metals.

Just about any light, thin soft plastic, such as a small curly-tail grub or Red Gill, can be used as a teaser. Lures that are too heavy can affect the swimming ability of the main lure by dragging it down. However, one of the most popular and effective teasers is a saltwater fly called a Deceiver. Typically tied with bucktail or Mylar strands, these flies appear bushy when dry, but thin out when wet. They present the perfect profile of a sand eel or glass minnow, and weigh practically nothing, so they won't change or hurt the action of your main lure.

This small striped bass passed up the metal lure on the end of this rig in favor of the small Red Gill teaser that better matched the bait size in the area. Photo: Melissa Pulicare

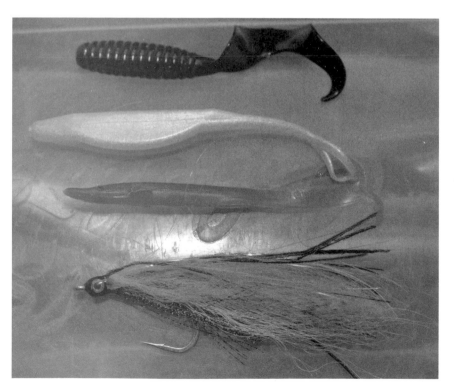

Almost any small, light soft-plastic lure can be used as a teaser, though flies, like the Deceiver shown at the bottom of this assortment, are favorites in the Northeast, as they represent small, slender baitfish very effectively.

Aside from greatly improving the odds that the fish you hook will end up in a photograph or on the dinner table, the ability to tie strong knots will increase your confidence every time you cast. When I'm fishing, I want to be certain that I'm prepared for a monster each time my lure touches down in the waves. To that end, even once you've mastered these knots, check the connection after 10 or 15 casts. Does it feel like there is abrasion on the line near the knot? Have any wraps come undone? These are things to be mindful of on the beach.

With any of the knots in this chapter, you want to put a strong amount of force on them after they're tied by pulling the line and lure or rig you've tied on in opposite directions to see if it slips. As a knot tightens, it can abrade the line or leader you're using, thus weakening the connection. You can avoid this abrasion by wetting a knot with saliva to create a little lubrication before cinching it tight. It's a good habit to start, as it will prolong the life and strength of knots, lines, and leaders. You may also want to put a tiny dab of Krazy Glue or Zap-A-Gap on a knot after tightening. It's not necessary most of the time, but it's all about your confidence. I know surfcasters who will not cast a lure tied on a knot that isn't coated in glue. But just remember that a bad knot covered with superglue is still a bad knot.

Improved Clinch Knot

The improved clinch knot is arguably one of the most, if not *the* most, widely used and versatile connections in fishing. But watch out, because the clinch can bite you. Tied properly it is very strong and highly reliable, but tie it incorrectly and it is one of the most likely knots to fail.

Its popularity stems from a number of factors other than strength. Those include its ability to be tied quickly, and its ability to be created in lines of varying diameters. The improved clinch can be used in all forms of surf fishing, as it is perfect for tying on a hook for use with bait, connecting swivels or snaps within a rig, or connecting any lure. One important point, however, is that I do not recommend tying an improved clinch with braided line. This is because the clinch's strength relies on wraps of line tightening down on the end of the line—known in tying terms as the tag end—and holding it in place. This works well with monofilament or fluorocarbon, as micro-abrasions within these wraps create friction when the knot is tightened. In this case, that slight bit of friction and the abrasive quality of these types of lines actually improves knot strength.

But braided line can be so thin and slick, even an improved clinch you think is securely snug can slip when it counts. As a broad rule of thumb, use an improved clinch when targeting fish weighing up to 20 pounds. It can certainly handle larger specimens, but if you know there is a good chance you'll be connecting with 30-plus-pound fish, I'd opt for a Palomar knot.

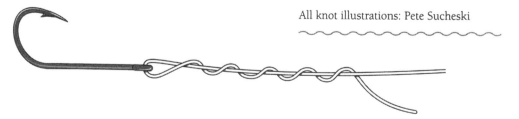

All knot illustrations: Pete Sucheski

Step 1: Pass the tag end through the eye of the hook, lure, or swivel you're tying on, drawing through about 5 inches of line. Make four to six wraps (the thicker the line, the fewer the wraps) around the line or leader with the tag end. You can do so either by winding the tag around the line, or spinning the hook, lure, or swivel you're tying on.

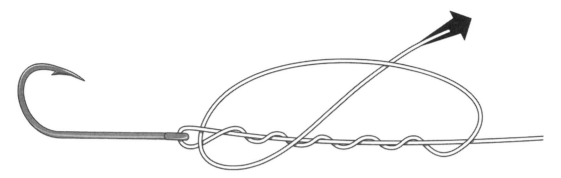

Step 2: Pass the tag end through the small loop created in front of the first wrap at the eye of the hook, lure, or swivel. Once through, pass the tag end back under the large loop it created on the way to the small front loop.

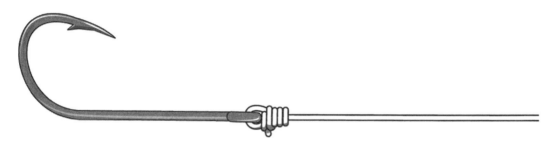

Step 3: Pull the hook, lure, or swivel and main line in opposite directions. The wraps will form into tight coils that draw down the line to lock the tag end in place. Once the knot is cinched tight and secure, trim the tag end close to the coils, leaving a small bit protruding. Do not trim the tag right up to the coils or the knot may slip.

Palomar Knot

Without question, the Palomar is one of the strongest knots you can tie. Its breaking strength is incredible, and unlike the improved clinch knot, the Palomar is safe to tie with braided line. With this being the case, I use it almost exclusively anytime I have to connect braid to any lure or piece of terminal tackle.

Whereas the improved clinch will slip if formed improperly, the Palomar will tighten down under the strain of a fish and sever itself in spots where the line overlaps within the knot. Of course, this problem is avoided when the knot is properly formed. Tied correctly, there is a much better chance your line will snap before the Palomar knot fails. This makes the Palomar an excellent all-around knot for connecting hooks, swivels, or any lure to your line, but when you're specifically targeting larger fish, the knot is a must for added confidence and security to ensure you'll put your trophy on the sand.

In most cases, leaders can be attached by using a Palomar or improved clinch knot to tie the length of leader to one end of a barrel swivel and the main line to the other. However, in certain scenarios you can benefit from skipping the swivel and joining the main line and leader with a uniknot-to-uniknot. Note that this connection should only be used with lines of relatively similar diameter, and would not work well for joining 10- and 80-pound line, as an example.

One major advantage is that the knot this splice creates is slim in profile, so you can reel it through the rod guides and recast without it catching and hindering distance or accuracy. This is handy when fishing with lures at night, as it's not always easy to see a barrel swivel in the dark. If you reel a swivel into the first guide of the rod, it will generally get stuck, requiring you to free it by hand before recasting.

Because of its profile, the uniknot-to-uniknot will also collect less seaweed or grass than a swivel, which can help you get more clean runs in dirty water conditions. And finally, when dealing with soft-striking species, such as flounder or croakers, cutting the swivel out of the equation and using directly joined lines can increase sensitivity, as the tap of a fish can be telegraphed up the line without getting muted by a swivel.

Finally, as discussed in chapter 2, braided line should not be wound directly onto a bare reel spool; it may slip. First wind on a bed of monofilament so the slick braid has something to grab, and then use the uniknot-to-uniknot splice to join the braid and mono together and continue filling the spool.

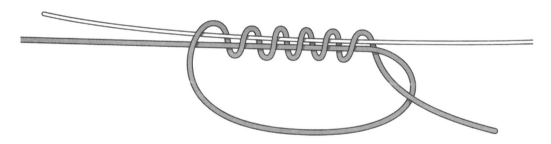

Step 1: Start by laying the end of the main line and end of the leader next to each other, overlapping them by a good 8 to 12 inches. Begin with either the main line or leader, wrapping it five times around itself and the other line.

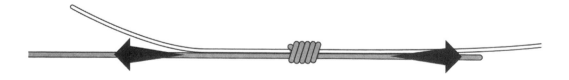

Step 2: Pull gently on the line you wrapped to draw the coils closer together over the other line. Don't cinch down these coils down too tightly.

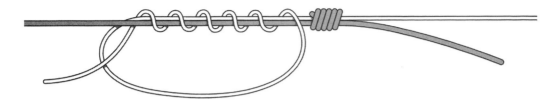

Step 3: Repeat steps 1 and 2 with the end of the other line.

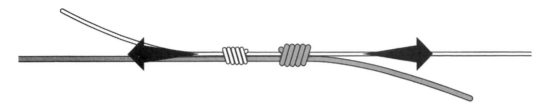

Step 4: Pull the main line and leader sharply in opposite directions.

Step 5: The wraps of each knot should tighten and the pair of coils should jam against each other. Once the knot is secure, trim the tag ends close to the coils.

Nonslip Mono Loop

The nonslip mono loop serves one main purpose, and that is to give more action to lures that don't have as much life-like movement on their own. A few examples of such lures would be bucktail jigs or soft-plastic finesse baits, even small diving plugs. These lures can greatly benefit from riding on a loop of line as opposed to being tied directly with a Palomar knot or improved clinch knot.

Straight knots like these mean the angler has to work the rod a little harder to make such lures wiggle and wobble to their full potential, but tie them on a loop and they can free-swing and slide as they rise and fall between cranks of the reel or jerks of the rod tip. I most often use the nonslip mono loop when targeting fish weighing up to 10 pounds. This is not because it won't hold larger fish, but I find this knot is strongest when tied in lighter lines of 10- to 20-pound-test. If I need a leader of 40- to 50-pound fluorocarbon, it usually means I'm after larger species and will opt for the Palomar knot or improved clinch.

As its name suggest, this knot is most reliable when tied with monofilament or fluorocarbon. I would not recommend tying it in braided line, as there is a good chance it might fail. The nonslip mono loop is an ideal connection that will improve catch rates when using smaller jigs and plugs for flounder, weakfish, sea trout, small red drum, and pompano.

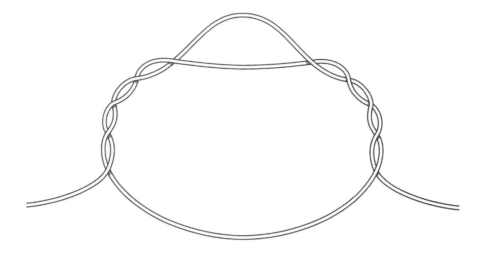

Step 1: First determine where on the leader you want the dropper loop to be positioned. Create a loop of your desired size in the leader at that point. Now make four wraps around one side of the loop with one end of the leader. With the other end of the leader, make four wraps around the other side of the loop. Use your fingers to spread the gap where the wraps on both sides meet.

Step 2: Pull the bottom of the loop up through the gap in the wraps.

Step 3: Pull both ends of the leader in opposite directions. During this step, I find it easiest to hold the loop being created in my mouth to stop it from shortening as the knot draws tight. Note that after completion, you can also snip one end of the loop close to the knot to create a longer single-strand dropper. This cut will not compromise the knot's strength.

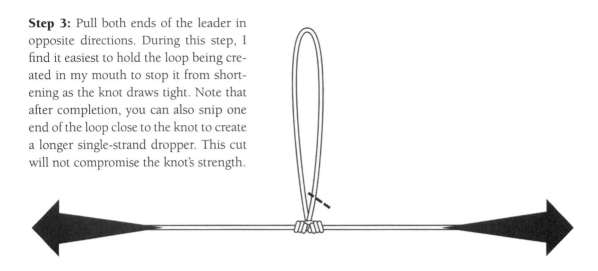

Snell Knot

Both the Palomar knot and improved clinch knot are effective for connecting a hook to a line or leader. However, many bait fishermen prefer to snell their hooks when creating bait rigs. The snell knot is very strong and will rarely pull when tied properly. It is also much more streamlined than the clinch or Palomar, which is useful when you need to feed a hook through a chunk of bait. But there is a reason not everyone uses a snell: It's tricky to tie.

Though there are a few methods for crafting this knot, I've always found the one below to be the easiest and the result stronger than other variations. Another appeal of the snell is that it can be tied with heavier leaders and maintain its strength. This is a knot worth practicing during the off season, but a must-know if you plan on baitfishing for larger species like red drum or striped bass that like big chunk baits and require stout leaders. Hooks must be snelled to the leader with this method before the leader is connected to a swivel or the main line.

Step 1: Feed the leader through the eye of the hook, stopping when there is approximately 6 inches remaining from the rear of the eye down past the hook bend. Bring the tag end around and pass it through the eye from the opposite direction. Pinch the spot on the shank where the leader overlaps to hold it in place. There should be enough line that a loop is created below the shank.

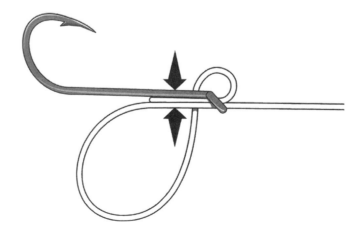

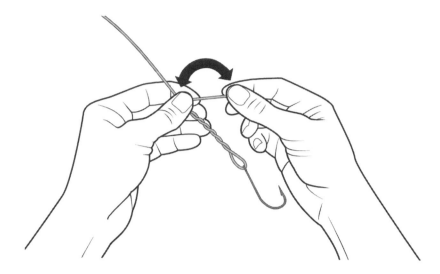

Step 3: When the twists have been locked off, do not clip the tag end. Clipping can produce a sharp snag that may potentially cut the fishing line or injure your hands if you grab it. Instead, rock the tag end back and forth where it meets the coils until it breaks on its own.

Shown here is the completed haywire twist.

Arbor Knot

The arbor knot isn't a connection that will come in handy on the water as much as during pre-trip tackle preparation. Its one purpose is for tying the end of your fishing line to the empty spool of your reel prior to winding on fresh line. The arbor will draw tighter than simple overhand knots and stop the line from sliding around the spool once you begin reeling.

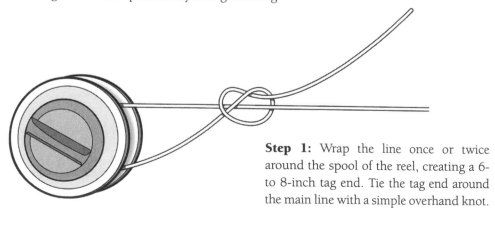

Step 1: Wrap the line once or twice around the spool of the reel, creating a 6- to 8-inch tag end. Tie the tag end around the main line with a simple overhand knot.

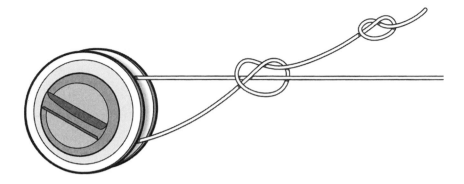

Step 2: Tie a second overhand knot near the tip of the tag end.

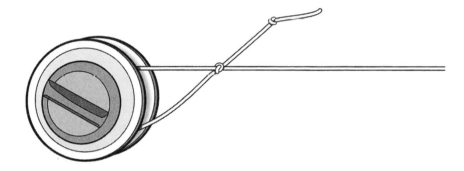

Step 3: Cinch both overhand knots tight. Now pull the main line away from the spool. The line will slip through the first overhand until the second overhand knot jams against the first on the spool. Trim the tag end close to the knot.

on the structure of the beach. They've ruined beach communities, permanently closed off inlets, and at the same time formed countless new points and islands. It is perpetual motion all year long, and therein lies a key difference between good fishing spots on the surf and on any other body of water. If you find a good stretch of deep water and are catching fish in it all season, it is very possible that the spot won't exist at all next year. Beaches are constantly changing. One storm that brings extra-violent surf can make a deep beach shallow in a matter of days. This is, of course, a blessing and a curse, since it also means new productive spots can open up at any time.

Tides Simplified

Tides, in simplest terms, are rises and falls of the ocean's level caused by both the rotation of the earth and gravitational pull of the sun and moon. Sounds complex? It is. But the "why" is not nearly as important for the angler to understand for using tides to catch more fish in the surf.

Most coasts experience two low and two high tides daily. There are approximately 12 hours between tides. However, the tide period varies each day; tide times are never set in stone and will change constantly. As an example, if high tide occurs at 8 in the morning, it will not occur at that same time forever. If high tide is at exactly 8:45 AM and 9:26 PM on Monday, by Friday the high tides would occur at approximately 11:45 AM and midnight Saturday. This was calculated using a roughly 20-minute time shift (add 20 minutes to the tide each day) in the 12-hour tidal period. It is far from an exact science, as in some areas there may be a half-hour difference, 10-minute difference, or hour difference. The best way to figure out the tidal swing in your area is to consult local tackle shops or go on the Internet. SaltwaterTides.com is a great website that allows you to choose your area and select dates for which you want tidal information. It gets you in the ballpark, but even these calculated times could vary based on wind, weather, and moon phase.

Whether the tide is high or low is often not as important as how the tide is moving. Any seasoned surfcaster will tell you that moving water is key. The beginning and end of the tide—also known as the top and bottom of a tide—are when either incoming or outgoing water stops moving and goes slack. Slack tide is generally considered the least productive point in any given tide, as the water flow is what moves baitfish and currents that gamefish follow up and down the beach. There are times when a slack tide offers advantages, but that is the exception, not the rule.

Tidal flow is strongest at the beginning of each tide and diminishes toward the end of the tide stage. Therefore, the beginning of the outgoing tide is favored for many species. In this stage, the water is high and begins rushing back out to sea. Likewise, the beginning of an incoming tide can be productive as the tidal surge pushes bait and fish back toward the beach. But here, too, productive tide phases constantly fluctuate. I can recall an entire striped bass season when the action started on one of my favorite beaches at the beginning of the outgoing tide and shut down completely two hours later. The next season, the bite in the same spot was at dead-low water for the first hour of the incoming tide. The more time you spend on the surf, the more you'll begin to recognize seasonal correlations between tides and good fishing at your favorite beaches.

Aside from figuring out the best fishing tide in your area, it is also important to know that tides have just as much, if not more, to do with shaping a beach as waves. These forces combined carve depressions, build up sandbars, and form channels that act as gamefish highways. Always take the time to examine the areas you intend to fish at all tidal stages. Even if the fishing is best at high tide, low tide phases can reveal structures that you may not have seen or been able to identify just by reading the waves.

Using the Moon

While the earth's rotation and the sun's gravitational pull both affect tides, no other factor has as much influence on them as the moon. This is important to keep in mind for a few reasons. First, new moon and full moon periods will cause higher and lower tides than average, as the gravitational pull of these moon phases is more extreme. This is good information to know, as it could mean that a spot you easily access at a normal high-tide level will be harder to reach. On the other hand, a spot that produces well at a normal low tide may not have enough water in it to hold fish during a full or new moon phase.

Because new and full moon phases cause more significant tide swings, the pull they create will also increase currents running along the beach. This can be a good or bad thing depending on the particular spot you're fishing. In some cases, increased tidal current can draw more bait into an area and bring more gamefish with it. But in spots where success depends on getting lures or baits near a piece of structure, heavy tidal flow can hinder your ability to keep your offering in the zone. Likewise, strong currents can make it more of a challenge to get a lure or bait to the proper depth. If fish are holding deep during full or new moon phase, it's often necessary to increase the weight of your lure or sinker.

It's important to understand how moonlight changes gamefish behavior. Large fish that are wary, notably striped bass and weakfish, are more inclined to feed close to the beach during the dark of night. Shadows and moonlight can make them more cautious. Therefore, many seasoned surfcasters opt to target trophy fish during new moon phases when the night sky is at its darkest. Interestingly, new and full moon periods can also make catching some species nearly impossible. Both snook and black drum spawning is triggered by these phases, so if you are planning to target either at these times, don't bother. When the moon is right for romance, these species leave the surf and head for bays and inlets to breed. A quick Internet search for moon phases will give you a plethora of current calendars you can use to track the moon.

Decoding the Waves

We've already discussed how waves behave in deep water, and how they stack and crash when they reach the shallow bottom near the beach. Now it's time to use that information to identify top fish-holding areas. Though there are situations where shallow water has an advantage, for the most part you need to find the depressions or troughs close to the beach, and you can do so just by watching the waves.

TROUGHS

On many beaches, a sandbar—a long sloping mound of sand—creates a trench or trough down the length of the beach. This bar, commonly referred to as the outer bar, is the first spot where incoming waves rise and break. Pick a wave breaking far out and follow it with your eyes. Study it closely as it

All beaches eventually drop off. This drop-off occurs right behind where waves first begin to break, in many cases just beyond the outer bar. Of course, this drop-off can be hundreds of yards from dry sand or within easy casting distance. On flat, shallow beaches where troughs and depression are not present, getting your bait or lure past the waves and into the deep water can mean the difference between catching fish and being shut out. Here's where that long, 10-foot rod comes in handy—but depending on the distance to the drop, it might not be enough reaching power.

On North Carolina's Outer Banks, surfcasters looking to beach monster red drum in the fall know that these fish follow the beach along the backside of the waves. It's not uncommon to see them wade 80 yards or more through chest-deep troughs to reach far-off sandbars that will put them within the proper casting distance of the fish. Wading far out to reach the drop should be done with care, as in some cases you may not hit water deeper than your ankles all the way out, while in others strong waves may be hitting you chest-high on the approach. Most often you'll find that you need to wade a bit to reach the drop, and then walk your rod back to the beach after the cast if using bait.

CHANGING CONTOURS

Understand that the tide will play heavily into your ability to reach productive casting zones. That's why it's important to study your favorite beaches at all tide stages. What you often learn is how the tide changes your access.

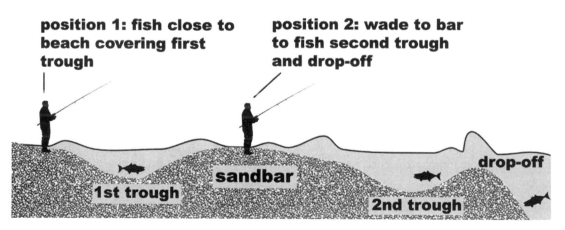

position 1: fish close to beach covering first trough

position 2: wade to bar to fish second trough and drop-off

drop-off

sandbar

1st trough

2nd trough

Tide will often dictate your best approach. At high tide, Position 1 allows you to cover the inshore trough. When the water drops at low tide, move to Position 2 to cover the offshore drop.

As an example, at high tide, you might fish from the beach, concentrating your efforts on a trough close to your feet. During this tide stage, it may be dangerous—or downright impossible—to attempt wading out farther. Likewise, it's not smart to wade through a trough without fishing it first. Some of my biggest surf-caught stripers have struck within 5 feet of the tip of my rod. Work close first, then let the tide dictate your next move.

As the tide falls, that first trough will shallow, allowing you to safely cross to the sandbar on the other side. Once there, you can now easily cast to a trough that has formed farther offshore, or reach the drop on the backside of the waves.

At high tide, the water in these troughs might be too deep to allow wading to the far side of the sandbar. At the same time, during high water, these same troughs can hold big fish right at your feet.

But keep this warning in mind before wading out far: The tide will eventually change again, and you don't want to end up caught in deep water. Wading out in the surf must revolve first and foremost around your comfort level. If something doesn't feel right to you, turn around and head back to the beach. Wading safety has much to do with gut instincts whether you're dealing with the surf or a trout stream. If the depth doesn't seem safe to you, if you don't like your footing, or if you just have a hunch that reaching an intended spot will put you in harm's way, bail out. No fish is worth risking injury or death.

FINDING THE RIPS

With a keen eye and a bit of info on how beach currents works, you can also identify underwater structure that may not even be visible at low tide. Underwater structure along seemingly flat beaches occurs more often on rocky coastlines, like those found in New England where rocks and boulders fall away from the shore. However, even a hump of sand or debris washed in by the waves can produce what is called a "rip." And rips are one of the most fish-producing types of formations you can find.

A rip forms when water moving under the surface suddenly smacks into an underwater obstruction. When the current hits, the obstruction forces water up to the surface, creating a patch of nervous, rippled water visible to the naked eye. A rip can be a few yards long when the underwater obstruction, perhaps a few rocks or an old dock piling, is small. But in areas of high current and rocky bottom, such as Montauk Point in New York, rips can go on for hundreds of yards and produce rather large standing waves.

The reason rips are so productive for anglers is that they act as natural bait catchers. Baitfish traveling with the current get caught in the rip, become disoriented, and are pushed up to the surface where gamefish await an easy meal. Rips frequently offer excellent action with topwater lures, as fish slash and attack anything that moves across the roiled surface. But that doesn't mean rips shouldn't

During this outing, there was so much seaweed in the water that it clung to the line during the retrieve. This much debris in the surf can make fishing completely unproductive. Photo: Melissa Pulicare

In dirty water, you have to focus on the fish's sense of smell and ability to pick up vibration with their lateral line. That means using strong-smelling baits and throwing lures that the fish can "feel" rather than see. Lures like soft-plastic shads with a paddle tail, lures that feature a spinner blade, or those that rattle will up catch rates in low-visibility conditions as they emit vibration fish can sense from a distance. Even in dirty water, gamefish can track such lures. Though baits naturally give off an odor fish can follow to the offering, it might be worth enhancing it further by dousing the bait in bunker oil, shrimp oil, Berkley's Gulp! attractant, or Smelly Jelly with a scent that matches the local forage.

There are, however, a few instances where dirty water is a desired surf condition. Most notably, surfcasters chasing pompano in Florida often seek out patches of cloudy water. Note that there is a difference between patches of cloudy water and an entire beach of "chocolate milk." These patches, formed by slightly rough surf, are preferred by pompano because they disorient crustaceans, allowing the fish to attack under the cover of poor water clarity. Likewise, hot spots for redtail surf perch in Oregon and Washington are often found in areas of dirty water.

"Dirty water tells you there is some kind of current blockage, usually a spit of shallower bottom," says veteran Northwest surfcaster Kelly Corcoran. "Troughs form behind these spits and the perch hang in them to feed. These troughs also protect the fish from fast current moving across the beach."

On the Texas Gulf coast, dirty water can be a surfcaster's friend as well, especially if kingfish—a long, toothy predator in the mackerel family—is the desired catch. Though kingfish are not a commonly surf-caught species, they frequently hunt where dirty water meets clean water, which is known as a "color break." If a color break occurs just beyond the waves, it can act as a magnet that draws kings right to the beach. Baitfish will hang on the dirty side of a break using the cloudy water as protection, while kingfish patrol the clean edge waiting for the bait to move into the water with higher visibility.

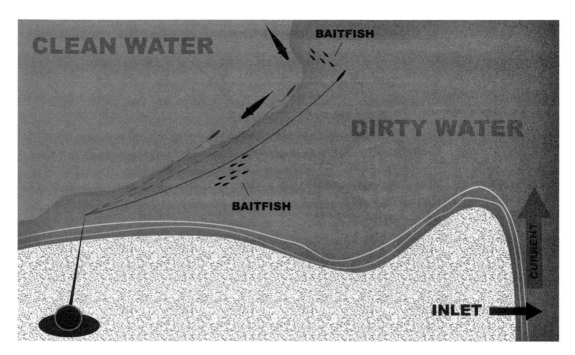

Gamefish will patrol a "color break" where clean water meets dirty water. Work a color break by casting lures into the dirty water and retrieving them along the clean edge.

Kingfish are not the only gamefish to use color breaks for hunting. Snook, striped bass, and bluefish are just a few others that will patrol a dirty water edge. However, color breaks that present themselves in a way that allows anglers on the beach to take advantage of them are not a common occurrence. Most often they will be found adjacent to bay-draining inlets. As the tide pulls dirty water out of the bay, it meets clean ocean water and mushrooms out, snaking in along the beach.

Birds: Fish Finders in the Sky

You can become an absolute ace at reading a beach and finding productive water by learning the nuances of deciphering the waves and tide, but sometimes Mother Nature makes the job of finding fish easier. Nothing is more pleasing to a surfcaster than walking up over the dunes and being greeted by massive flocks of birds working the surf line. The cawing and screeching, clattering and flapping is music to our ears. The species of birds that are working the surf will change with geography, but their presence is as exciting to a sea trout hunter on the Gulf coast as it is to a striper hunter in Rhode Island. Birds point out the fish.

When a flock of birds is diving, dipping low, and flying erratically in a tight cluster, what is usually happening is that gamefish working under the surface are attacking a school of baitfish. In an attempt to escape the slaughter, the baitfish will swim up and often break the surface. When this happens the birds can grab an easy meal. This is known in surf-speak as a "bird blitz," and although a blitz can stay stationary for a long time, more often than not you'll see the birds moving up or down the

Picking up the scent from a moving school of baitfish doesn't occur often, but smelling the aftermath of an attack on baitfish is rather common. When gamefish move through a school of bait, cutting and slashing as they go, the oils in that bait are released into the water, sometimes creating a slick on the surface. These slicks can have an odor reminiscent of watermelon, and the narrower a slick, the more recently it was made. The wider the slick, the more time it's had to disperse. With that in mind, it is actually possible to follow a slick down the beach like an arrow, to feeding fish. This, however, mainly occurs when the water is very calm with limited wave action.

Surfers and Surf Fishermen

Surfers and anglers have historically butted heads over who has the right-of-way on the beach. It's true that when surfers are out in large numbers, not only is it hard to cast around them, but the productivity of the spot will suffer as well. Unfortunately, much the same structures, winds, and tides good for surfcasters appeal to surfers. But I thought it was worth sharing a story that may change your attitude toward wave riders, or at least stop you from blowing a fuse if they're parked in your favorite spot.

Though surfers can seem like a nuisance, they get farther off the beach than fishermen and often spot bait or schools of gamefish that you can't see. Talk to them, as their insight can occasionally help you out.
Photo: Darren Dorris

Years ago, I drove two hours to fish near one of my favorite jetties—only to arrive and find a dozen surfers bobbing in the swells combing over the deep hole I intended to fish. Frustrated, I sauntered down the beach, looking for another spot, though my heart was broken. About an hour later, having caught nothing, I walked back near the surfers just as one of them was heading to his car.

"Did you get any of those big bluefish?" he asked.

I was shocked. "No. I haven't caught anything or even seen a hint of bait," I replied.

"Go down the beach the other direction," he said. "When we got here there was a bunch of baitfish right where we're surfing, but we spooked it out. It's stacked up on a sandbar just south of us now and we keep seeing blues flashing as they come in to grab some."

I thanked him and headed down where he instructed. I fired a long cast with a metal lure and connected right away. Had the surfers not been out there, I would have never seen any evidence of these fish from my view on the beach. Surfers spend lots of time waiting for waves at or just beyond the reach of a good cast, which means they sometimes spot bait and gamefish that you can't. This wasn't an isolated incident.

A few seasons later I had come up short on striped bass on a beach in northern New Jersey. When I saw a surfer get out of the water, this time I made the approach.

"See anything out there?"

"Yup," he said as he dried himself off. "They're coming. Looks like stripers rolling. They were way out there an hour ago, but they're starting to get a little closer. I'd stick around if I were you."

I did, and an hour later those bass were almost rolling at my feet. Seeing that the beach can be an overwhelming place to figure out, sometimes it's better to make friends rather than enemies with surfers.

Chapter 7

Surf Fishing and the Weather

Fishing by the Weather Report

There is an old belief that fish bite better in the rain. That's not untrue, but more realistically, the low barometric pressure associated with rain is what makes them feed more heavily. It's also been said that fish don't eat on a sunny day at high noon. Well, if the wind is right and baitfish are stacked up on the beach, gamefish in the surf don't really care what time it happens to be. But weather can play a huge role in productivity on the beach, so having a basic understanding of how wind, pressure, and temperature affect the fish and fishing conditions will only help you pick your days wisely. Of course, weather is a very complex subject, but have no fear. You need not have a background in meteorology to figure out how to use it to you advantage.

Sunny skies and tranquil seas do not always offer the best conditions for the fish, even if they're best for the fisherman. Rough surf and wind can actually be a beach angler's friend.

Many people look for a sunny, warm, bluebird day to plan a fishing trip. If you're bringing the family along, hoping for this weather report may not be a bad thing, as introducing kids to the sport revolves heavily around them being comfortable on the water. This is not to suggest that you won't catch anything or that only miserable weather conditions breed good surf action. Rather, it sheds light on that fact that just because a particular day happens to be appealing to a fisherman doesn't mean it's as appealing to the fish. Weather is just one more piece of the puzzle that should fit into place when a serious outing is in the works. I even know surfcasters who will fake sick at the office or shirk family obligations simply because the latest weather report says the wind will change to a more favorable direction in the afternoon. When it comes to surf success, perhaps no other factor is as important as the wind.

The Wind

Before diving into how wind affects surf fishing, let's clear up how wind direction is designated, as I've found the weather report often confuses novice anglers. A prevailing wind is classified by the direction it is blowing *from,* not blowing toward. This designation is often misread, as rookies assume a north wind is blowing south to north, when in fact it's the other way around. Wind is not a bad thing on the beach, and it's one more reason why surf fishermen have somewhat of an advantage over boaters. A strong wind may make offshore conditions too rough for them, but that same wind could produce epic action from the sand.

The most productive wind direction is all relative to location, as what's best on one shoreline can be totally wrong 50 miles up the coast. Prime directions can also change by season, but there are no doubt staple producers in every region. To better understand how location and wind correlate, refer to the illustration of the New Jersey and Long Island, New York, coastlines. The example set here will apply to any area, as points, capes, and shoreline orientation will alter what is considered a good wind direction.

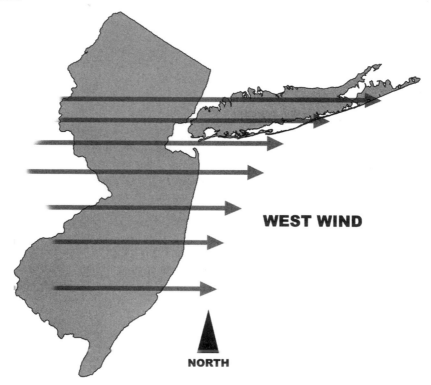

This illustration depicts the west wind blowing over land out to the ocean. On East Coast shorelines running north to south, a west wind will typically produce calm beach conditions with small waves and a flat sea surface beyond. On the West Coast, an east wind would have the same effect. However, as you'll notice, Long Island's oceanfront shoreline runs east to west, so a west wind will blow straight down the beach and not generate the same calm.

On north-to-south coastlines, a west wind can be very productive, particularly in the Northeast during the fall when bluefish, stripers, and pelagic species are migrating south. Both adult and peanut bunker will actually swim into the wind, as opposed to other bait that swims with it. That means a westerly blow can potentially put bunker and the gamefish chasing them a short cast away. Calm conditions associated with this wind direction also make it excellent for topwater lure presentations, as there is usually little wave action to muffle the splash and bubble trail these artificials produce.

Even a very stiff west wind can have little effect on surfcasters, whereas hard gusts directly from the east can make casting a challenge. I've driven to the beach in 30-plus-mile-an-hour west winds, my truck getting blown all over the road, only to walk out onto the beach an feel little evidence

On the East Coast, a west wind that blows over land onto the ocean typically produces calm beach conditions with a flat surface and minimal waves.

Adult and peanut bunker swim into the wind, so a calm west-wind day can bring them right to your feet where gamefish follow and attack. Photo: Stan Kosinski

of the gusts. Oceanfront homes, trees, and even dunes can be enough to knock down a west wind and push it over your head. Despite a hard wind on higher ground, the first few hundred yards of surf can still be pancake-flat.

On the East Coast, an east wind can push bait that's hanging offshore onto the beach, though an easterly that's too stiff can make casting a challenge seeing that it would be blowing directly in your face on a north-to-south coastline. This is where a metal lure becomes your best ally. What is classically considered the best throughout much of the Northeast and mid-Atlantic states is wind blowing from the northeast. Light to moderate northeast wind especially makes for great fishing conditions, as it will push bait to the beach, have you casting at an angle to the blow, and roil the surf to disorient baitfish without making it too rough fish effectively. At the same time, there are instances when hard northeast winds can create incredible action in the surf, particularly a day or two before a nor'easter on the East Coast. One theory as to why the approach of inclement weather turns on a bite is because fish anticipate strong winds dirtying the water, thus making it more difficult to find food.

Though light to moderate northeast wind is a favorite of Northeast surfcasters, rough northeast winds can also produce amazing fishing. This photo was taken at New York's Montauk Point the day before a nor'easter pounded the coast.

On the Atlantic coast, a south wind for the most part is considered the least favorable wind for surf fishing, though exceptions do occur in some niche areas. One main problem with a south wind is that it causes upwelling, whereby colder, denser water is pushed up from the depths, rapidly cooling the surface temperature. In some cases, this can be a blessing that extends fishing seasons. As an example, frequent south winds from Maryland through New Jersey in late June can keep the inshore water cooler, therefore more suitable to striped bass that may stick around longer before heading north for the rest of the summer. However, south winds generally present poor surf conditions on north-to-south shorelines, as they can coincide with strong waves and also dirty the water. Some anglers, particularly from Virginia through Maryland, prefer this dirty water during the summer months for species like croakers and kingfish, though by and large, overly rough surf combined with poor water clarity spells tough fishing.

While a south wind will push cold water to the surface, sustained north winds will knock it back down deep and raise surface temperatures. A decent north-wind period can really help to kick off spring seasons along much of the East Coast, as most bait and gamefish movements are based on rising temperature this time of year. East and west winds can move water temperatures up and down, though to a lesser extent than north and south winds. These winds typically push surface water more than anything, which can help or hurt anglers depending on the season. For example, according to Florida surf expert Mike Conner, pompano fishermen hope for sustained west winds in Georgia and the Carolinas as fall turns to winter. Although the air temperature may be cooling this time of year, surf temperatures in these regions can remain relatively warm. A west wind will blow the warm surface water out to sea, thus prompting pompano cruising the wave line to head south, right onto the lines of waiting Florida anglers. However, this wind may be a blessing to Central Florida surfcasters, but can end the pompano season for Carolina and Georgia fishermen. Likewise, this same effect can be a nuisance in the summer or fall when a good Spanish mackerel, false albacore, or bonito bite has taken shape on the beach. These species are less tolerant of quick temperature changes, so a sustained west wind can send them offshore quickly. With that said, any sustained winds have a negative effect on a fishery in some way. There needs to be fairly consistent change to maintain balance. A day or two of west wind will not usually cool water temperatures so drastically that it alters fishing, just like a day or two of south wind, especially if it's light, doesn't automatically mean the surf will chill off to the point of bad fishing. Even a favored wind like the northeast can be a problem if it persists too long. The surf can get rough and warm, and fish not adapted to these conditions may move up or down the coast, or offshore, permanently.

What can alter surf conditions drastically and rapidly are major storm systems like hurricanes. Surfcasters often say that a hurricane can make or break an entire fall season, and there's a lot of truth to the theory. If the fishing has been slow, the wind and rough seas associated with a hurricane can jump-start the action. If the fishing is already good, a hurricane can alter the conditions so quickly, the fish move on and the season gets cut short. Long periods of strong winds, a hurricane, or a nor'easter have the most critical effects during transitional times toward the end of a season. In the spring as many seasons begin to get under way, major weather events may delay the arrival of gamefish by a week or two, but because the water and air are naturally heating anyway, they don't really have the potential to stop a migration or cause fish to skip over an area.

Understand that there is really no such thing as the "wrong wind," just wind that is more or less favorable for success. Hectic schedules may only allow you to hit the beach on certain days a few times a season, and I wouldn't skip a day over the wind direction if it's not easy for you to make a trip. In truth, I've caught plenty of fish during wind conditions that don't normally coincide with prime fishing. Likewise, don't automatically rule out a day that is forecast to have stronger winds. Naturally, gale-force onshore winds can make fishing unsafe, but a stiff blow coming at an angle onto the beach can be worth taking a little extra salt spray in the face.

Barometric Pressure

Barometric pressure—also known as air pressure or atmospheric pressure—may sound like a complicated subject, but it can be broken down pretty easily and I believe it's essential for an angler to comprehend, even though there are many theories and opinions on how drastically it affects fishing productivity. In simplest terms, barometric pressure is the pressure exerted on a given area of the earth's surface by the weight of the air. This pressure also pushes on the surface of the ocean. One thing that most fishing experts agree on is that barometric pressure has little if any effect on deep-water saltwater fish, as they are already dealing with drastic water pressure far greater than air pressure. But the surf in most areas is less than 20 feet deep. Therefore, air pressure has more potential to alter fish behavior.

Much the same as a moving tide is generally more important than whether it's high or low, barometric pressure benefits a surfcaster most when it's rising, falling, or fluctuating throughout the day. Long periods of high or low pressure can slow feeding. High pressure is associated with weather favored by beachgoers, which is something to keep in mind when hitting the surf in the summer. Those weekend spans of sun and cloudless skies might be great for swimming, but they are not necessarily as good for fishing.

Long periods of high barometric pressure produce clear, sunny skies great for beachgoers, but not often as favorable for surfcasters. Photo: Rick Bach

One theory as to why long high-pressure periods slow the fishing is that the air pressure pushes on a fish's swim bladder, expanding it and making the fish feel full. Although there is much debate to as to whether or not that's really the case, many anglers will slow down presentations with lures during high-pressure periods, or constantly change retrieve styles, adding subtle movements. If fish feel full, therefore making them less likely to strike, many believe that slowing down so they don't have to chase, or creating a slightly different action will turn on a bite. It is also believed that high-pressure periods push fish toward cover or into deeper water. I believe this has less to do with actual high pressure than the clear skies with which it's associated. Fish don't like to be exposed, and many also like to ambush prey, which is more difficult when bright sun lights up the shallow surf. This is much more important on calm beaches, such as those throughout the Gulf, where red drum and sea trout will hold in one place instead of roaming the surf line. During high-pressure periods, it's wise to seek these fish in deeper depressions or around any kind of beach structure that might provide some cover. But throughout the Atlantic, species like bluefish and even striped bass when they're chasing bait hard won't all stack up around jetties or push to deep water. Wave action is actually a form of cover that roils the sand and churns the water so much that even on the brightest day, gamefish in the surf line won't feel completely exposed.

Low barometric pressure is associated with cloud cover, rain, and storms, and just like high pressure, long periods of it can slow feeding activity. But perhaps there is no more favorable pressure situation than a falling barometer. If the weatherman says there is a rain system moving into your area, action on the beach can be stellar starting approximately 24 hours before that front moves in. Barometric pressure can change very quickly. Even a passing storm can drop the pressure significantly, and it will start rising again as soon as it has passed through. Minutes before the storm hits, fish can go on a feeding tear. Of course, safety comes first, and I'd never recommend standing on the beach holding a fishing rod during a storm. But if you do happen to ride one out in your truck, or can get to the beach immediately after a storm passes, the switch from low to rising pressure can also get fish chowing down.

A rainbow appears over the beach in Delaware after a passing storm. Falling barometric pressure associated with approaching rain can make gamefish highly active. Photo: Floyd Morton

Not only do fish seem to feed most heavily when the pressure is falling, they also tend to lose a lot of their wariness. This makes them less likely to scrutinize baits and lures, and more likely to react to movement alone. Many anglers fishing a falling barometer are quick to tie on topwater lures, as this is arguably one of the best times to draw surface strikes. While lures may need to be slowed down during high-pressure periods, falling pressure can mean that a speedy, erratic retrieve will garner more reaction bites.

While falling pressure can provide outstanding fishing, what's more important on an every-day basis is fluctuating pressure. On a clear day, even if not occurring during a long period of high pressure, air pressure will increase to some extent as the sun moves higher in the sky. Low light and less boat traffic make early morning and evening peak times to fish the surf, but the daily pressure at these times of day also factors into the equation. I've witnessed redfish attacking anything that moved at first light, only to refuse every offering at noon. As I was sight fishing, I could literally see my lure move past the fish and do nothing but spook them or go unnoticed. The air and water temperature hadn't changed at all, but my guide suggested that the barometric pressure went stagnant. The very next day from late morning into the afternoon, it would be bright and sunny, and then there would be fleeting periods of cloud cover. The redfish never tired of hitting our lures. This was in water less than 10 feet deep, and though the conditions between the two days weren't incredibly different, the pressure on day two constantly rose and fell instead if remaining flat. Just as a slack tide offers the least productive fishing for many species, air pressure that remains constant during the day is what plays a role in that midday lull anglers talk so much about. But unlike the effects of wind on fishing productivity, which are more calculable and constant, barometric pressure plays a lesser role overall. Is it a good thing to keep in mind when choosing a fishing day? Absolutely, but if a forecast calls for a light northeast wind in October, I'm going fishing even if the pressure is high. During a hard south wind with steadily falling pressure, I'd think twice, because I don't personally believe the pressure will outweigh the negative effects of that particular wind.

Cold Fronts and Warm Fronts

While cold and warm fronts don't play as big a role for saltwater anglers chasing fish in deep offshore waters, they can alter a bite for the surfcaster. The effect air temperature has on water temperature largely revolves around depth and current. As an example, the water temperature of a small pond or lake can be changed significantly over a few days by sudden rises or drops in air temperature. But it will take longer for air temperature to alter the water temperature of a moving stream or river. Like-wise, ocean currents are constantly pushing water around. Even during the winter, eddies can spin off the Gulf Stream—a huge warm-water current running far offshore of the Atlantic coast—and bring pockets of heated seawater closer to shore. Although the surf is always churning, these warm currents rarely have any effect on water along the beach. That's largely because as they move inshore, the water begins to shallow, and shallow water is far more affected by air temperature. Given that the surf is not very deep, following warm and cold fronts can help you catch more fish.

Warm and cold fronts tend to affect surf temperatures more during transitional times of year. In the middle of the summer, a cold snap is not likely to be drastic enough to move fish offshore to warmer water. But in the fall, if striped bass are feeding in the surf and a drastic cold front comes through, it can be enough to make them seek more favorable water temperatures farther off the beach or by moving up or down the coast. In the spring when the surf is just waking up in many areas, warm fronts are an obvious blessing.

As bays and estuaries are shallower than the ocean, they'll heat much more quickly as winter turns to spring. Bays with dark mud bottom heat especially quickly, as the mud will trap and hold heat more efficiently than sand or rock. During spring warm fronts, fishing the surf close to an inlet during a falling tide can help you catch your first fish of the year. Though the air temperature may not raise the water temperature on the beach, the outflow of heated bay water can bump it up a few degrees and turn on the fish.

Cold fronts are often associated with low pressure, and while the water temperature drops they can induce may cause fish to push out of the surf, the period from 24 hours right up to a few hours before a cold front hits can provide excellent fishing. Fish can sense the change in atmosphere, and if they're foraging on bait in the surf, they will try to get their fill before a cold front moves that bait or forces them to move off to deeper water. Because cold fronts typically move through an area more quickly than warm fronts, fishing can also perk up right after one passes and air pressure begins to rise.

During a cold front, don't assume that the surf is suddenly void of life. Many gamefish species will remain within reach of a surfcaster's line, though a drop in temperature may cause them to slow down and feed much less. When this happens, fishing baits still on the bottom can be the most effective approach, though pay close attention to your line, as strikes can be subtler. Lures can still be effective, though you'd be wise to fish those that maintain enticing action during slow retrieves or while being hopped and paused along the bottom.

The Rain and the Surf

When it comes to surf fishing, rain doesn't mean much other than you being wet on the beach. In fresh water, it is widely believed that the pitter-patter of raindrops on the surface can stir fish like trout and largemouth bass to feed, but in the surf this is not quite the case. Between wave action and the fact that saltwater gamefish always have the option to head out to deeper water, rain isn't likely to induce a bite directly, or make gamefish think they are actually hearing bait on the surface. But rain can play a key role in the surf, especially around inlet mouths.

Many baitfish species have a higher tolerance for and are actually attracted to fresh water. "Sweetwater," as saltwater anglers sometimes refer it to, has more nutrients than salt water. Even certain gamefish, such as black drum, striped bass, tarpon, and snook, have a natural inclination to gravitate toward freshwater influxes. But any species of gamefish can be found near freshwater outflows considering they can create the perfect food chain. Microorganisms on which baitfish feed are drawn to fresh water. Baitfish move in, and gamefish are often right behind them. Though natural freshwater outflows dumping directly into the surf are not that common on the east coast, a few days of heavy rain can create this effect.

As inland creeks and rivers flood with excess rainwater, a larger-than-average push of fresh water will end up in bay and estuary systems. Depending on the proximity of freshwater entry points to an inlet, this can cause a flow of water with decreased salinity to pour out into the ocean. It doesn't take a huge drop in salinity to attract baitfish to the outflow, and the higher the salinity of the bay sys-

Freshwater drainage pipes that spill into the surf can be a hot spot after rainy periods, as the fresh water attracts baitfish—and gamefish aren't usually far behind.
Photo: James Myatt

tem, the more effect the introduction of fresh water can have on the fishery. This is particularly important in South Texas, as the Laguna Madre—the long bay system behind Padre Island National Seashore—is one of the saltiest bodies of water on the planet. Bay anglers look forward to periods of rain, which decrease the salinity and attract gamefish from the Gulf deeper into the bay. But the system also benefits surf anglers fishing the oceanfront beaches of Padre Island, particularly around inlets like those found across the bay from Port Mansfield. Surfcasters here can catch bay-bound fish moving into the inlets. Likewise, during times of drought, fish holding farther back in the bay will move closer to or just outside the passes where the salinity level is less excessive. This scenario can be amplified in locations where the mouth of a river serves as an inlet with a small or narrow bay system. The area around the mouth of Florida's St. Johns River and New Jersey's Manasquan River are just two examples where a massive influx of fresh water can cause a stir in activity along the surf.

As previously noted, it's not very common to find natural sources of 100 percent pure fresh water dumping into the surf, but thanks to technology and infrastructure, there are man-made substitutes as good as a spring stream careening down the dunes into the waves. Many beach communities, particularly those on barrier islands, need to get rid of rainwater somehow. While inland towns rely on storm drains to empty into streams or drainage ditches, many shore towns drain rainwater directly into the ocean via pipelines on the beach. Fish around a pipeline after a heavy rain, and good things are likely to happen. In fact, some of my fondest surf fishing memories are of a beach with a very small drainage pipe up near the dunes. When fresh water was rushing out, it created a short river through the sand, right into the wash. The rainwater would often create a patch of cloudy surf, and never once did I fish there after a rainstorm where there wasn't some type of baitfish splashing and flashing through that cloud. I didn't always catch the stripers I was after, but I scored more often than I struck out. Freshwater drainage pipes typically won't produce any better than other spots when no water is flowing, but if you find one, don't forget where it is and be there next time it rains.

Chapter 8

Primary Surf Species

The Key Players

On every coast there are a great many species of fish that can be caught from the beach, but in each region you'll find those that are the most common, the most prized, and the most abundant targets for surf anglers. In the Northwest, it is possible to catch steelhead from oceanfront beaches, as these huge seagoing rainbow trout migrate to river mouths. But I wouldn't advise you to book a flight to Washington or Oregon looking for them. Catching one is a rare occurrence, and you're more likely to luck into a steelhead than find one on purpose. Throughout the Atlantic states, sea robins, skates, and spiny dogfish are banes of the surfcaster. Clas-

sified as "trash fish," these species steal bait, ruin rigs, and let you down when you think you've tied into a nice striper or drum. It is the rare species and the unfortunate surf by-catches that you'll come to learn on your own.

Chronicled here are the primary gamefish targets of the surf from Washington to California, Texas to Florida, and Georgia to New England. Consider this a quick reference guide to their habits and range that you can use to figure out what's biting on any beach, any time of year. In chapter 11, you'll find information on a few fish unique to rocky beaches and jetties, and in chapter 9 the elusive pelagic species are covered separately as different skills and techniques are required for catching them. But in this chapter, all the fish can be caught from main oceanfront—or Gulf-front—beaches with the baits, rigs, and lures covered thus far. Just be sure to check local seasons, regulations, bag limits, and size limits on all species before hitting the sand.

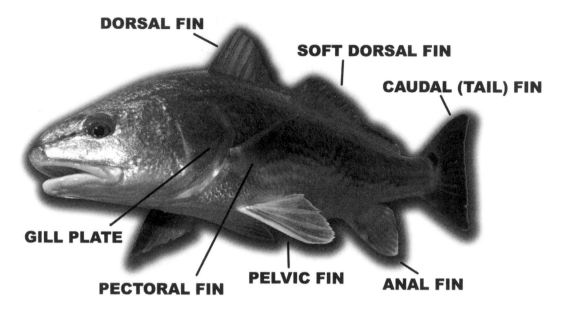

Understanding the basic exterior anatomy of a fish will better help you identify the species you catch, as well as make the gamefish descriptions provided in the chapter easier to follow. Consult this illustration as a reference for locating spots, bars, and unique fin structure noted in the gamefish reference guide.

Atlantic Croaker

Common Names: Croaker

Description: Croakers are silver or gold in color, often with wavy lines or faint spots on their sides. This fish's mouth is positioned on the underside of its head, making it well adapted to feeding on the bottom.

Range: Atlantic coast from southern New England to Florida; Gulf coast from Florida to Texas.

Croakers may be among the smallest gamefish found in the surf, yet they are perhaps one of the most important. These fish are abundant throughout the Atlantic and Gulf, and they are an easy species for anglers of all ages to catch. In the Northeast, croaker numbers are strongest from midsummer through midfall, while farther south and in the Gulf, the species thrives in the waves spring through fall, generally moving offshore during the winter. What makes these fish so appealing is that there isn't a lot of specialized tackle needed to catch them, and while a 3-pounder would be a monster, they are prized for their mild flavor and great texture.

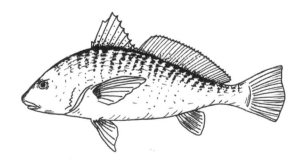

All fish illustrations: Laura Braciale

Croakers are one of the most abundant surf species along the Gulf and Atlantic coasts. Though not monsters, they are a fantastic panfish and can be caught in great numbers.
Photo: Darren Dorris

All you need to catch croakers is a small hook, weight, and a tiny piece of clam, squid, or shrimp. They'll also attack small bucktail jigs, soft-plastic grubs, and occasionally small metal lures when schools are particularly thick. Croakers are frequently caught in greater numbers at night, and when the waves are loaded with them, you can hear them "drumming" or "croaking"—hence the name—by beating their abdominal muscles against their swim bladders. While croakers can be taken on lighter tackle, I've had the most success sticking to a 10-foot rod, as they often follow troughs farther of the beach that require a long cast to reach. If you're looking to bend the rods on summer vacation with the family, not taking surf outings too seriously, there is a good chance you can find croakers on whatever beach you're visiting.

Barred Surf Perch

Common Names: Surf Perch
Description: Barred surf perch have rounded bodies with silver base coloration. Their name derives from the vertical bars on their sides that can range from yellow, to gold, to coppery brown.
Range: Pacific Coast from Central to Southern California.

Although barred surf perch top out around 15 inches, they are nonetheless an important gamefish for Southern California surfcasters. Both willing takers and tasty panfish, these fish provide year-round action, though December and January are considered peak months for abundance. For larger fish, San Diego expert Paul Sharman cites the spring as a great time to fish because heavier female perch move in close to give birth to live young.

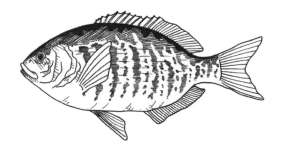

Though average barred surf perch measures between 8 and 10 inches, this fish is a particularly large example of the species taken from the California surf.
Photo: Paul Sharman

Surf perch do offer opportunities for artificials enthusiasts to cash in, with small curly-tail grubs and several smaller offerings from Berkley's Gulp! line producing well. Sharman notes that grubs that are brown with red glitter flakes—a color pattern sometimes referred to as "motor oil"—work particularly well. However, more fish fall to bait than anything else. Live sand crabs are a favorite forage item and make up about 90 percent of the surf perch's diet. Small pieces of clam or sea worm are also good baits should sand crabs be in short supply.

High–low rigs with small hooks are common for barred surf perch, though slide rigs that use light egg sinkers work well, too. Depending on water clarity, leader sizes can vary anywhere from 8- to 20-pound test, with fluorocarbon being the material of choice. In some cases when fish are being extra-finicky, Sharman will use leaders as light as 2-pound-test and greatly reduce his hook size. Because surf perch have fairly small mouths to begin with, it's important to use low-profile hooks with a short gap. One of Sharman's favorite styles is the Mosquito Hook produced by Owner.

Black Drum

Common Names: Striped Drum, Drumfish

Description: Black drum appear brown to silvery gray in color, with smaller fish sometimes exhibiting light bars across their backs. Drum have whisker-like barbels under their lower jaw, and fish over 40 pounds can develop a bulging, knotty head and back. Their mouths are located on the underside of their heads.

Range: Atlantic coast from New York to Florida; Gulf coast from Florida to Texas.

Black drum weighing more than 80 pounds are not incredibly uncommon in the surf, though the average fish throughout their range will weigh in between 15 and 40 pounds. Some of the heaviest species are taken from beaches between southern

New Jersey and Maryland during spawning months of May and June, though exceptionally large speci- mens are also caught along Gulf beaches. Smaller drum can be found in the surf, spring through early fall on the Atlantic coast, and year-round in the Gulf. The new and full moon periods in May and June are what draw true giants in from offshore to spawn in bays throughout the mid-Atlantic, while in the Gulf, spawning occurs primarily from February to April. As these fish migrate inshore, they'll spend time feeding along the oceanfront beaches before moving through inlets and passes.

Black drum are bottom feeders, and potent baits, such as fresh clams, sea worms, or bunker chunks, produce best in the Atlantic. High–low rigs, slide rigs, and standard bait rigs that use stout leaders work well. In the Gulf, dead shrimp and mullet are popular baits. Oddly, drum in the Gulf are more prone to hitting artificial lures, like bucktail jigs and shrimp imitations, though in the Northeast they tend to lazily rove over the bottom looking for a meal they need not chase.

These fish are strong fighters, though they often don't provide the same line-ripping runs as other gamefish. The exception here is when you hook into a true giant weighing 40 pounds or more, as they'll use their body weight to hold their ground, making it feel more like you're pulling against a sunken pile of bricks than a fish. Drum weighing less than 20 pounds make excellent table fare, while the flesh of larger fish can become coarse and tough. One of the most popular recipes in the Northeast is drum Parmesan.

Bluefish

Common Names: Blue, Snapper (Juvenile), Gator, Chopper, Slammer, Tailor
Description: Smaller bluefish tend to be vibrant silver, while larger fish can turn dark blue-green.
Bluefish also have a bright yellow eye and forked tail.
Range: Atlantic coast from New England to Florida; Gulf coast from Florida to Texas.

Bluefish are one of the most prevalent surf species from New England through North Carolina, with some of the largest fish—up to 20 pounds—primarily taken from Massachu- setts through Maryland. In this region blues of all sizes are available from early spring through late fall, sometimes straggling into the winter

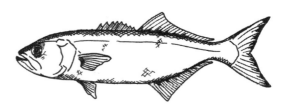

months depending on how fast the water temperature drops. As the Northeast fish migrate south for the season, Virginia, North Carolina, and South Carolina experience a push of larger fish before they move offshore. Florida also sees a spike in bluefish activity during the winter, but here a 10-pound specimen would be considered very large. Along the Gulf coast from Florida to Texas, bluefish make an occasional appearance for surfcasters, but they generally weigh less than 5 pounds, although en- counters with heavier fish aren't impossible. But no matter where you find bluefish, know that they very rarely travel alone. This caveat keeps them closely associated with blitzes, as they'll move in like a wolf pack obliterating any hapless bait school in their path. Bluefish are so voracious, they'll eat until stuffed, regurgitate, and continue to feed. However, they do move very quickly, so by the time you land one, the rest of the school may have pressed on. If you're fishing two or three baited lines at once, don't be shocked if all the rods get hit at the same time when blues come through.

Surf guide Floyd Morton hoists up a Delaware bluefish. Specimens this size are brutal fighters and a challenging opponent for surfcasters.
Photo: Floyd Morton

In the Northeast, surfcasters have a love–hate relationship with bluefish. On the one hand, they are as hard fighting a fish as you could hope for, with larger blues making line-peeling runs and giving your arms a workout. They are incredibly aggressive fish that will hit almost any lure with explosive force, especially topwaters. On the other hand, bluefish have a brutish habit of chasing other gamefish out of the area by overpowering them in number and decimating baitfish schools in a matter of minutes. This can be an annoyance when you're trying to catch striped bass or weakfish, as blues are equally quick to eat a chunk bait sitting on the bottom. Their sharp teeth account for many lure and rig bite-offs, and even if your leader doesn't sever, it will often be so abraded that you need to change it.

Of course, if you're targeting bluefish specifically (which I do frequently), adding a piece of steel wire ahead of your hooks or lures will guard against their teeth. Always remove the hooks with pliers, and if you're using plugs and metal lures, changing treble hooks to single hooks can make that job easier. Even though the species as a whole has a reputation for being poor table fare, bluefish weighing 1 to 5 pounds are excellent when made fresh. The trick is to cut the gills and bleed them immediately, then make sure they're kept on ice. Larger fish are very oily, though their edibility is a matter of opinion, as some people find them delightful.

California Halibut

Common Names: California Flounder

Description: Halibut can change their tone based on the color of the bottom. Most commonly they are tan with blotchy white and brown spots, but they can appear lighter or darker.

Range: Pacific Coast from Southern Oregon to San Diego, California.

Halibut are a flat fish and one of the main species targeted in the Southern California surf, though they do straggle north to southern Oregon. These fish are available throughout the year, but according to San Diego surf expert Paul Sharman, the winter months see larger fish lying within range of surfcasters. While California halibut can reach 50 pounds, 6- to 20-pound fish are most common from the beach.

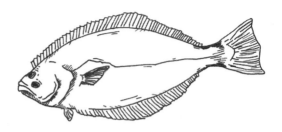

Halibut, like most other flatfish, are very aggressive, but they don't often chase lures like other species. Still, bucktail jigs and soft-plastic swimbaits will get inhaled quickly should they find themselves in close striking distance of a halibut. To that end, it becomes important to move around, working many holes and troughs rather than casting to the same area over and over. Many Southern California surfcasters chase halibut with lighter lines and rods to make casting small lures easier and to give them better action, but you can also target these fish with heavier outfits and dead baits.

Squid, mackerel, and sardines are all popular bait choices for halibut. When the grunion—a small silver baitfish—migrates up to the beach to spawn between March and August, halibut are frequently hot on their trail. Like their northern cousins the Pacific halibut, the California variety makes an exceptional meal.

Cobia

Common Names: Ling
Description: Cobia have a shark-like shape with a flatter head and dark brown coloring. Some smaller cobia have a dark stripe that runs down the length of their body.
Range: Atlantic coast from Maryland to Florida; Gulf coast from Florida to Texas.

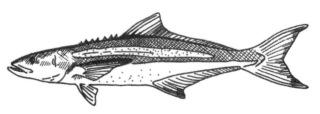

Catching cobia from the surf is not easy, as these fish are primarily found offshore in open water. However, in some areas they make fairly regular appearances in the surf during certain times of the year. Perhaps the most popular place to target them is the Virginia coast through North Carolina's Outer Banks, with the strongest action starting in June, then becoming more sporadic throughout the summer. Likewise, the northern Gulf coast from Florida through Louisiana sees cobia migrating close to shore during the spring, though finding them within casting range of the beach is not as typical as in the mid-Atlantic.

Cobia average 15 to 40 pounds from the beach, but these fish can top the 100-pound mark. Outer Banks surf guide Rob Alderman has actually led clients to 90-plus-pounders. Although it takes nothing more than a fresh chunk of bunker sitting still on the bottom to entice cobia, the real fun for diehards is sight fishing for them. Alderman will stand on the roof of his truck to gain elevation, hoping to spot cobia in the waves. When he does, bucktail jigs, metal lures, and various soft plastics will

Cobia fall frequently to simple chunk baits on the bottom, though sight fishing for them as they cruise in the waves is considered one of surf fishing's ultimate thrills. Photo: Ric Burnley

take these fish. But if you're lucky enough to have some on hand, a live eel is perhaps the best bait for cobia.

No matter how big the cobia, it's wise to beef leaders up to 40- or 50-pound test, as they are one of the most sporting fighters, making sizzling runs and often continuing to thrash violently once on the beach. Cobia landed in small boats have actually been known to cause serious damage to anglers, engines, and tackle as they flop and kick on deck. Putting up with a cobia's bad attitude is worth it, however, considering that they are fine eating fish whether cooked fresh or smoked. Always be sure to bleed cobia immediately by cutting the gills, and keep them well iced.

Corbina

Common Names: California Whiting, Sucker

Description: Corbina—members of the croaker family—have an elongated body that's silvery gray with light diagonal bars across the back. Corbina have a single barbel under their lower jaw. A corbina's mouth is located on the underside of its head.

Range: Pacific Coast from Santa Barbara to San Diego, California.

Corbina are often compared to bonefish, a species found on shallow warm-water flats in tropical locations, as they can feed so close to the beach, you can sometimes spot their backs stick-

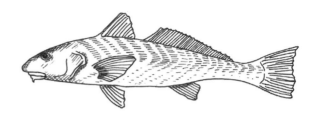

ing out of the water while they forage in the sand. These fish rarely measure more than 24 inches, making them a very appealing light-tackle target. But despite their size, corbina put a serious bend in the rod, often engaging the drag as they run. It's possible to catch corbina all year, but the summer months bring peak action.

You can hook corbina by presenting sand crabs or shrimp in shallow troughs and depressions close to shore, but sight fishing for them is a favorite approach among the Southern California surf crowd. Slide rigs using light egg sinkers are a favorite bait-delivery method. Like bonefish, corbina are notoriously wary, making a stealthy approach necessary. So as not to spook them while casting, anglers will actually kneel to shorten their profile and shadow. The trick is to land your bait in front of a moving fish without spooking it, but that's easier said than done. One way this is accomplished is by casting up- or downcurrent of the fish and letting the waves and tidal flow pull your bait to it.

These fish are incredibly line-shy, so it's important to use light fluorocarbon leaders that they won't recognize as easily and that won't make your offering appear unnatural. Corbina also hit baits very lightly. It will often feel like wave pressure pushing the bait as opposed to a strike. To help compensate, be sure to keep your rod tip high and line tight. It will increase your chances of picking up this subtle bump. Corbina are a good eating fish, though since they can be difficult prizes to catch and numbers fluctuate year to year, many anglers opt for catch-and-release.

Flounder

Common Names: Northern: Summer Flounder, Fluke; Southern: Southern Fluke

Description: Northern, southern, and Gulf flounder all flatfish that have tan to dark brown coloration depending on the color of the bottom. All species have mottled white spots. What separates them are distinct darker spots called ocelli. Northern flounder have five or more, southern flounder have none, and Gulf flounder have three.

Range: Atlantic coast from New England to Florida; Gulf coast from Florida to Texas.

While the names of these three flounder species seem to designate their geographic location, there is actually significant overlap in the range of these flatfish. Northern flounder, commonly called "fluke," are most abundant between New England and North Carolina, though they do stray as far south as North Florida. Both southern and Gulf flounder can be caught from Virginia, around Florida, all the way to the Gulf coast of Texas. Though these species look very similar, their sizes vary quite a bit.

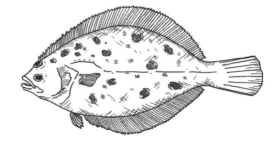

Northern flounder commonly hit the 10-pound mark, and it's not unheard of to catch them to 15 pounds. Southern flounder average 3 to 5 pounds, though here, too, 10-plus-pounders are not

terribly uncommon. Gulf flounder are the runts of the family, rarely weighing more than 5 pounds. But what these fish share despite their size difference is an acute predatory instinct that makes them voracious feeders, even though many people assume they're lazy since they lie on the bottom.

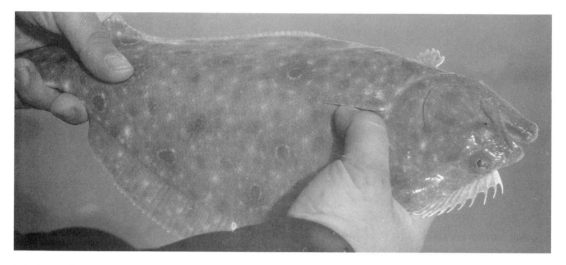

The distinctly larger darks spots, called ocelli, are what distinguish this northern flounder, or "fluke," from its cousin the southern flounder. Photo: Melissa Pulicare

All species of flounder can be caught from the shallow surf. A widespread misconception is that the biggest flounder are only hooked in deep water offshore, but it just isn't so. During the summer months in the Northeast, flounder are a popular target for surf anglers who like to fish a little more actively. While you can simply cast out a bait rig with squid, live mud minnows, or mackerel strips and catch them, those anglers moving around and hopping bait-tipped bucktail jigs across the bottom have more success. That's because flounder don't roam as much as red drum or bluefish, so waiting for them to come to you is less productive. Some anglers also use a standard bait rig adorned with a bucktail-dressed

While just as aggressive and very similar in appearance to the northern flounder, this southern flounder lacks the larger dark ocellus spots.

hook tipped with a bait strip and perhaps a flashy spinner blade on the leader. Rigs like this are matched with a lighter, rounded sinker and reeled slowly across the bottom.

In the southern and Gulf States, flounder frequently fall to soft-plastic shrimp and baitfish imitations jigged along the bottom. A spoon or small metal lure will produce as well, though it's not always necessary to keep contact with the bottom. Flounder are actually very aggressive and will rise up to attack prey, or chase it a considerable distance before striking. Believe it or not, I once watched a flounder in Texas swim up and take a swipe at a topwater popper. It may not be a usual occurrence, but it just goes to show that these fish don't always sit and wait for a meal to pass in front of their mouths.

With all species, don't assume you always need to reach the deepest drop-off or find the perfect trough. While it won't hurt to do so, flounder will also sit in a few inches of water close to where the waves lap the beach. Don't cast over them. Even if you found a nice trough, work right near your feet first. In the Northeast, flounder arrive in the spring and can remain in the surf through late fall. A similar pattern can be found in the mid-Atlantic states, while in Florida and along the Gulf coast, fall provides peak action as fish leave the bays in preparation for spawning offshore in winter. All flounder species make excellent table fare.

Kingfish

Common Names: Whiting, Sea Mullet

Description: Northern, southern, and Gulf kingfish share similar body styles with a wider head tapering into a thinner tail section. They also all have a single barbel under their chin, and their mouth is on the underside of their head. Southern and Gulf kings are silver or light brown, though the former exhibits faint yellow bars across their backs. Northern kingfish are darker with a single long dorsal spine not shared by the others. They can have bronze to deep brown coloration with black bars on their backs.

Range: Atlantic coast from southern New England to Florida; Gulf coast from Florida to Texas.

Because kingfish rarely best the 2-pound mark, these species are not prized for their fight as much as their excellence as a food fish. It may take a coolerful of these little scrappers to get a fish fry going, but they are all very delicious. Like Atlantic croakers, kingfish are great targets for kids, and they require minimal tackle. Although these are a great light-tackle species, they often follow troughs and narrow cuts that

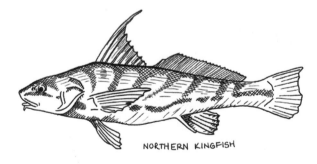

NORTHERN KINGFISH

can be far enough off the beach that a long rod and heavier weight is required to cover the distance. Kingfish are not typically classified as willing takers of lures, though there are some occasions when they will hit small bucktail jigs or soft-plastic grubs. This most often occurs on very calm days when the fish are close and you can see them. Kings have a very subtle strike, which can make lure fishing a challenge unless you actually watch them eat your offering.

The southern kingfish, shown here, does not have the long dorsal spine of its northern relative, and is also more silver in color.

The best way to fish for them is with a high–low rig that has colorful floats on the dropper leaders. Small-gap offset gold hooks are common on prepackaged rigs. Squid strips, sand fleas, shrimp pieces, cut mullet, and clam pieces are all top baits throughout their range, though tiny pieces of fresh sea worms can prove utterly deadly. Kingfish are also not picky about eating a variety of artificial baits, such as Berkley Gulp!, as discussed in chapter 3. Because kings are apt to pick a hook clean without the strike even registering in the rod tip, it is important to keep slight but constant tension on the line. Many anglers chasing these species won't leave a baited rod in a sand spike, as holding it will increase chances of feeling the nibble.

Kingfish seasons change by region, with action in the Northeast heaviest from late spring through midfall, though lulls often occur during the hottest months. Maryland, Virginia, and the Carolinas experience excellent fishing in the early spring, though kingfish are around in all but the coldest months of the year. In the Gulf, these fish are available year-round, though many areas, Texas in particular, see the most abundant surf catches during the winter.

Pompano

Common Names: Florida Pompano, Carolina Pompano

Description: Pompano have round bodies with silver sides and yellow coloring on their throats. They are often confused with permit, which have a dark spot under the pectoral fins absent on the pompano.

Range: Atlantic coast from Delaware to Florida; Gulf coast from Florida to Texas.

This member of the jack family is one of the most sought-after surf species in Florida and the Gulf states, though good fishing can be found from the Carolinas down to Georgia. Every once in a great while, a surfcaster will catch a pompano as far north as New York, though it's far from typical. While this species doesn't grow to epic proportions, they can get up to 7 pounds and are exceptional fighters regardless of size.

The Atlantic coast of Florida from Jupiter to Jacksonville is arguably the most prime hunting ground for serious pompano anglers. Late fall through early spring marks the peak season, though it is possible to catch them on occasion during the summer. Farther north, Georgia and the Carolinas see action spring and summer, but the best fishing usually begins in September and lasts through midfall. These fish then push south to Florida, providing the winter action. On the northern Gulf coast from the Florida Panhandle to North Texas, spring and early summer are prime pompano times, though fish are available all year. On the South Texas coast, pompano don't have the same prestige bestowed upon them as they do in Florida, though surfcasters who do chase them fare well in the winter months.

Pompano may not be the biggest fish in the ocean, but they are scrappy fighters and make excellent table fare.
Photo: Mike Conner

Without question, live or frozen sand fleas fished on high–low rigs with floats are the best bait for pompano, though shrimp or squid will work as well. Most pompano anglers agree that slightly off-color water produces the most fish, as this coloration is associated with surf action that stirs the bottom. Crystal-clear water is generally considered a hindrance on the Atlantic coast of Florida, but it can occasionally provide sight-fishing opportunities.

Pompano will attack small nylon or bucktail jigs, though according to Florida surf expert Mike Conner, using them is a more common practice on the northern Gulf beaches than the Atlantic oceanfront. This is mainly because pompano foraging in the rougher surf are more interested in grubbing the bottom for crustaceans than chasing small baitfish or shrimp mimicked by jigs. These fish can also cruise farther off the beach on the Atlantic side, making them hard to reach with a small, light lure. To that end, even though pompano may not be massive, a 10- to 12-foot rod is the stick of choice for presenting baits in the distant troughs. On the Gulf shores, pompano will frequently work closer to the beach, and surf conditions are calmer in general. As far as table quality is concerned, pompano are one of the finest fish you can put on your dinner plate.

Red Drum

Common Names: Redfish, Channel Bass, Puppy Drum (juvenile to approximately 24 inches)

Description: Red drum have a large mouth positioned on the underside of their sloping heads. Coloration can vary greatly, from copper to bronze, gold to tan, and even silvery-gray in some areas during certain times of the year. The most distinguishing mark of the red drum is a black spot at the base of the tail that acts as a false eye used for tricking predators into attacking from the rear so the fish can flee. While most drum have just one spot, multispot fish are not at all uncommon.

Range: Atlantic coast from Maryland to Florida; Gulf coast from Florida to Texas.

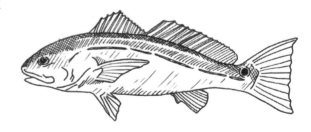

From calm Gulf beaches to the roaring shores of the mid-Atlantic, red drum are one of the most widespread and heavily chased species. There is nothing not to love about them. Whether you are catching 20-inch "puppy" drum or 40-pound "bulls," they are one of the hardest-fighting fish within reach of a surfcaster's line. When you set the hook on a monster red, it is nothing short of being connected to a Mack truck. They will eat anything from a chunk of dead bait to a fast-moving topwater lure. Depending on where you're fishing, they can be a breeze to catch or the ultimate challenge.

From Maryland to North Carolina, the presence of bull red drum in the surf is seasonal. But it is these runs that keep anglers on edge as they wait for the action to begin. As with many other gamefish, bunker and mullet migrations coincide with the heaviest drum migrations, creating perfect predator-and-prey harmony. The Atlantic states experience two major drum runs every year, one in the spring when they move in from their offshore breeding grounds, then another in the fall when they pour back out of the bay systems to head offshore again. In both spring and fall, bunker are moving down the coastline; in fall massive amounts of mullet enter the picture as well. In the northern reaches of their range, mainly Maryland through North Carolina, drum action slows dramatically during the summer as the water temperature rises. During the winter months, depending on how cold it gets, anglers fishing North Carolina's Outer Banks can still find smaller fish feeding in the surf.

Farther down the coast from South Carolina into northern Florida, spring and fall are also peak seasons for surf drum, though in these areas fish will winter over in back bays. While beachfront landings tend to dwindle as reds head for inland refuges, it isn't outside the realm of possibility to hook them through the winter depending on ocean water temperature. Through much of the Gulf, red drum are available year-round, but action with bulls, especially from North Texas through Alabama, can be excellent during the winter months. South Texas, Padre Island National Seashore in particular, provides terrific red drum fishing opportunities all year, with action often best near inlet mouths.

This night-caught red drum is the epitome of a "bull." Fish this size require stout tackle, as their fighting spirit is tough to break. Photo: Ric Burnley

Because red drum feed along beaches that range from glass-flat to incredibly rough, tackle and approaches vary greatly by region. In their North Atlantic reaches, anglers targeting bulls rely on stout rods that are at least 10 feet long to fire large sinkers, big bait chunks, or heavy lures to distant troughs and drop-offs. In Florida, calmer shorelines offer better conditions to scale down tackle and use smaller artificial lures. Although many Gulf beaches are relatively calm, tackle is dictated not so much by the surf conditions as the size of the prevalent fish. When bulls are running hard, long rods and heavier rigs get the nod here. However, on the same beaches where this tackle may have been necessary during the winter, summer conditions may call for a 7-foot rod and light jigs, as smaller fish abound.

When conditions are right, you can find red drum grubbing for food in the shallow surf with their tails protruding from the water. "Tailing" is more often seen on the calmer beaches of Florida and the Gulf than in the mid-Atlantic.

Wherever true bulls are found, most anglers throwing rigs with large mullet or bunker chunks favor 30- to 60-pound fluorocarbon leader. Circle or J-hooks ranging from 5/0 to 10/0 are the most widely used. Hook size and leader strength can be reduced if you're using dead shrimp or small mullet for "puppy" drum. One unique behavior of red drum not shared by other frequent surf dwellers is "tailing." When they're feeding on the bottom in shallow surf, it's possible to spot their tails protruding from the water. While this behavior is most common on Florida and Gulf beaches, every so often you'll find tailing fishing on the oceanfront shores of the mid-Atlantic.

Bull red drum action is generally more productive on beaches with deeper water, as they tend to follow the offshore slope of the first sandbar, or run in troughs between bars. This can make presenting baits and lures a challenge. Along North Carolina's Outer Banks, die-hard drum fishermen will often wade chest-deep through close troughs to send a cast to distant channels or over the offshore drop. It can be a dangerous game, especially when the surf is rough. But this is not to say that big reds never come in close. If you're on a beach where the only deep troughs and cuts happen to run closer to the water's edge, bulls can be a short cast away. If you are more interested in targeting quantity over quality, the Gulf beaches from Florida to South Texas can provide nonstop action with smaller fish when all the conditions, including the presence of baitfish, come together. While size and bag limits are very different from state to state, red drum is one of the most delicious fish you can eat.

Redtail Surf Perch

Common Names: Rosy Surf Perch, Oregon Porgy, Redtail Seaperch

Description: While named for its purplish red tail, the redtail surf perch may also exhibit this coloring on the soft dorsal fin and anal fin. Its body is round and compressed with mostly silver coloration. Faint red or brown bars are visible along the sides of the body.

Range: Pacific Coast from Northern California to Washington.

Of all the US coastlines, that of the Northwest is arguably the least associated with surf fishing. In Washington and Oregon, there is no abundance of brute species like the red drum or bluefish that bend rods deeply in the Gulf and Atlantic, with the exception of occasional striped bass in Oregon. However, that is not to say there isn't a devoted cult of surfcasters in this region. Their numbers are quite strong, and the fish they chase most are redtail surf perch.

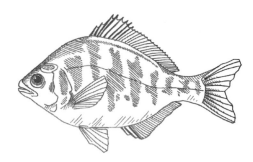

While many people associate the Northwest beachfront with high headlands and rocky outcroppings, Washington surf expert Kelly Corcoran says that for the most part, the beaches are flat and sandy. This provides ideal habitat for redtails, which are available all year. However, if you're looking to catch bigger perch with the most consistency, spring offers prime shots as larger fish come in to spawn. But keep in mind, "large" for this species would be 3 pounds. While redtails may not be giants, their pursuers value them for their fine eating quality.

The Northwest surf may not offer shots at monster fish, but what it lacks in brute species, it makes up for with redtail surf perch—a species chased throughout Oregon and Washington that's prized for its flavor on the table.
Photo: Kelly Corcoran

Spring may be a great time to target this species, but according to Corcoran, season doesn't mean a whole lot if there happens to be a razor clam dig on the beach. Thousands of people can storm the surf line on designated digging days during the winter to fill a bucket with these meaty seafood delicacies. Digs occur at low tide, and in the process, countless shells are broken, sending clam juice and scent into the waves. Corcoran rarely misses an opportunity to fish the first high tide after a dig, as the perch move in to feed on leftover clam bits en masse. The best bait during this time is a razor clam neck, which gets discarded during the clam-cleaning process.

When digs aren't in progress, sand shrimp and ghost shrimp are the go-to baits, although Corcoran puts a lot of stock in squid because of its strong smell. The Northwest surf is typically stained, so with the limited visibility, scent plays an important role. High–low rigs are standard for perch, and Corcoran finds that the addition of an iridescent round float on his dropper leaders, positioned just ahead of the hooks, ups catch rates significantly. While there are some opportunities to catch redtails on artificials, such as small Berkley Gulp! grubs, most anglers find bait more productive. Because getting an offering far off the beach can be the key to success, light jigs are reserved for scenarios where the perch happen to be feeding very close.

Traditionally, an incoming tide has always been the favorite of Northwest surfcasters, but Corcoran actually prefers a falling tide. The difference between high and low tide in this part of the country can be as much as 6 feet; tidal pull is very strong. On the outgoing tide, Corcoran's rig gets pulled farther offshore as opposed to getting pushed in, making it necessary to constantly reel in slack to maintain a tight line. Redtails follow troughs and depressions as they forage, and unlike other surf species that are constantly on the move, perch will hold in a hole or cut for as long as a food source is present. Though the surf is typically cloudy in Washington and Oregon, patches of extra-dirty water are sure signs that currents are hitting a sandbar and stirring the bottom. These areas are prime for perch, as the wave action exposes and disorients the shrimp these fish love to eat.

Snook

Common Names: Lineside, Robalo

Description: Snook have a tapered head, silver or gold coloration, and yellow-tinted fins. But what makes this species so identifiable is the dark black stripe that runs down their bodies following the lateral line.

Range: Atlantic coast from Georgia to Florida; Gulf coasts of Florida and South Texas.

Snook have less tolerance for cooler water temperatures than other species covered thus far. These fish are found most abundantly in Florida from St. Augustine to Miami on the Atlantic coast, and Clearwater to Naples on the Gulf coast. Though snook can be caught on the Gulf coast from the Florida Panhandle to North Texas, they're not incredibly common.

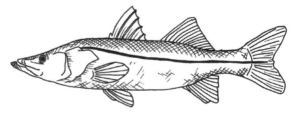

The overall number of snook on the southern Gulf coast of Texas does not quite match that of Florida, though Padre Island National Seashore does see decent snook activity, especially around inlet mouths. In the Atlantic, this species can creep as far north as the Georgia coast.

Snook average between 5 and 20 pounds, though they can best the 40-pound mark. Depending on the conditions and presence of bait, they can be incredibly aggressive and strike lures savagely. However, they also have finicky tendencies, following lures without hitting or paying no mind to offerings drawn right across their faces. Of course, it's partly the art involved in tricking them that makes snook so appealing to surfcasters.

Snook move out of estuaries and begin feeding along the beaches in June. This usually coincides with the water temperature in the surf hitting 80 degrees. Though the summer months are excellent for snook, fall provides some of the best opportunities in Florida on the Atlantic and Gulf coasts, according to Florida snook expert Terry Gibson. This time of year they follow migrating mullet out of the bays and estuaries and onto the beaches. In South Texas, snook can be caught in the waves throughout the summer, though here, too, fall mullet migrations draw them out of the bays into the surf.

Snook have a cult-like following among Florida surfcasters, as they can frequently be caught while sight fishing. Photo: Courtesy of Riop.com

A snook's gill plate is razor-sharp, so even for smaller specimens, most anglers opt for 30- to 40-pound fluorocarbon leaders for abrasion resistance. But sometimes these fish can be leader-shy, forcing you to using thinner leader to draw a strike. If you have to resort to this tactic, it's wise to keep your drag set slightly lighter than normal to hedge the chance of the leader stretching too tightly, making it more susceptible to being cut off on the gill plate.

During the fall, live mullet are the favorite bait, but large shrimp and sardines work as well. Most surf anglers cast live mullet from the beach, but many opt to fish lures, as snook will strike a wide variety of baitfish and shrimp imitators. Some of the most popular include MirrOlure suspending twitchbaits, D.O.A. shrimp, bucktail jigs, and soft-plastic finesse-style baitfish imitations. When the surf is roiled, snook can respond well to topwater lures, as well as noisy plugs that feature internal rattles.

These fish frequently follow troughs and depressions in a zigzag pattern, shooting into shallower areas to grab a meal, then darting back to the deeper water. When the surf is calm and clear, it's not uncommon to spot moving fish. This gives you the chance to present a lure ahead of them and actually see the strike. Any hardcore snook surfcaster will tell you it's an addictive experience.

When mullet are particularly thick, the key to success lies in getting under the bait, according to Gibson. "Species like bluefish will attack the mullet full-force in the fall," he says. "But big snook will just hang near the bottom waiting for dead mullet to sink or the blues to push a few down." If you see a school of mullet getting hammered by bluefish, don't hesitate to send a dead mullet or a bluefish chunk deep. Even these dead baits will score surf snook, according to Gibson, but for the best success, rigs should feature a float near the hook to keep the offering just off the bottom. Snook make excellent table fare, though most serious anglers opt to catch and release. Snook also breed from May through September, and the largest fish are always female. Handle them with care when removing the hook, making every effort not to take them out of the water; the heaviest fish are most important to future populations.

Spotted Sea Trout

Common Names: Speckled Sea Trout, Speck, Trout

Description: Spotted sea trout can have a base coloration ranging from silver, to gold, to gray with purple twinges. Their bodies, dorsal fins, and tails are covered in many dark spots. Sea trout have a large mouth and two fangs at the tip of the top jaw.

Range: Atlantic coast from Maryland to Florida; Gulf coast from Florida to Texas.

Sea trout are willing and aggressive takers in the surf, and much like red drum, they are widely available along much of the Atlantic and Gulf coasts. On average, sea trout will weigh anywhere from 1 to 3 pounds, with 5- to 10-pound fish considered trophies in many areas. Their size range makes them a great target for anglers looking to stray from long, heavy rods in favor of lighter tackle.

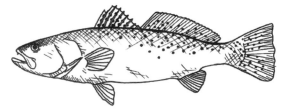

As with other popular species, their presence in the surf zone often coincides with baitfish migrations, making fall one of the most productive times to catch them along much of the Atlantic coast. While they can be pulled from the waves during the summer months, most trout spend the hot season tucked up in back bays and estuaries. In South Carolina, Georgia, and the northern part of Florida, sea trout will winter in the backcountry, making shots at them on oceanfront beaches limited that time of year. The exception comes along the Gulf coast from Alabama through North

Spotted sea trout offer great opportunity to scale down your tackle and have some fun on lighter gear. They're known for their aggressive strikes and affinity for topwater lures. Photo: Ric Burnley

Texas. In these regions, sea trout are a popular year-round target, with peaks occurring in both spring and fall. On the southern Texas coast, the winter months can offer good trout fishing along the beach.

Although larger sea trout typically fall to live bait or lures, it is possible to successfully catch this species on fresh dead baits. In the Atlantic, squid strips, shrimp, and even cut sea worms are popular choices, while shrimp is used as dead bait most heavily on the Florida and Gulf coasts. High–low rigs with small floats, as well as slide rigs with small egg sinkers, are popular bait-delivery methods for trout.

In situations where the beach is calm and trout are feeding close, tossing a weightless live scaled sardine, peanut bunker, or mud minnow can be highly productive, while a mud minnow on a jighead is a simple yet very effective approach that lets you achieve a little more casting distance. Fishing live or dead baits under a popping cork is also a staple approach for this species.

Sea trout can be found on flat, shallow beaches, as well as in troughs and depressions throughout their range. Because their mouths are soft and thin, light drag settings are ideal, while 10- to 20-pound leader material works best with the smaller lures these fish prefer. Suspending twitch-baits, soft-plastic paddle-tail or finesse-style baitfish imitations, shrimp imitations, and topwater lures are all productive. In the topwater category, sea trout seem drawn to walk-the-dog, Spook-style lures more than poppers. Many anglers believe that since trout are highly sound-oriented hunters, a Spook's "click" is more appealing than a popper's "chug." Frequent and explosive surface strikes contribute in no small way to this species' popularity, though their quality as table fare helps, too.

Striped Bass

Common Names: Striper, Rockfish

Description: Striped bass are silver in coloration, though their backs can vary from dark gray to olive green. Eight or nine vivid, unbroken black stripes run down their sides, and they feature a large mouth capable of swallowing bigger forage in a single gulp.

Range: Atlantic coast from New England to North Carolina; Pacific coast from San Francisco, California, to southern Oregon.

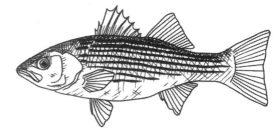

Perhaps no other species is more associated with the surf than striped bass. This is because unlike other species that visit the shoreline during certain times of year, but also spend time offshore or in back bays, stripers are naturally adapted to living tight to the coastline. In fact, it's rare to catch one more than 5 miles offshore. They are just as comfortable feeding along rocky, boulder-strewn beaches as they are over long spans of soft sand. They can be found on the far side of deep drop-offs, in troughs tight to the beach, and in some cases in less than 2 feet of water on shallow expanses of oceanfront. Northeast striper surf anglers make up one of fishing's most recognized cults, but bass are just as accessible to the beginner as they are the seasoned pro.

Striped bass are associated with surfcasting more than any other species, as they naturally prefer to hunt close to the beach. Stripers will also fall to a wide variety of offerings, from dead baits sitting still to fast-moving lures.

One thing that makes this species so popular is their willingness to feed on near-countless of-ferings. Clams and bunker chunks sitting idle on the bottom are just as likely to land a monster striper as a fast-moving pencil popper. Striped bass can be moody, but when they're working a school of bait hard, you can easily find yourself in a situation where you connect on practically every cast. The most exciting part is, it's not impossible for each of those fish to weigh 20 pounds or more.

The average surf-caught striper falls in the 8- to 30-pound range, but 40-, 50-, and 60-pound-ers are taken from key locations with shocking regularity. Is it easy to find, fool, and land a 60-pound striper? Not particularly, especially if you're looking for it specifically. Fish this size often fall to the most dedicated anglers, but in truth, you could catch one simply by happenstance on your first surf trip on a simple clam bait. As stripers patrol the beach both solo and in schools, you just never know exactly what size bass is going to encounter your offering. Clams, bunker chunks, live eels, whole dead mullet, and whole sea worms are thought of as the best big-bass baits, though squid strips, cut sea worms, and even sand crabs are all fine choices for smaller bass often referred to as "schoolies."

Provided you match the most prevalent bait source in size and profile, striped bass are not terribly picky about lure styles, gladly smacking everything from bucktail jigs, to poppers, to metals, to diving swimmers with some incredible force. Regardless of size, what follows is a worthy fight full of dogging dives and hard runs as the bass attempt to flee to deeper water. Stripers are also pretty cunning, and if there's a rock or other debris in the area, they'll run right for it trying to wrap and break your line.

Remember that a 40-pound striper is approxi-mately 20 to 25 years old. The chance that it has encountered lures and been caught before is practically 100 percent. Therefore, if you do hook a genuine "cow," don't expect it to give up easily. You're dealing with a wise old fish.

There are resident striped bass along their entire Atlantic coast range, though during the warm summer months, these fish will typi-cally retreat to back bays and feed most heav-ily during the night. However, these smaller residents will be the first hooked on clams and sea worms as early as March. Exceptions occur from Maine through Rhode Island, as the water is cooler in summer, and this stretch of coast makes up the traditional summering grounds of the migratory fish, though abundance fluc-tuates yearly. The best striper fishing coincides with migrations of both bass and baitfish, like bunker and mullet. In the spring, fish pushing

This bass is about average size for late-fall clammers in the Northeast and upper mid-Atlantic states. Photo: Melissa Pulicare

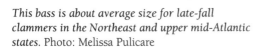

north from North Carolina and Virginia terrorize bunker schools off the beach as they move. In the fall, as the bass head back down to their southern wintering grounds, action throughout the Northeast and upper mid-Atlantic states heats up once again. During the winter, surfcasters from Virginia to North Carolina can see tremendous action with large bass, though their presence in the surf varies yearly as the fish may opt to winter a few miles offshore, never moving into the surf line. But don't set your watch by any of these seasons. Instead, consider them a general guide; water temperature and the presence of bait can swing productive times in any direction. As an example, decades ago, striper fishing was generally over by Thanksgiving in New Jersey. But now, when the water stays warm, some of the best beach action in recent years has occurred well into January. Likewise, cooler water temperatures in the summer can keep bass lingering from New Jersey to Maryland into July. Where edibility is concerned, striped bass are terrific. However, size and bag limits change drastically from state to state. Smaller fish are generally considered better for the table.

Striped bass were introduced to the West Coast in the late 1800s. Juvenile fish were netted in New Jersey and transported by train to the San Francisco Bay, and though the species thrived, striper fishing is a bit different here than on the East Coast. For starters, while bass are found from San Francisco through Oregon, the most consistent fishery occurs in the inland river and delta systems. There just is not the same kind of oceanfront migration as on the East Coast; instead the bass move into the surf for certain periods of time, then retreat back inland. Spring and summer mark the height of surf productivity, though fish topping the 25-pound mark are infrequent, with the average fish ranging from 5 to 10 pounds. Just like on the East Coast, diving birds can be sure signs of feeding stripers pushing baitfish to the surface. While eastern stripers can be hooked right in the wash close to the beach, West Coast bass require a long cast more often than not. Therefore, metal lures and heavier jigs that imitate sardines and anchovies are top producers, though live sea worms are also popular baits.

Tarpon

Common Names: Silver King, Sabalo

Description: Tarpon are hulky fish with broad heads and very large mouths. These fish are pure silver and easily identified by their wide circular scales and long trailing ray on their dorsal fin.

Range: Atlantic coast from South Carolina to Florida; Gulf coast from Florida to Texas.

Simply stated, catching a tarpon from the beach is no easy feat, mostly because finding them within casting range can be tricky. But these fish are important to cover nonetheless, because should you encounter a pod of them rolling and breaking the surface while you're chasing another species, you won't want to miss out on the chance to hook one . . . of course, you'd better hope your gear is up to the task.

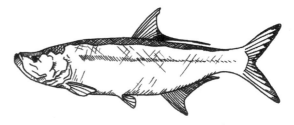

Tarpon grow to 200 pounds, though 30- to 100-pounders are caught most frequently from the beach. While they are available during the late summer in South Carolina and Georgia, as well as throughout the Gulf of Mexico, prime surf fishing opportunities exist mainly on both Florida coasts and the coast of South Texas. Peak times to find "poons" running the beach are late spring and during the fall months when mullet begin moving out of the bay into the ocean and Gulf. Rarely will you hook one blind casting, as they tend to make their presence known by crashing bait pods, rolling their backs out of the water, and gulping for air (tarpon can actually bring their heads out of the water and take a breath). When tarpon are around, anglers will constantly move up and down the beach trying to get ahead of a pod and present offerings in front of them.

Tarpon may not be the easiest species to catch from the beach, but if you do hook one, get ready for the fight of a lifetime. Here, a good-sized tarpon jumps close to the surf line on Florida's Gulf coast.

During the mullet run, a live specimen is by far the best bait for tarpon, though some anglers will actually rig a small live bluefish when they're available. Small blue claw crabs fished under a popping cork can also turn on a tarpon. Artificial lures work well, with large bucktail jigs, various diving and lipless plugs, soft-plastic baitfish imitations, and metal spoons all being excellent choices for matching live mullet. Because tarpon make fearsome runs, I wouldn't recommend casting to them with a reel spooled with less than 300 yards of line. Also, tarpon have incredibly hard mouths, so you need a rod with backbone to really drive the points in when you set the hook. Even if you've gotten this far, the fight's not over.

Tarpon are notorious jumpers. Even large fish flip through the air with ease, shaking and rattling their heads as they plunge back down. It is often during a jump that the hook pops loose because the angler keeps tension on the line. When a tarpon goes skyward, you have to bow the rod, lowering it quickly to cause slack between the rod tip and the fish. Finally, as the inside of a tarpon's mouth feels like heavy-grit sandpaper, 60- to 100-pound leader material is an absolute must to thwart abrasion. Tarpon have absolutely no value as a food fish.

Weakfish

Common Names: Weakie, Northern Sea Trout

Description: Weakfish are almost identical in body shape to their southern relatives the spotted sea trout. The major difference is in coloration and dot pattern. Weakfish have a silver to light gold base coloration, often with a dark back and tinges of purple on their sides. Small black dots run in horizontal vertical lines from their back to the center of their body, though fins rarely exhibit a dot pattern.

Range: Atlantic coast from southern New England to Central Florida.

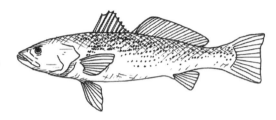

While the weakfish's range extends to Central Florida, they are most abundant in the coastal waters of Massachusetts through North Carolina. But their range can be narrowed further considering they are most often targeted in the surf from New York to Delaware. These fish are very cyclical, with a few good years of great numbers followed by a few years of low catch rates throughout the Northeast. That said, upswings and downswings don't stop dedicated surfcasters from hunting for them, particularly in the spring when the biggest fish—dubbed "tiderunners"—move into the bay systems to spawn. These heavy hitters can be intercepted on the beachfront or from rock jetties as they make their way into the backwaters.

Weakfish provide action all summer long and well into the fall throughout much of their range, though northeastern surfcasters can expect to pick through plenty of little "spikes" to get to the occasional keeper-sized fish. While the tiderunners can be very picky about baits and mealtimes, often feeding at very specific tidal stages, spikes will readily grab a wide variety of baits and lures. Live mud minnows, squid strips, grass shrimp, and whole fresh dead peanut bunker are some of their favorites, while anything from small curly-tail grubs to metal lures will prove to be productive lure choices. As far as lure color is concerned, Northeast weakfish have always been partial to bright pink, though you can't go wrong with a small white bucktail jig tipped with a fresh squid or mackerel strip.

Like striped bass, some of the largest weakfish go on the hunt at night, making small black plugs worked through troughs and depressions highly effective when mullet or peanut bunker are present in the surf. Rat-L-Trap lipless crankbaits are also a go-to lure, as like spotted sea trout, weakfish react very well to sound. Smell is important, too. Many skilled weakfish anglers insist on coating soft-plastic lures and plugs with shedder crab oil. The term *shedder crab* refers to blue claw crabs in their soft-shell stage. They are quite possibly the best bait for weakfish whether fished live or dead and cut into pieces. Though they can be pricey, shedder crabs are available in bait shops when they're in season. As for weakfish on the table, they are fine eating, with mild white flesh that takes well to almost any cooking method.

Weakfish, northern cousins of the spotted sea trout, are popular surf targets from Maryland through New England. They fall to a number of artificial lures and baits and can weigh in at over 15 pounds. Photo: Darren Dorris

Chapter 9

Pelagic Pursuits

Speed Demons in the Surf

The word *pelagic* is defined by *Merriam-Webster's* as, "of, relating to, or living or occurring in the open sea." It's a pretty broad term, but surfcasters say it with reverence. To anglers, it refers to those species that are found only in the oceanic depths. Tuna, marlin, and swordfish are just a few examples. They are species that by definition have no business showing up within reach of a surfcaster's line. Yet some true pelagic mackerel and tuna family members make a grand appearance on the beach year after year. When you hook one, you are treated to one of the most hand-shaking, arm-aching fights you can get with both feet on the sand. But to make that happen, you've got to understand what factors need to come together, and how these fish behave. They are not common catches you'll luck into with regularity, except in a few key areas along the Atlantic coast. However, I can state with certainty that these fish can pop up on any beach within their range.

Finding pelagics is only half the battle. You have to be ready for them. The right lure needs to be tied on and primed to fire. Your reel better have a full spool. You'd better be able to cast accurately, because you will often spot them for a split second, and then suddenly they'll be half a mile up the beach. Members of the tuna and mackerel families move constantly. Whereas striped bass and weakfish will often linger in a trough or hole, waiting for a meal to come to them, pelagics do not rest. When they're feeding, they do not slow down. Of course, they don't slow down when you hook one, either, which is part of the fun.

If you're very lucky, inshore pelagics will hammer a large school of bait within your reach, circling, cutting through, and slashing at the baitfish until the food is gone. When this happens, birds form frenzies in the sky, and you might get multiple shots at the fish. But more often, a small school will shoot down the beach like lightning, giving you one chance to connect at best. All you may see is a tail break the surface. Perhaps one push of bait. Even just a single boil will tip you off to speed demons in the surf. Catch one and you're addicted for life. Have I gotten your attention? Good. Now let's meet the players.

False Albacore

Of the three major pelagic species to show up within a surfcaster's range, false albacore are the largest. They are also the strongest fighters, capable of spooling a reel quickly if your line is low, or breaking a rod if your drag is set too tight. This species also goes by the names "albie," "little tunny," and "bonito" throughout the southern Atlantic and Gulf coasts. While these fish show up on the beach in Florida and South Texas, the Atlantic coast from Massachusetts through North Carolina makes up their primary surf range. To draw an even tighter bead on these targets, the island of Martha's Vineyard in Massachusetts through Cape May, New Jersey, is arguably ground zero for false albacore from the sand.

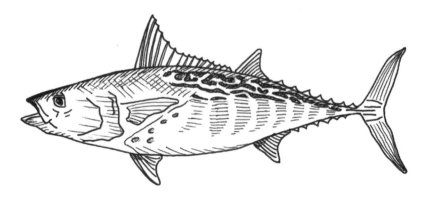

Aside from the ability to reach to 25-pound mark, what false albacore have that other surf-caught pelagics lack is a relatively big mouth. Generally speaking, inshore pelagic species feed most heavily on rain bait, and while that's often the case with albacore, they have been known to upsize. One of their favorite meals is actually herring, though they also feed on squid and occasionally crustaceans.

The most identifiable features of false albacore are the squiggly striations high on their sides that fade into the dark-blue coloration on their backs. These markings help them blend in to the water

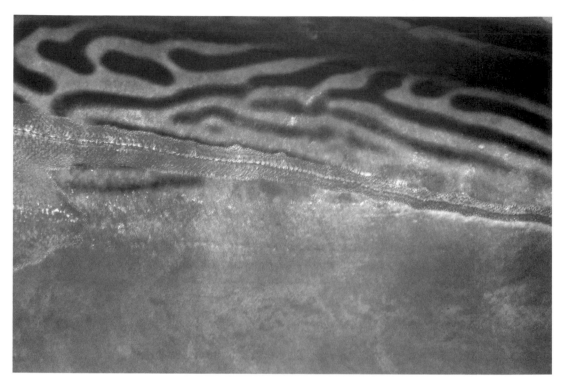

Pelagic species that can be taken in the surf not only provide thrilling fight, but are some of the most beautiful fish that swim. Shown here is a close-up of false albacore striation marks.

fish are naturally prone to feeding near the shoreline throughout the year, even on relatively shallow beaches.

Whether or not you start a hunt in a location like Hatteras or Montauk, distance casting is a factor that weighs heavily into the pelagic game. Anglers who move out to the tip of rock jetties often get more shots at these species than fishermen working the sand, though I have seen bonito snapping rain bait within 5 feet of the end of my rod on the main beach. It's been my experience overall that the most consistent productivity coincides with calm-wind days and minimal wave action, as pelagics are less likely to move within casting range when the surf is roaring. This doesn't have much to do with a dislike of rough waves; rather, these conditions limit pelagics' ability to perform one of their preferred feeding rituals.

Remember that pelagic species travel in schools. Though you may only spot a tail or two breaking the surface, assume that there are more fish around. Pelagics will often corral a school of bait by circling it, forming the bait into a tight ball. Then a few fish at a time will peel out of the school and slice through the bait, grabbing a few bites in the process. This can happen with 10 pelagics and a school of bait no wider around than a kitchen table, or this can occur on a massive scale with ¼ mile of bait getting attacked by hundreds of fish. But for this ideal feeding harmony to come together, the water needs to be calm, as heavy wave action will disperse the bait, making it harder to find and therefore harder to control.

These peanut bunker are being corralled by false albacore along the edge of the surf line. Calm conditions offer better chances of finding this kind of scenario within range of your casts. Photo: Stan Kosinski

Pelagics that are corralling bait absolutely offer the best opportunity for you to connect, as they are preoccupied with one school of forage that they can keep working until it's gone. The problem is that a surfcaster is more likely to encounter cruising fish that zip up and down the wave line with incredible speed. Pelagics are easily spooked, and nothing will send them packing back to deeper water faster than too much boat traffic. When false albacore and bonito are close to the beach, boat anglers looking for light-tackle fun will often patrol the water just beyond the waves. Whereas this noise can sometimes push species like striped bass and bluefish closer to the beach, 9 times out of 10 pelagics will dive and bolt offshore. This is why some of the most successful surf anglers who chase them are on the beach in the dark, ready to make their first cast the second the sun peeks over the horizon.

Catching pelagics is all about utilizing windows of opportunity. The early-morning hours are one window, when the ocean is calm and not yet filled with engine noise from boats chasing schools of breaking fish. Tide swings can also provide windows. There are surely going to be no pelagics on a beach where no bait is present, but they can show up in the blink of an eye when an outgoing tide starts drawing rain bait or peanut bunker out of an inlet into the open ocean. With a steady food source being a main component of successful fishing, the fall months are going to provide the best action along the Atlantic coast for bonito and false albacore.

Both of these species migrate south and offshore for the winter months, but they need to pack on pounds for their journey. When the water temperature begins to drop in mid- to late September, two things happen. First, baitfish migrations begin, with spearing, mullet, and peanut bunker making their way out of the bays into the ocean. Second, pelagics that have been happily thriving 5 to 20 miles

Atlantic bonito may not be as big as false albacore, but they are brute fighters nonetheless. The best beach action for this species typically coincides with their fall migration in the Northeast as they feed heavily before heading south. Photo: Dave Skok/dwskok.com

offshore all summer are signaled by the drop in water temperature to go on a feeding tear. They know that there will be steady foraging opportunities closer to shore and will move in to hunt. But there can be a noticeable difference in feeding behavior as fall wears on.

"The first false albacore and bonito that show up early in the season can be finicky," says noted New York surfcaster Alberto Knie. "If you notice, in September, fish are most responsive to lures that perfectly match and move like the bait they're eating. But as it gets later in the fall, they suddenly start hitting almost anything that will fit in their mouths."

Knie's observation holds true because pelagics, like many other gamefish, go on a gluttonous feeding tear just before heading south in the fall. Of course, the fish will continue to feed as they migrate, so action that's furious one day in Montauk can turn to good action in New Jersey the next day. Pelagics will rarely stick around in water temperatures below 60 degrees, with 67- to 64-degree water being optimal for finding them close to the beach. But some years, water temperature aside, pelagics can come within a surfcaster's range for only a day or two, even in prime locations. Much of winning this game revolves around simply being in the right place at the right time and fishing frequently. If your buddy calls with a great pelagic report at 6 AM, don't expect them to be there at 6:30 . . . or the next morning, for that matter.

The fall months are also an excellent time to catch Spanish mackerel from Virginia to Texas. In Florida, it is possible to find these fish year-round, with even the winter months providing shots from the beach in the southern end of the state. The early-spring months see these fish begin to push up both the Florida coasts in a northward migration. As the water cools in the fall, Spanish migrate south again, offering surfcasters a second shot at roving schools. Throughout the Gulf, the summer season provides the best chances to hook these speedy mackerel from the sand, though between Alabama and North Texas, they are not targeted as passionately as they are in Florida. In South Texas, however, anglers fishing along Padre Island National Seashore frequently chase them throughout the summer, with fall baitfish migrations starting in September drawing in both greater numbers and bigger fish.

Tactics and Tackle for Beach Pelagics

"Whenever anyone is fishing Cape Hatteras, even if they're here for the red drum run, I always recommend having a lighter 9-foot rod rigged with a metal lure on hand," says Outer Banks surf expert Rob Alderman. "If Spanish mackerel or false albacore come through, you need something that will fire a small lure far and fast."

Though Alderman may be talking about just one area where pelagics frequently come into range of the beach, his suggestion applies anywhere they are found. The surfcaster who's parked on the sand with two baited lines out for striped bass or red drum has as much opportunity to catch these species as the angler chasing them specifically, but the key is preparedness. The pelagics don't offer the luxury of time. If you're watching baited lines, see a pod of albacore break the surface, and think you'll be able to rig a metal and catch them, it most likely won't happen. Unless there is a mass blitz in progress, plan on one good shot at roving pelagics.

Whenever casting to pelagics, it's important to lead the fish by putting lures ahead of them. Fast-moving species like this false albacore aren't likely to turn around for a lure that's behind them. Photo: Dave Skok/dwskok.com

With that in mind, anytime you line up a cast to moving fish, aim high and try to land your lure out in front of them. The technique is called "leading," and it can make or break a shot at false albacore or bonito. Since these fish are constantly on the go, if they're in pursuit of a school of bait, they'll have so much forward momentum that they're not likely to turn around to chase your lure. These fish will be looking ahead, so you essentially need to create a collision between them and your lure. And just as the pelagic species swim with bolts of speed, so should your offering.

All pelagic species are almost 100 percent reaction-strikers. They don't have the time to study a lure like a weakfish or striped bass that may follow at a distance before committing to the take. Pelagics see movement and react, and the faster that movement, the more likely you are to draw a strike. When your lure touches down, flip the bail closed and start cranking as fast as you can. While pelagics may be swimming a few feet under the surface, they're not usually eating right off the bottom in the surf, so lures need not sink very deep in most cases.

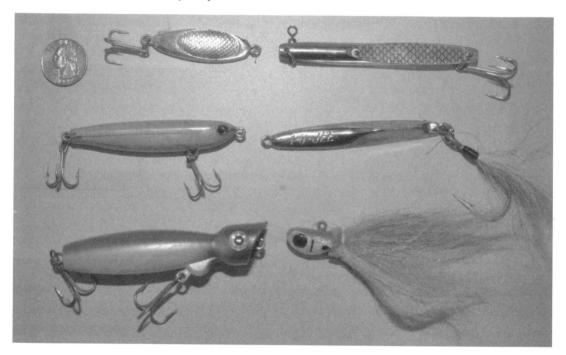

This collection of lures represents those that most frequently take pelagics in the surf. Note that they're relatively small in length and profile to match the rain bait on which these fish most frequently feed.

The retrieve speed combined with a pelagic's proclivity to react to shiny bait species make metal lures the all-around top producers. Not to mention, they are also the most likely lure to reach fish feeding a little farther out. Because pelagics feed so heavily on rain bait, thin-profile metals, such as Deadly Dicks and Point Jude Po-Jees, are going to outproduce most other lures on most days. As most metals have a streamlined, compact shape, they can be ripped through the water at high speed without sacrificing action. Likewise, smaller bucktail jigs are a close second for taking pelagics: A quick retrieve matched with a shaking rod tip produces a flutter that's hard for them to resist.

On occasion, especially during mid- to late fall when Atlantic pelagics are pushing south, small topwater lures can draw some highly memorable strikes. When choosing topwaters, opt for those that can be worked very quickly and still maintain their action. As an example, a Spook-style lure could work well, but if the fish are reacting best to fast-moving prey, you may not be able to maintain the proper side-to-side cadence during a very quick retrieve. Poppers are arguably the best topwater lures for pelagics, simply because they can be worked a bit sloppy on a speedy retrieve, but still splash and gurgle enough to make a fish hit. Small diving and lipless plugs work well, too, though casting distance can become an issue when the fish are cruising beyond the waves. These lures are much more popular with anglers in prime Spanish mackerel territory, especially along the Gulf coast, where the fish feed very close to shore and the water is typically more calm. But if there is one lure that is a staple of the southern and Gulf Spanish mackerel fishery, it's the Got-Cha plug.

Got-Cha plugs are very simple lures consisting of a slanted lead head and tubular plastic body. Though they may not be complex, they are a staple for Spanish mackerel in the southern Atlantic and Gulf states.

Got-Chas are incredibly simple lures, qualifying as a cross between a jig and a plug. The slanted leadhead is fitted into a tapered, tubular plastic body. While I've often shaken my head at these ugly little offerings, they have a unique action when you jerk the rod tip during the retrieve, causing them to rise and fall. At the same time, they can be brought back with a straight retrieve and produce just as well. One point of note relating to Got-Chas is that because they sink quickly, they are best used on beaches with some deeper water; shallow beaches won't provide enough depth for them to achieve their famous rise-and-fall action. There are many Got-Cha colors available, though the original (and still one of the most productive) is the classic red head with a white body. While these lures account for loads of landed Spanish mackerel, they'll just as quickly snap up the same small metals and bucktails favored by false albacore and bonito.

Once you've got a lure selected, you can worry about setting your drag. As soon as you set the hook, all pelagics are going to take off like a bullet. If you can get through the first run, you're halfway there. To that end, it is very important to keep your drag set lighter than normal; these fish have a habit of hitting a lure so fast, the hook only catches the inside of their lip, making it vulnerable to pulling

Like the other pelagic species, Spanish mackerel are suckers for metal lures. This one fell to a small AVA Diamond Jig. Photo: Darren Dorris

free. Avoid the temptation to crank the drag down or horse a fish in, as you can easily end up with a broken rod. To minimize the amount of line a fish runs off, always follow it as it moves down the beach. You also never want to give a pelagic any slack; keep the same amount of pressure on the rod whether you're reeling or just holding it and letting the fish run. But don't reel against the drag, as this can create line twists. Just be ready to reel as fast as you can when a fish turns and runs at you. You've got to pick up the slack very fast in order to put the pressure back on.

A final tackle element that's very important is leader. With bonito and Spanish mackerel, teeth become an issue. For the most part, metal lures and Got-Chas will rarely be swallowed, thereby

Though they're not very large fish, bonito have very sharp teeth. You can adjust for this by using 30- or 40-pound fluorocarbon leaders when casting small lures.

making it difficult for the fish to reach and sever the leader. But sometimes the trick to success is downsizing to very small offerings. If that's the case, fluorocarbon leader is a must. Though bonito and Spanish aren't particularly large fish, it's worth using 30- to 40-pound leader material just for its abrasion resistance. It can be hassle to keep changing leaders, though catch rates can be noticeably higher when using fluorocarbon as opposed to a wire leader. Because wire is stiff, it can also cause a loss of action with some lures. False albacore have teeth as well, but they are much smaller and will rarely cut through 30- or 40-pound fluorocarbon.

Surf Pelagics on the Table

While it might be fair to say that none of the pelagic species available to the surfcaster are as prized as relatives like the bluefin tuna, wahoo, or yellowfin tuna, there is still fine dining to be had with these fish depending on your personal taste. For starters, though the false albacore seems like it would provide a meal for the whole family, I promise the family will never speak to you again if you cook one. The name says it all. These fish can be confused with "true" albacore, which have white, mild meat. I have heard whispers and murmurs that some people find false albacore an excellent source of homemade sashimi, though I can't say I'd recommend trying it. I've sliced up my share of them for use as bait strips, and the meat is so blood- and oil-rich, it can appear almost black. I'd say catch-and-release is the way to go.

Many people say the same thing about Atlantic bonito, though I find them very good to eat. Bonito are an acquired taste, and while they are not oily like a false albacore, they do have a fishier

A few racks of Atlantic bonito fillets come out of the wood smoker.

flavor, though I personally would not call it overpowering. To help quell that taste, bonito benefit from a marinade. My favorite is soy sauce, garlic, ginger, rice wine vinegar, and lime juice. I'll coat the fillets in sesame seeds after marinating and put them on the grill or in the broiler. Bonito doesn't work as well cooked with traditional whitefish recipes, so if you like your fish with butter, lemon, and herbs, bonito may not be for you. It is, however, an excellent fish for smoking. I like to do so with applewood, then serve the fish on a bagel with cream cheese, or mince the meat and mix it with cream cheese to make a smoked fish dip.

Of all the pelagics, Spanish mackerel is easily the most valued as a food fish. It has mild flavor and light pink or white flesh that takes well to many cooking methods. As with bonito, I find that an Asian marinade or citrus dressing works best when Spanish mackerel is grilled. However, this fish is more suitable to frying or baking if those are your preferred methods. Though the practice of preparing sushi at home may not be incredibly widespread, Spanish mackerel cost top dollar in restaurants when served raw. Naturally, if you plan to eat it this way, utmost care has to be taken to maintain maximum freshness. I've actually had sashimi from fresh-caught Spanish mackerel, and must say it was better than that of the best sushi restaurant in town.

Chapter 10

Skills of the Surf Angler

"What Do I Do Now?"

I still get a laugh every time I think back to a surf trip with a friend from college. Nick wasn't that passionate an angler, but after hearing me talk about what a good fall it had been for striped bass, he begged to come along. So I scrounged up an extra pair of waders and a dry top, picked him up at the dorm at 3:30 in the morning, and off we went. The entire ride to the beach I prepped him on how to work a paddle-tail shad, slowly bumping the bottom and slightly shaking the rod tip. We talked about how to hold the rod and set the hook. We went over what the bite would feel like. When it came time to start casting, he caught on pretty quickly, and once I knew he was doing okay, I walked down the beach to give him some space. Ten minutes later, I glanced down toward him and saw his rod doubled over. He looked back at me frantically and cried, "What do I do now?"

There are many scenarios in surf fishing that might have you asking yourself what to do next. After all, hooking the fish is only part of the game. Aside from fighting and landing a fish, what do you do if that fish has teeth? How do you properly release a fish? What should you do if you accidentally stick a hook in your arm? If you decide to keep a fish, how do you care for the catch and clean it for the table? Having the knowledge to answer all these questions makes a surfcaster well rounded, and ultimately safer and more successful on the sand.

Fighting and Landing Big Fish

On a boat, you have the luxury of bringing a fish up vertically from the depths. Usually there is a nice, big landing net waiting for the capture. In the surf, a fight can be a little more involved, especially when dealing with large specimens. When fish aren't in deep water where they can freely dive when

Landing a big fish in the surf is not as straightforward as cranking and pulling with all your might. The trick is learning to use the waves to your advantage when it comes to the endgame. Photo: Darren Dorris

hooked, they have nowhere to go except out. To that end, a big fish hooked in the surf will do its best to escape to deep water beyond the waves. Small species will come to the beach with relative ease, but should you hook into a heavy cobia, striped bass, or red drum, there are some maneuvers you should keep in mind.

One big mistake that causes anglers to lose a lot of fish is not moving with their catch. If the bruiser you've just set the hook on is peeling line up or down the beach, the last thing you want to do is stand in one spot. Always follow your fish and reel as you walk. You need to take up slack constantly to maintain steady pressure. Despite what you might see freshwater anglers do on TV, don't angle your rod to the side or low to the water. The less line you have in the water, the less chance there is of wave action moving that line and potentially loosening the hook's hold. Use the length of a surf rod to your advantage and keep it high and arched throughout the fight. Moving also helps you keep a shorter length of line between you and the fish, thereby reducing the amount of seaweed your line can collect.

The most critical point in landing a big fish on the beach is when it gets into the very shallow wash. Once that fish's belly hits the sand, your line will go slack. Even if you've maintained solid pressure during the battle, just one instant of slack can cause the hook to come loose. When a fish is shallow, use the waves to your advantage by surfing the catch to your feet. Don't try to horse the fish across the shallow bottom. Instead, keep pressure on the line and wait for an incoming wave to lift the fish off the bottom. As the wave rolls in, back up the beach while reeling. If the wave recedes and the fish still isn't within your reach, wait for the next wave and surf it again. Once the fish is close you'll want to wait for the wash to draw out, leaving the fish beached. Now you can run down and grab the trophy by the tail or under the gills and drag it away from the water. Just remember that if you intend to release the fish, you should never hold it by the gills or drag it too far from the wash.

Properly Releasing Fish

Just as there is an art to fighting and landing large fish in the surf, there is art in a proper release. Given size and bag limits on gamefish, plus the conservation ethic that has infected anglers, you are obviously not going to be able to or want to keep every fish you catch. But nothing is more upsetting than watching anglers outright mistreat a catch that won't be kept. I've seen people kick black drum back into the wash and throw undersized flounder over a shoulder. Such practices make little sense to me—you're harming a flounder that might be legal next season, or potentially killing a drum that someone else might like to hook. Proper releasing skills are a must.

If a fish is to be let go, ideally you won't have to handle it very much. For starters, make every effort once a fish is beaten to kneel down and work with it on the wet sand or in the shallow wash. Grabbing a fish and raising it to your chest only adds unneeded stress. Try to remove the hook with pliers without roughly handling the catch. Never grab by the gills a fish that you intend to release. Species without sharp teeth, such as snook and striped bass, can be gently held by the lower lip for stabilization if necessary.

When releasing a fish, gently cradle it in the water, supporting the head by placing one hand below and behind the gills, and using the other to support the tail: Photo: Dave Skok/ dwskok.com

If the hook is buried deep, a hook disgorger can come in handy. These tools feature a long rod with a hooked or rounded end designed to slide down your line and rest in the hook's bend. Once in place, a quick pop should dislodge the hook. But if the hook is truly buried and the fish is not legal to keep, clip the line immediately as close to the hook's eye as possible. It will be the best chance the fish has for survival.

Once the hook has been removed, gently cradle the catch, supporting the head just under the gills with one hand and the base of the tail with the other. Move the fish to water just deep enough for it to swim and slowly rock it back and forth. This gets water moving across the gills and aids revival. The fish should kick naturally and swim off strong.

Some of the best advice I ever heard regarding releasing fish came from good friend and *Field & Stream* editor-at-large Kirk Deeter. He told me that once a fish is landed and you're about to begin the release process, hold your breath. About the same time that you start getting uncomfortable, assume the fish is ready for a breath, too. This trick really teaches you to work quickly and effectively when releasing a catch.

Dealing with Toothy Fish

You may have seen largemouth bass anglers on television fight a fish, then reach down and pull it from the water by the lip. Don't try that in the surf. While there are some routinely surf-caught species with no teeth, the majority have chompers. Fish like sea trout, flounder, weakfish, and even croakers have little teeth. But bonito, bluefish, and Spanish mackerel have bigger ones, and none of these species will be shy about trying to take a bite of your hand while you're removing the hook.

If you catch a toothy species that you intend to keep, grabbing the fish under the gills is a fine way to secure it for hook removal. This hold often calms the catch, or at least reduces its ability to flop and wriggle. The hand under the gills is now out of harm's way, leaving your other hand free to carefully remove the hook with pliers or a disgorger. If you're going to release the fish, keep it in the shallow wash and carefully place your hand behind its head for stabilization. Do not grab and squeeze, but apply just enough pressure to keep the head still while you remove the hook with your other hand.

Some anglers that frequently tussle with bluefish carry a BogaGrip, a tool that helps land and release fish with teeth without the need to grab or hold the catch with bare hands. Bogas feature two

BogaGrips allow you to land and unhook toothy fish while keeping your hands clear of their mouths.

spring-loaded steel pinchers that lock onto a fish's bottom jaw. Once locked, you can support the fish on the Boga, keeping one hand well away from the mouth while using the other to remove the hook with pliers. BogaGrips also feature a built-in scale that allows you to weigh the catch before it hits the cooler or swims free.

Caring for Your Catch

As I've noted the food value of each species described in chapters 8 and 9, some basic information on cleaning and caring for your catch will surely come in handy if you plan to fish for your dinner. Keeping your catch cold once landed is a no-brainer for maintaining its fresh taste on the table, but if you're the kind of surfcaster who prefers being mobile and covering lots of ground, carrying a cooler full of ice is not very feasible. In colder regions like the Northeast and Northwest, fish left on the beach will stay cool long enough to make it back to a cooler of ice in your car. But during the summer or in warmer regions, nothing will spoil a catch faster than heat.

One trick is to bury your fish in the sand, mark the spot, and return for it later. The idea here is to dig deep enough to reach cooler, moist sand, which will lower the temperature of the fish and help keep it from drying out. If this seems like too much of a hassle, at the very least carry a length of cord to create a stringer. Run the cord through the gills and out the fish's mouth. Now you simply let your catch drag in the water, which will be cooler than the air, if only by a few degrees.

Fish that are oil-rich, particularly cobia and bluefish, should be bled out immediately. Once a fish expires, its blood can actually taint the meat, making it less palatable. However, proper bleeding means the fish pumps out all its blood on its own. Simply puncturing the head or gills will generally cause the fish to die before all the blood is gone. My favorite way to bleed a catch is to sever one or two gills with either my knife or the cutters on my pliers. As the fish dies, it will continue to attempt breathing and pump out its blood through the cut gills. It's not a pretty process, but if you are going to kill a fish for the table, you may as well be sure it tastes as good as possible instead of being unhappy with the flavor and potentially wasting the catch. Some anglers insist that almost every species needs bleeding, but I disagree. White-fleshed species like sea trout, flounder, and striped bass maintain excellent flavor without being bled.

Basic Filleting

Although small- to medium-sized fish can be sliced from just forward of the anal fin to the chin, gutted, and cooked whole, most people prefer to dine on boneless fillets. I happen to be one of them, so presented here is a guide to basic filleting. In this reference, an Atlantic croaker is on the cutting board. But no matter what size or species of fish you're filleting, a sharp, flexible fillet knife is a must. Dull blades can quickly ruin your catch, or at least make it more difficult to get the maximum amount of meat off the fish. Blades should measure at least 8 inches for fish up to approximately 30 inches long. Any bigger than that, and you'll want a longer blade to easily work with the wider body and thicker girth.

All Fillet Step Photos: Melissa Pulicare

Step 1: Slice the fish diagonally across the head, passing the knife behind the pectoral fin and ending at the stomach. Be careful not to sever the head. You should feel the knife hit the spine as you cut. Once it does so, you know that the incision is deep enough. Done correctly, the spine will remain intact during the filleting process.

Step 2: Holding the tail to stabilize the fish, make a small cut at the base of the tail. Now work the knife under the meat, turning the blade so it's parallel to the cutting board. This is where blade flexibility becomes very important. A stiff blade will not allow you to achieve the proper cutting angle.

Step 3: Working toward the head, slide the knife under the meat using the spine as a guide. If the blade resists, it means the edge is hitting the spine and should be angled upward slightly. The spine should be making contact with the back of the blade as it moves. If no contact is made, you might be cutting too shallow and will end up losing a lot of meat. To keep the fish stable, continue to slide your fingers along the spine under the flap of meat. Try to avoid stopping and starting. Working in one clean pass will produce better fillets. This is why making sure your knife is razor sharp before starting is critical.

Step 4: Once you reach the head, angle the blade up and finish the cut by pulling the knife through the first incision made in step 1. The fillet should fall away from the body easily. Repeat steps 1 through 4 on the other side of the fish.

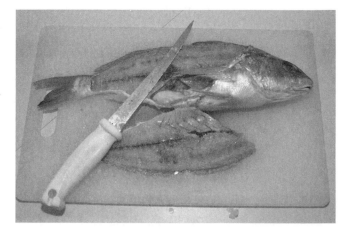

Step 5: If you prefer to cook your fillets with the skin on, you can remove the scales with your knife by scraping against their grain. When complete, the fillet would be ready for the oven. I prefer to skin the fillets. To do so, start by laying the fillet skin-side down on the cutting board. Make a small cut at the thin tail end, and work your knife at an angle between the skin and the meat.

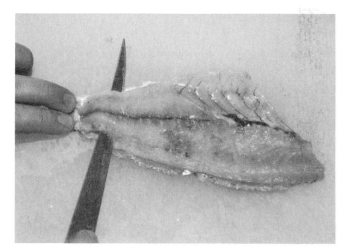

Step 6: With the same motion used to remove the fillet from the body, slide the blade smoothly along the backside of the skin. If your knife is sharp, there should be no sawing motion involved. As in step 3, slide your fingers forward behind the blade to stabilize the skin until the knife passes through cleanly and the two pieces are separated.

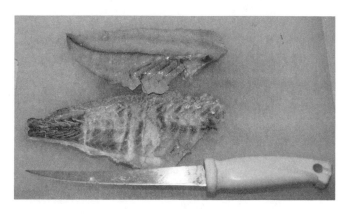

Step 7: The final step—which is not always necessary—is to cut away the rib cage at the front of the fillet. The meat between the ribs is typically thin and worth discarding unless you don't mind a bone or two in your fillet—which defeats the purpose in my opinion. With the fillet trimmed to your liking, you can vacuum-seal and freeze it or keep it in the refrigerator for a few days before cooking, though

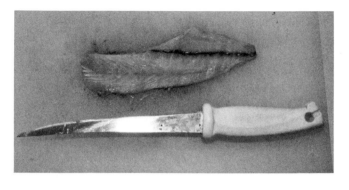

I'd recommend covering it as fish can absorb flavors and odors from other foods. Also, never rinse a fillet off with fresh water—even if there are few scales or blood on it—until just before you're ready to cook. When you do rinse it, the colder the water the better. Fresh water will quickly cause the flesh of saltwater species to turn mushy.

Hooking—and Unhooking—Yourself

Fish long enough, put in some years, and sooner or later you will get hooked. It's an inevitability that just needs to be accepted by an angler. You might think, *I'm too careful to ever hook myself*. Trust me, it happens when you least expect it, and often you're hooked by someone else who isn't so careful. It happens on windy days as your lure swings prior to a cast. It happens when a fish flops during the unhooking process, sending the other treble hook on the lure into your skin. It's a matter of when, not if. The question you need to answer after getting hooked is whether or not the hook can be removed on the beach or if you need to seek medical attention. Depth of the point, location, and hook size all factor into this decision.

There is a difference between getting poked and getting hooked. "Poked" typically means the point breaks your skin, but it doesn't dig in past the barb. In this case, it's easily removed with no more worry than a little pinch and drop of blood. It's when a hook lodges in past the barb that the situation can get more serious, as the hook won't simply back out. When this happens, prep the hook for removal right away. Clip the line or leader as close to the hook eye as possible to relieve any tension. If you've been hooked with a lure, carefully separate the hook from the lure body either by opening the split ring on the hook or clipping the hook free with cutters. If you're dealing with a treble hook, once free of the lure, clip off the remaining hook points. Anytime you or a friend gets hooked in the face, especially near the eye, leave immediately for the closest emergency medical facility, regardless of the size of the hook. Likewise, if you're dealing with a hook that's too thick in diameter to be clipped with pliers or cutters, it's best to let a doctor undertake the removal.

Small- to medium-sized lighter-gauge hooks can often be safely removed on the beach, as most hookings occur in the hands or arms. If the hook is embedded shallow just under the skin, sometimes the easiest and most painless way to remove it is to keep pushing the hook up until it exits your skin. Then you can clip the point below the barb and back out the shank through the entrance hole. If the hook is deeply buried past the barb, you're going to need some assistance, and it won't be particularly pleasant. Still, there is a tried-and-true method for getting the hook out efficiently and leaving you in good enough shape to continue fishing.

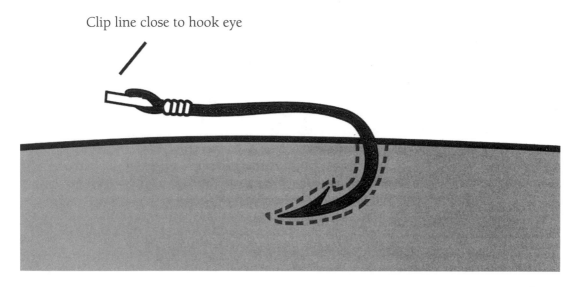

Clip line close to hook eye

Step 1: Clip the line as close to the hook eye as possible. As noted, when dealing with lures and treble hooks, first separate the lure body from the hook and clip off the remaining hook points.

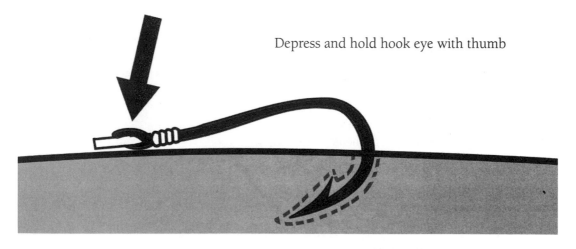

Depress and hold hook eye with thumb

Step 2: With your thumb, depress the hook eye and keep it held down. This angles the point and helps realign it with the track it followed going in. This is important, as it will reduce the amount of resistance created by the barb as it exits.

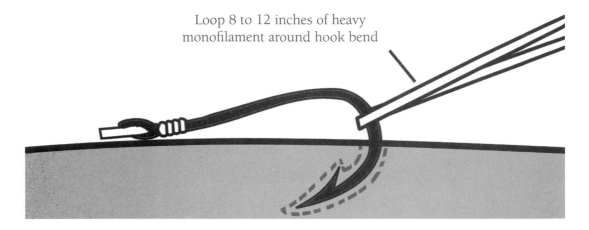

Loop 8 to 12 inches of heavy
monofilament around hook bend

Step 3: Have a friend or fellow angler loop an 8- to 12-inch piece of heavy monofilament around the bend of the hook. I always carry a piece of 80-pound-test mono for just this purpose. If none is available, cut a longer length of light mono from your reel and double or triple it up before looping. If the hook is stuck somewhere other than your hand or arm, you can perform this step on your own.

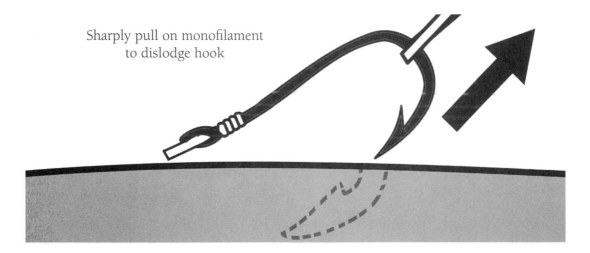

Sharply pull on monofilament
to dislodge hook

Step 4: Have the other person sharply jerk the line while your thumb is still depressing the hook eye. The person responsible for pulling should not hesitate or tug gently. One quick pop should back out the hook relatively smoothly, causing the least amount of pain and barb damage.

Once the hook is free, apply antiseptic ointment and small bandage or piece of waterproof tape. If you don't have these items in your vehicle's first-aid kit, or aren't fishing near your vehicle, rinse the wound off with salt water and treat it immediately once you get to the car or back home. One final note of importance: Rusty hooks can potentially lead to tetanus, so it's wise to make sure your vaccinations are up to date. If they're not and you get stuck with a rusted hook, it's worth popping into the doctor's office to make sure everything is okay and you're fit to hit the beach again.

Chapter 11

Fishing the Rocks

Attacking Jetties and Rocky Shorelines

So far, we've discussed the approach you'll want to take to successfully land gamefish from the beach. In this case, "beach" refers to the main oceanfront shoreline, be it composed of sand, pebbles, or mud. But on many of these beaches, you'll find rock jetties jutting out into the water. If it seems to make sense that fishing from the end of a jetty would be productive, you're right. Likewise, fishing around jetties from the sand can significantly increase your catch rates.

There are also many beaches, particularly from New England to New York, that are notoriously rocky, and boulders and rock piles near the beach provide structure that many gamefish species can't resist. Most of the time, these kinds of shorelines are best fished with lures, simply because sinkers can get easily snagged, and you'll end up losing a lot of bait rigs. But there is more to change in your approach than just fishing style. The rocks that make up famous beaches like those at Montauk Point in New York and many Rhode Island beaches are often referred to as "greased bowling balls" by local surfcasters. They can pose a serious challenge to the angler. Therefore, fishing rocky surf is not quite so simple as grabbing your rod and heading out, but the payoff can be phenomenal. Before we dive into the fishing tactics that will make you successful on rocky beaches and jetties, let's first look at some of the gear you'll need.

Fishing on rock jetties can help you gain offshore distance, as well as provide shots at fish you might not have gotten from the sand. But it also requires a bit of specialized gear and a few lessons in safety.

Gear Up for the Rocks

Before strolling out onto a jetty or rocky beach, understand that some safety concerns come into play once you leave the sand. While it's true that jetties and boulder points can provide some of the best surf action, it's also fair to say that fishing them is not as casual as planting a couple sand spikes on the beach. This doesn't mean that the rocks are always complex, but there is a certain level of commitment that comes with fishing them, most of which revolves around paying close attention to your surroundings at all times. There are also a few pieces of specialized gear no "rock hopper" should be without. By far the most important is a pair of jetty cleats.

Any rocks or hard surfaces that are constantly wet with or submerged in salt water will develop a thin coat of algae. In most cases, you'll spot a brown or green film on the rock, but sometimes this slime can be tough to see with the naked eye. Even if you think there is none on the rocks you want to fish, take no chances. Jetty cleats strap onto your wader boots and have sharp metal or carbide spikes on the soles. Though it may seem counterproductive to walk on slippery rocks with little spikes, you need to understand how they work.

Notice the thin layer of algae on this rock. It's this slimy film that causes more injuries than anything else in surf fishing.

The spikes penetrate through this slime and make contact with the actual rock surface, giving you sure footing. If you were to attempt walking on these rocks with flat soles, the bottom of your foot would simply slide across the algae. Considering that fishing jetties often goes hand in hand with facing crashing waves, having spikes to keep you planted reduces your risk of getting washed off. Believe me, falling on jetties can result in serious injury or death. One of the most popular and affordable brand of spikes are those from Korkers (www.korkers.com). Their jetty cleats feature screw-in spikes that make changing or replacing them easy and convenient. Cleats are so important to anglers throughout New England, specifically on the coasts of Rhode Island and at Montauk Point, they'll go one step farther by duct-taping them to their boots after strapping them on. If you were to wade a little way out or walk to the end of a jetty and lose a cleat, you could be in serious trouble.

However, jetty cleats shouldn't be viewed as a means to run as fast as you can to the end of the rocks. It's critical that you mind your footing at all times and give some thought to your next step. Never rush across the rocks, and always try to find the flattest possible spots before setting your foot down. As you fish jetties and rocky beaches more often, you'll quickly learn what feels right as you walk. Rocks and boulders that are slanted can be the most dangerous. Likewise, it's never smart to jump from rock to rock. If the gap between boulders on a jetty is too wide to easily step across, find another way around.

Though scattered submerged boulders on rocky coastlines offer the advantage of height, I would recommend staying off them until you build confidence on the rocks. Even with cleats on, standing on boulders puts your center of gravity higher, thereby making you more inclined to slip

Cleats are an absolute must when fishing a jetty or rocky coastline. The spike on the soles will penetrate through algae to give you more stable footing.

when facing incoming waves. Instead, fish next to large boulders, bracing your legs behind or along their sides to increase your stability. When moving over rocky bottom, it's safer to shuffle your feet than lift your legs, as losing contact with the bottom makes you more vulnerable to slipping or losing your balance when a wave washes in. Try not to cross one leg over the other as you move, and always make sure one leg is firmly planted before shifting the other.

Though it's already been established that a headlamp is a must for fishing in the dark, consider buying a lamp that's waterproof and that has an indicator or "strobe" setting if you plan to fish the rocks. With this setting, the light will flash on and off rapidly. Remember that jetties, those along inlets especially, are most likely going to have current running down their sides from tidal push and pull. So if you happen to slip or get knocked off, you might not be able to simply climb out in the same spot you went in. If you can remember to quickly turn on the strobe setting of your headlamp, other anglers on the rocks can better mark your location in the water should you start getting pulled by the current. It's a very frightening scenario, but unfortunately one that happens all too often in the world of surfcasting.

Landing and Releasing Fish Safely from a Jetty

One of the most dangerous times for jetty anglers to make a mistake is during the landing of a fish. I've seen seasoned fishermen suddenly lose their wits and scramble to lower rocks when a fish is on the line, slipping and getting seriously injured. Remember that the closer to the water a rock is positioned, the more algae-covered and slick it will be. Never forget that safety comes before any fish. Successfully landing fish off a jetty simply boils down to good planning and keeping your cool.

Before standing on large submerged boulders, get used to the feel of walking on smaller rocks. If you're a novice angler, you're best off using rocks like this one to brace your legs against until you're confident in your balance. Photo: Rick Bach

Right off the bat, many dedicated rock hoppers opt to fish rods with a little extra backbone for lifting small to medium-sized specimens straight out of the water. But when dealing with heavier fish, it is often necessary to scope out a landing zone before you start casting. Look for angled rocks close to the water that may help you slide a fish up, or find outcroppings in the rocks that fill with water as waves roll in. You can play a fish into one of these outcroppings and use the water to your advantage, letting a rising swell lift the fish to where you can grab it more effectively. You may also find a spot that will allow you to safely descend lower to the water when it comes time for a landing. This makes daylight scouting of a jetty you intend to fish at night very important. The more familiar you are with the rocks, the safer and more successful you'll be in the end.

Depending on how far out you happen to be, it's also possible to walk a hooked fish back to the beach to land it, though this is more the exception than the rule. You may want to do so for a true trophy, but you certainly aren't going to walk every fish you hook back to the stand, weaving around other anglers as you make your way.

Should you intend to release a catch from a high jetty, gently cradling it in the water until it catches its breath is not always an option. But there is a release method that is safer for the fish and gives them the best chance for healthy survival. Once you have a fish off the hook, support the head under the gills with one hand while holding the tail with the other just as you would a fish in the shallow wash prior to release on the beach. With one swift motion, throw the fish off the jetty like a spear, headfirst. The idea is to quickly send a flush of water over the gills when the fish splashes down. Think of it as a shot of caffeine that should jump-start the fish's breathing. It's not as reliable as gently reviving a fish in the water, but your safety comes first, and this method gives fish the best odds for fighting another day.

Two Uses for Jetty Gaffs

Another tool specific to the jetty angler is a long-handled landing gaff. Jetty gaffs are typically made of Calcutta reeds measuring 8 to 12 feet long and have a barbless hook at one end that measures anywhere from 3 to 5 inches across. Most of these gaffs are homemade with material from tackle shops and hardware stores. When a fish is near the rocks, these long gaffs allow you to snag the fish and haul it up. Of course, catch-and-release is no longer an option once you gaff a fish. I often carry a gaff out on the rocks, but will only use it if I hook a fish I know is of legal size, I'm sure I want to keep it, and I've decided there is no other way to safely land it. Be sure to check regulations before using a jetty gaff in your local area. Gaffing regulations often vary by state and species.

Long jetty gaffs not only are helpful for landing large fish from high rocks, but can also increase safety by offering something to grab if they're wedged between rocks and a strong wave washes over.

Even if you never use a jetty gaff to land a catch, they have another use that could save your life, and actually once saved me from potential disaster. When you carry a gaff onto the jetty, wedge the butt end deeply between two rocks and fish close by. Should a wave break on a jetty that threatens to knock you off, you can grab the gaff and hang on to it as the wave passes. A few years ago while fishing a jetty near Asbury Park, New Jersey, I crouched down to rig a lure just as a slightly larger-than-average wave smacked into the rocks. Had I been standing, I would have taken the hit with little ado, but my center of gravity was low, and the wave took my feet right out from under me. Luckily, I grabbed my gaff, which was secured in the rocks next to me. I got wet, but I didn't get washed off.

Other Safety Measures

In the boat-fishing world, there is a practice known as "filing a float plan," but in my opinion it applies just as much to surfcasters, especially those who frequent rocky beaches or jetties. *Float plan* is nothing but a fancy term for telling someone your intentions for the day. This is particularly important for fishermen heading out to the rocks alone. Before leaving, make sure someone knows where you plan to fish, and what time you'll be back. Thanks to cell phones, your return time can always be changed if the fishing is on fire, but should you not call in an extension and not show up, it lets someone know that things may have gone awry.

Even if you're fishing with a friend during broad daylight, every so often look to make sure he or she is still standing upright and on the jetty. It may seem trivial, but I can remember just a few years ago when a solo jetty jumper was knocked into the water at New Jersey's Barnegat Inlet and clung to a rock, trying to avoid being pulled out to sea, for over two hours before he was rescued. If I'm fishing a jetty in the dark, I'll occasionally turn on my headlamp and face my friend, who will flick on his light as a signal that he's still standing. Even shouting "hey" every once in a while will work. You might be surprised at how difficult it can be to see someone just 20 feet away on a dark jetty when the waves are breaking.

Because some of the best jetty fishing can occur on rougher days, it's important to keep in constant communication with your fishing partner on the rocks, or let someone know when you plan to be home if you're fishing alone.
Photo: Darren Dorris

Though this view from the lighthouse of Montauk, New York's, Turtle Cove may make it look easily maneuverable, the rock fields just a few feet out in the surf can be dangerous if you're not prepared to navigate them.
Photo: Rick Bach

Of course, it's not as if every time you walk out onto a jetty, waves will be breaking at knee level and the wind will be whipping. On a calm day, fishing a jetty can be no different than standing on a tranquil lakeshore. But the reason there is so much emphasis placed on jetty and rocky beach safety is because some species, particularly striped bass and bluefish, feed more heavily along a jetty during rough conditions. Roiled surface action compounded by waves will disorient schools of baitfish. Gamefish will pin the bait against a jetty, cutting of its escape route, and keep attacking until the food source has been exhausted. No matter what, never turn your back on incoming waves if they are breaking hard.

Approaching Beachfront Jetties

In any kind of fishing, structure plays a vital role. Though we've already discussed in chapter 6 that "beach structure" can simply be a sandy trough underwater, jetties offer pros and beginners alike the chance to skip reading the beach and focus their efforts on a clearly visible target. By the way, you don't necessarily have to walk out onto a jetty to cash in on its benefits. The first step in attacking a jetty is understanding where and when fish will use this prime structure to feed.

Surfcaster Chris Foster works the deep pocket along a short beachfront jetty. These holes are an excellent location to find both roving gamefish that herd bait against the jetty, and predators lying in ambush, waiting for an easy meal to come to them.

The purpose of a jetty is to slow beach erosion by acting as a barrier against wave action moving too much sand away from a given area. As sand is pushed down the surf line, it will stop when it meets the rocks. Therefore, what you'll often find around a jetty is that the side that takes the brunt of the wave action will be shallower, as moving sand is constantly being stacked up. On the other side of the jetty, wave action will move sand away, creating a deep depression. These holes that form in the corner where a jetty meets the beach are often called "pockets" by surf anglers, and they offer fantastic fishing opportunities. You can usually identify the deeper side of a jetty by noting how incoming waves behave, much like you would when identifying a main beach trough. Barring tremendously rough surf, waves should roll into the pocket and diminish. Given the nature of how waves crash into a jetty, with the exception of very calm days, the surface may not completely flatten. But the shallow side of a jetty will usually feature more whitewater and inbound waves combing through, colliding harder with the rocks.

Pockets present the perfect feeding location for almost any gamefish. Striped bass, weakfish, bluefish, and snook are just a few species that love to herd a school of baitfish into a jetty pocket, where the buffet line can go on for hours. Likewise, a stiff offshore wind can also blow baitfish into a pocket. The bait becomes trapped against the rocks, and gamefish will, in some cases, continue to feed until the school is decimated. But even if you don't find a mass of bait trapped in a pocket, it doesn't mean there is no bait present. It's ironic, but baitfish perceive safety in deep water and against structure, so they are naturally drawn to pockets. This also makes a pocket the ideal location to find ambush predators. Though striped bass and weakfish will corral bait schools, they will also hunker down and wait for a meal to come to them. Surf anglers chasing flounder that lie in wait for a baitfish to swim by find some their biggest fish in jetty pockets. Though you can fish a pocket from any point along a jetty, it's smart to start by working close from the beach before walking out onto the rocks.

Gamefish patrolling or ambushing in a jetty pocket can be found consistently in a few different areas. They will cruise the inshore edge of the drop-off closest to the beach waiting for baitfish to stray out of the pocket into the waves, or get pushed out of the deeper water into the surf line. You can also find gamefish holding tight to the rocks, as the boulders provide cover that allows them to stay in one position more easily than out in the current or waves. Don't overlook the outside edge of a pocket, either, especially at the point where the waves just begin to build and roll. The first swell will kick up the sand and expose sand eels or crustaceans as it moves. Species like flounder and sea trout will hang right along the downward slope of the pocket and pick off this forage. Just remember that the productivity of a jetty pocket is strongly related to tidal stage. At dead-low tide, there might not be enough water to make a pocket worthwhile to gamefish. As a general rule, pockets fish best at the very end of the incoming tide and during the first few hours of the outgoing. With the former, baitfish will theoretically move in as the water rises, with gamefish following. During the outgoing tide, bait holding the pocket will be drawn out to sea into the mouths of predators waiting on the perimeter.

The tip of a beachfront jetty is just as important as the pocket, and in some respects offers gamefish an even better point of ambush. As the tide flushes out, baitfish holding along the sides of a jetty for cover will get flushed with the water, right past fish waiting at the tip. As water moves around a jetty, sometimes a calm eddy can form at the end, also providing a spot for gamefish to hold out of the main current. This eddy can actually span out off the tip of the rocks a fair distance, so don't assume that every strike will come right along the boulders. One of the best approaches to fishing the end of a

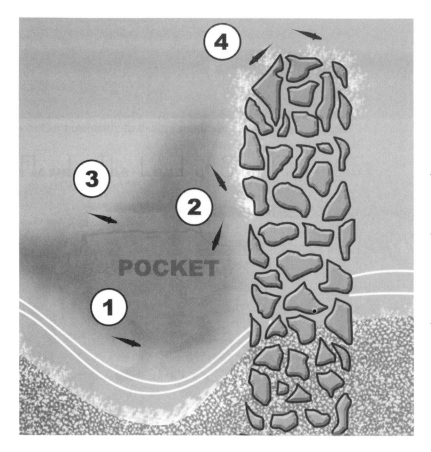

If gamefish aren't notice-ably attacking bait schools along a jetty, look for fish in these four spots: 1. Patrolling the inshore edge of the jetty pocket, 2. Holding tight along the jetty, waiting for a meal to come to them, 3. Cruis-ing or holding along the outside edge of a pocket, 4. Stationed at the tip of a jetty, waiting for bait to flush down the side of the rocks as the tide falls.

jetty can be using the outgoing tidal sweep to bring your lures naturally to waiting gamefish. Artificials like bucktail jigs and diving plugs should be cast slightly off to the side of the tip and worked slowly, allowing current and waves to swing them around the front of the jetty. Of course, a direct cast off the end and a retrieve that brings your offering straight back will also produce very well.

Baitfish constantly change their position in the water column to compensate for the chop-pier conditions often associated with jetties. Predators holding near the bottom around the rocks are not necessarily looking to feed low, but rather waiting for bait to swim overhead. This makes jetties a particularly good place to work topwater lures. Gamefish that may not rise to a popper or Spook-style lure down the beach are more likely to shoot up and smack one around the rocks. When working a topwater, always end your retrieve as close to the rocks as possible. You'd be shocked at just how close gamefish will sit to the boulders. Likewise, many gamefish will follow a lure from off the tip or out in the pocket and strike just before you're about to lift the lure out of the water. These close attacks, which are not limited to topwater lures, can be heart-stopping, and anglers who aren't ready for them frequently miss the fish.

One of the heaviest striped bass I ever caught from a jetty hit in this manner, startling me so badly I almost lost my rod. While retrieving a popper, I stopped the lure just at the edge of the rocks and began digging in my tackle bag looking for something else to throw. The popper was just bobbing

Gamefish can be more inclined to strike a topwater lure around a jetty than elsewhere on the beach. This striped bass fell to a Creek Chub Knuckle-Head popper worked tight to the rocks.

along, tapping the boulders, when the bass came up and engulfed it, literally creating a vacuum hole in the surface of the water. The rod was only loosely tucked under my arm, but luckily I got a solid grip fast and ended up landing the 33-pound fish. It just goes to show you that sometimes stopping a topwater lure or plug for a few beats can draw a strike faster than working a steady retrieve.

Fishing Inlet Jetties and Broken Jetties

If there is one rule that applies to surf fishing on any coast anywhere in the world, it is that some of the best action occurs in close proximity to an inlet, or pass, as they're referred to in the southern and Gulf states. Inlets provide access to bay or estuary systems, and most experience strong currents at different stages of the tide. As the water rushes in, gamefish follow baitfish headed for the bay. As the water rushes out—typically a peak time to fish an inlet—gamefish will commonly station at the mouth to await forage getting pulled out of the bay into open water. Whenever you're in doubt about where to fish, if there's an inlet nearby, it is often your best bet for finding action, even if the rest of the beach shows no sign of life. A large percentage of inlets are flanked by jetties or rock walls that help stop them from silting in, which could make them hazardous and difficult for boats to navigate. It's these jetties that can be doubly productive for anglers, as they offer the same fishy haunts as beachfront jetties, but also access to a key holding area unique to inlets.

That holding area is the mouth of an inlet, and fishing can be on fire here during a dropping tide. Gamefish, notably striped bass, snook, and even tarpon, will stage at an inlet mouth with their heads pointed upcurrent, waiting for mullet, shrimp, or sardines to flush out of the bay. It is not uncommon to also find tidal rips at the mouth of an inlet, which as discussed in chapter 6, can explode

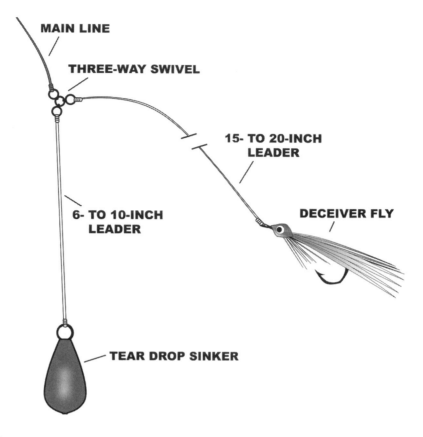

This rig, thought to have been developed in Delaware, uses a teardrop sinker to drag a fly on a long leader down an inlet. It is an incredibly effective way to match small, thin baitfish in a fast-moving inlet without the hassle of trying to get small lures to the proper depth and achieve the perfect arching swing.

at the end is tied a teardrop sinker weighing whatever you think is appropriate to keep contact with the bottom in the inlet current at hand. This rig is cast upcurrent and simply allowed to bounce across the bottom in a sweeping arc as it gets pulled up or down the inlet, depending on the tide.

The round sinker helps lessen snags and also won't dig into the bottom to anchor the bait. A pyramid weight, for example, wouldn't be nearly as effective with this rig. As the teardrop sinker swings and tumbles over the bottom, the fly drags behind it at a distance, portraying a stray baitfish swimming with the current. Though you can jig the rod with this presentation, it's not entirely necessary. Just hold the rod higher to reduce line drag, follow your line with the rod as it moves, and let the offering swing until it's parallel with the jetty. When a fish strikes, the swing will simply stop and you'll feel the weight.

If you would prefer to fish an inlet with bait, there are two approaches that will work. The first is the dead-stick method, whereby you use a sinker heavy enough to hold your bait in one place. This can be a challenge, especially when tidal flow is at its strongest, but it can also be a very productive method for many species that move in and out with the tide. Just be careful that there isn't too much grass or seaweed riding inlet currents, as it will cling to your line and either drag the bait out of place or cover the offering and make it nearly impossible for fish to find.

The second approach that typically works better in inlets is using rounded bank sinkers that will slowly thump along the bottom as they swing. In the Northeast, live eels, whole sea worms, squid strips, and mackerel strips work really well in inlets for everything from striped bass to weakfish. Baits like clams and large baitfish chunks are generally not going to be as productive, as the current can pull soft baits right off the hook, and chunks have a tendency to spin. However, large live baits, such as bunker, spot, or mullet, drifted down an inlet with no added weight can be absolutely lethal on gamefish stacked near the mouth. With this method, instead of locking the reel after casting, let the water take line off so the bait swims naturally. When you see an increase in line speed, lock up and set the hook, because your bait just got inhaled.

This small tarpon fell to a shrimp-tipped bucktail below a popping cork on Florida's Ponce Inlet jetty.

In the southern and Gulf states, inlet mouths are sometimes fished with baits under popping corks for suspended predators waiting for meals to drift down. This is particularly popular with live mullet and shrimp, and works well on tarpon, sea trout, even red drum. Suspending a bait-tipped bucktail jig under a popping cork also entices myriad gamefish species. Though it's not a method put into practice as frequently in the mid-Atlantic through Northeast, I've fooled many stripers and weakfish working a bucktail under a popping cork upcurrent along the side of a jetty, making a few forward pops, and then letting the cork float back for a couple of seconds. The strike frequently comes on the drop-back.

Breaks between jetties provide a phenomenal ambush point for many gamefish. Photo: Stan Kosinski

There is another type of jetty feature—though one that's a little tougher to find—that can be an incredibly productive place to hook a wide range of gamefish. I'm talking about jetty breaks: spots where another small rock pile is located off the tip of a jetty, and a channel runs between the two. Jetty breaks constantly have a flow of water running through them at all tidal stages. Both inlet and beach-front jetties can have breaks, and presenting a lure so it moves across the mouth of the break can draw savage strikes from any predators lying in wait within the cut.

Some breaks are man-made, but others can form naturally from years of waves pounding the rocks. In either case, expect there to be some rocks on the bottom between the end of the main jetty and broken piece. Work heavy lures like bucktails and metals with care, as snags can be common. Given that sand and silt are always washing in and out of jetty cuts, the water between them isn't usually too deep, which makes them ideal for topwater lure enthusiasts. Much like jetty pockets, gamefish use cuts to trap bait, as the roiled action of the cut disorients any forage that flushes in.

Uniquely Rocky Fish

Fishing on and around jetties can increase your productivity with almost any gamefish by creating prime holding areas and allowing you to get a little farther off the beach. But most gamefish spend only limited time around jetties at certain tidal stages, when a particular baitfish migration is under way, or when a school of baitfish is close by and easy to herd against the rocks. Still, there are two species of fish that set up permanent residence on rocky coastlines and around jetties. In a way, these fish are largely overlooked by the surf fishing majority, not because they don't offer a sporting challenge, but because catching them means making them the specific goal of a trip, as they are not likely to simply bite a baited line cast out in the surf. These species require a little extra effort and a slightly modified approach, but the payoff can be excellent.

Of the two rock dwellers that make themselves available to surf anglers, tautog are perhaps targeted most often. Because of their rather ugly appearance, it wasn't that long ago when tautog—otherwise known as "blackfish" or simply "'tog"—were considered a trash fish throughout much of their range from southern Maine to North Carolina. In truth, these fish, despite their blunt heads, stubby pointed teeth, and gray-black bodies, are one of the finest eating in the Atlantic. Plus, they are a genuine challenge to hook and put up a serious fight.

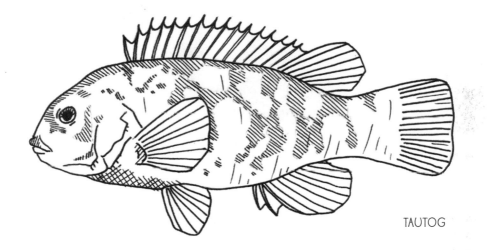

TAUTOG

Tautog are not open-water fish, which is why you'll very rarely hook one along the main beach. Offshore, 'tog anglers target deep wrecks and rock piles, but never open, sandy bottom. These fish prefer to hide within structure, largely because mussels and crabs make up the bulk of their diet. Their large front teeth and powerful jaws are designed to crack shells, and their thick, rubbery lips act as protection when ramming the rocks to break mussels loose. Only one time in my life have I seen a 'tog caught on an artificial lure, that being a metal jig. I promise it was a complete fluke. By nature, tautog simply don't chase baitfish like other species. Considering their diet, green crabs, white-legged crabs, sand fleas, grass shrimp, and small clam pieces about cover the bait choices. Some anglers swear by Berkley Gulp! artificial crabs, and I have seen them work effectively, though natural crabs are probably the most consistent bait you can use. And therein lies another reason why tautog don't share the popularity of other species: It's not always easy to find a bait shop that carries fresh crabs. Clams work well, but there are those days when 'tog simply will not touch them.

Tautog will back into holes and crevices between rocks and wait for forage to move past the opening. What these fish are not likely to do is swim out of their holes a great distance in pursuit of a meal. When a feeding opportunity presents itself, a 'tog will come out of its lair, grab the forage, and quickly retreat. It is this behavior that makes them such a worthy opponent for jetty anglers, as the

Green crabs are easily one of the most productive baits for tautog around a rock jetty.

whole process unfolds in an instant. If you're not prepared for the strike, tautog will frustrate you in a hurry. The first steps to success are proper rigging and proper bait size.

Unless live crabs are very small, you'll want to cut them into quarters with your knife or poultry shears (this does not apply to sand fleas, which should be fished whole). Be sure to remove all the legs and claws, as tautog can nibble at them or pull them off the body without getting the hook. 'Tog don't have very large mouths, so try to limit crab body pieces to no bigger than roughly 2 inches across, even if that means cutting a quartered crab body down into even smaller sections. When hooking a piece of crab, I prefer to make sure the point penetrates the shell once going in and again coming out to keep it exposed. I find that an exposed hook point increases my catch rates, though some anglers prefer to run the point through the shell and leave it hidden inside the bait. Clam pieces should be just large enough to cover the hook up to the bend, with the point remaining hidden in the bait. Because clams are soft, a sharp hookset will easily drive the point through the bait and into the fish's mouth.

The best rig you can use for tautog on the rocks is a variation on the high–low rig with changes made to accommodate this fish's striking style. Though you can use two hooks for 'tog, remember that your bait is going to be sitting among the rocks, and a second hook can sometimes cause more hang-ups than successes. To the end, the entire rig is designed with minimal terminal tackle to help reduce snags, as well as increase your chances of ripping a tautog out from its hole when it runs back in with your bait.

Start with a 20-inch length of 30- to 40-pound monofilament or fluorocarbon leader material. Though the average jetty 'tog will weigh 2 to 10 pounds, the stout leader is purely for abrasion resistance. First tie a dropper loop, being sure to make it no longer than 5 inches and positioning it around 6 inches from one end of the leader. Keeping the dropper loop low and close to the sinker helps your bait stay right on the bottom. Next, run the loop through the eye and around a long-shank hook with a relatively small gap. Long-shank hooks help stop tautog from swallowing the hook and severing the leader. Using a Palomar knot, tie a bank sinker or teardrop sinker on the leader below the dropper loop.

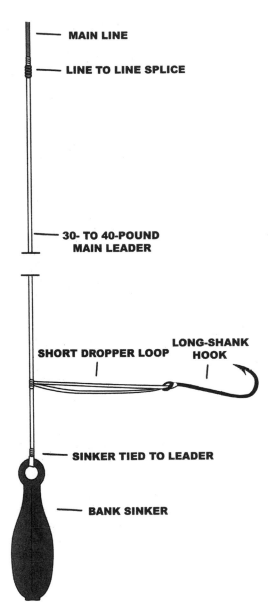

MAIN LINE

LINE TO LINE SPLICE

30- TO 40-POUND MAIN LEADER

SHORT DROPPER LOOP   **LONG-SHANK HOOK**

SINKER TIED TO LEADER

BANK SINKER

The low placement of the dropper loop in this tautog rig keeps the bait lying on the bottom, while splices connecting the leader and main line help boost sensitivity. By minimizing terminal tackle, like snaps and swivels, there is less to get hung up in the rocks.

Because these sinker styles are round, they'll hang up in the rocks a lot less than pyramid sinkers. Finally, connect the other end of the leader to the main line via a uniknot-to-uniknot splice. If you prefer, you can use a barrel swivel at the top of the leader for this connection, but again, this is one more piece of terminal tackle that can get stuck in the rocks. Also, I find that connecting the main line directly to the leader increases my ability to feel the 'tog strike by allowing the thump to telegraph straight up the line without being muted by a swivel.

Fishing for tautog doesn't require much casting. In fact, a major key to success is keeping your line tight at all times. Therefore, if you were to send your rig a mile down the jetty, wave action, wind, and current would likely create too much slack to allow you to feel the bite. 'Tog strike very quickly, and if there are many in the area, it's not the least bit uncommon for your bait to get taken the second it hits bottom. This kind of fishing is often done at rod's length, meaning you literally extend your rod off the jetty and drop straight down. A short flick is all right, especially if there are some submerged boulders off to the side of the main jetty. You want your bait to stay as still as possible among the rocks while you keep constant tension on the line. To do so, you may find it necessary to slightly raise and lower the rod tip, or reel in slack as waves move your bait. If you don't get a bite quickly, you can lift the sinker off the bottom and drag it a few feet. Tautog don't move too much, so what often happens is that the bait will be sitting just out of their range, and then the drag brings it closer to their hole where they'll attack.

There are literally hundreds of opinions on the best way to set the hook when a 'tog strikes. Some anglers like to give the fish time to "walk away" with the bait before striking. For me, this method results in more rigs snagged up in 'tog holes than anything else. Other anglers lift the rod high over their heads when they set the hook. I find this works well in deep water offshore, from a boat, but not in the shallows around a jetty. So, all I can do is explain the method that works best for me. You may develop your own technique for tricking these bait stealers, but I promise it will take a good amount of lost rigs before you find your groove.

Tautog may not be the most attractive fish, but these rock dwellers offer a real challenge to anglers and make excellent table fare. Photo: Darren Dorris

A hooked tautog instinctively wants to retreat into its lair, so the high-hookset method may work well for initially pulling them off the bottom, but as soon as the rod is lowered and the fish feels the slack, back between the rocks it goes. So as not to give the fish any slack, I make sure to reel at the same time I set the hook. The upward swing gets the fish out of the rocks, while reeling is taking in extra line, thus shortening the fish's lead and ability get back in the hole. I'll only raise the rod to shoulder height on the set, and I'll strike the instant I feel the first bump. Keep in mind that tautog are very subtle biters. Even a 10-plus-pound specimen won't always slam a bait. I know many anglers who are late on the hookset, or don't set at all, because they say, "That was just a little one nibbling." That "little one" could have been a 20-pound 'tog-o-saurus.

Tautog are available throughout their range in all but the coldest months of the year, when they migrate offshore. In the spring when the water temperature begins to climb above 50 degrees, tautog move inshore to spawn, making their first appearance along oceanfront and inlet jetties. A good number of fish will remain here during the summer months, though fishing for them this time of year can be slow, as most 'tog seek cooler water offshore. By far, September through early December is considered the peak time to find tautog within range of surfcasters.

Found from Maryland, around Florida, all the way to Texas, the sheepshead can be considered the tautog's southern Atlantic and Gulf counterpart. Though these fish have much in common, there are some differences that change the fishing approach. Sheepshead gravitate to jetties and rock walls because they, like 'tog, feed most heavily on mollusks, crustaceans, and shrimp. However, rather than wedge themselves between rocks to ambush prey, sheepshead are free swimmers that patrol the perimeter of the jetty. Unlike tautog, sheepshead will chase a meal, making it possible to catch them on small shrimp- and crab-imitating lures. Little bucktails, curly-tail grubs, and many other low-profile soft plastics fished on a light jighead will catch sheepshead, though it should be noted that sometimes these fish need to be worked up to attack a lure. Many anglers will carry a bucket of shrimp, crushed mussels, or crushed clams and toss handfuls off the jetty. Once the sheepshead have begun to feed, they'll pitch artificials among the clouds of descending chum.

SHEEPSHEAD

The average sheepshead will top out around 10 pounds, though larger fish are not uncommon. This species is named for its rows of teeth that look very similar to a sheep's, but are more often compared to human teeth. These chompers are designed to crush hard-shell forage just like a tautog's, but sheepshead are not opposed to chasing baitfish on occasion. Sheepshead have gray to yellow bodies with dark vertical bars along their sides. The spines of their dorsal fins are also very thick and sharp, which you should try very hard to remember when grabbing one to remove the hook.

Another similarity that tautog and sheepshead share is their ability to pick a hook clean in an instant. A bite can be very hard to detect, as a sheepshead will grab a bait and not move, instead staying in one place and crushing the offering in its teeth. The trick becomes being able to recognize when a fish is mouthing a bait, as they can chew the bait off the hook without you feeling anything. Most seasoned sheepshead anglers employ the lift method, where they slowly raise the rod about 2 feet to feel for pressure or weight. As with 'tog fishing, it's very important to keep your bait still and your line tight to better detect a pickup. If there is weight on the line during the lift, set the hook hard and fast. Of course, this is a challenge in and of itself.

Because of their thick teeth, setting the hook on a sheepshead isn't always easy. Therefore, a rod with a stiffer tip can make all the difference in driving the hook point into their mouths. Fiddler crabs, shrimp, clams, and even pieces of sea worm are all tops for enticing this species. Baits should be fished on a high–low rig, and because sheepshead can be found in open water along the sides of a jetty instead of down in the jagged rocks, surf anglers more commonly use double hooks and a barrel swivel to connect the main line and leader. Slide rigs that use a small to medium egg sinker are also popular for sheepshead, though their productivity is largely based on the jaggedness of the bottom since this rig is a bit more prone to hanging up.

Sheepshead can be caught year-round throughout Florida and much of the Gulf, but the winter months tend to see a spike in fish size and numbers. February and March provide particularly solid action from the Florida Panhandle across to South Texas, though the spring spawning season is also a very good time to fish, as most offshore sheepshead move in close to breed. While tautog can be caught during practically any tidal stage, hardcore sheepshead anglers favor slack tide and the outgoing tide for peak productivity.

Staying Legal on the Rocks

Before heading out onto any jetty, you should know that not all are legally fishable. Though they may be part of a public beach, some states don't allow anglers to walk out onto the rocks. The main reason is safety, both because a jetty may be particularly hazardous and because local and state governments do not want to be liable for any injuries that occur. Jetty closures can also come down to a township level for the same reasons. With that in mind, it's of the utmost importance that you research the jetty you intend to fish to make sure you're in the right.

There is much argument over jetty closures, and one that comes to mind is that of the Rudee Inlet Jetty in Virginia. It is illegal to fish these rocks, yet you will find plenty of online reports from anglers who do it anyway. While a large percentage of surf anglers feel that no jetty on a public beach should be off limits, I have to advocate staying within the law when it comes to fishing. Just because you see someone else working a jetty doesn't mean they are doing so legally. Angling groups have actually gotten into heated debates with mayors and councilors over such closures. Just remember that any angler breaking the law is a poor reflection on fishermen as a whole. It is those surfcasters who disregard closed jetties and private beaches that essentially lead to more access loss in the end.

Chapter 12

Surf Fishing by Region

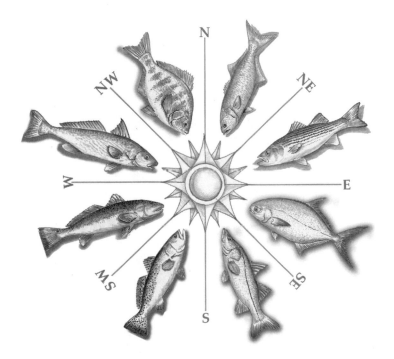

The Great Northeast

With the exception of North Carolina's Outer Banks, no area in the country is more synonymous with surf fishing than the Northeast, and no other area receives as many visiting anglers coming solely to cast from the sand. There are several reasons for this, but the biggest just may be that unlike other coasts with seasonal runs of large fish, it is possible to catch trophy gamefish from spring to early winter somewhere between Maine and New Jersey. States like Massachusetts, Rhode Island, and New York also have surfcasting history that dates back over 100 years. Techniques were pioneered along these shores. This is in no small way thanks to the popularity of the striped bass, which is easily one of the most—if not the most—coveted and heavily chased species that swims in the waves. Stripers plague the minds of anglers in this region, and though they are available all the way to Maine, their abundance in the northern reaches of the coast fluctuates from year to year.

All Map Illustrations: Susan Daly

Throughout the Northeast, no other gamefish is more sought after in the surf than the striped bass.

MAINE AND NEW HAMPSHIRE

While surf fishing in Maine does not receive the same attention as it does from Cape Cod in Massachusetts on south, spots like York Beach and Two Lights State Park in the southern end of the state can provide shots at stripers and bluefish during the summer months. In fact, recent seasons in Maine have produced some very large bass. North of Cape Elizabeth, Maine's coast becomes jagged and disjointed by islands, making surf opportunities very limited. Likewise, the short 18-mile stretch of New Hampshire that touches the Atlantic is not much talked about as a surf destination, though places like Hampton Beach, Sawyers Beach, and Seabrook Beach, especially near the mouth of Seabrook Inlet, can all produce bass and bluefish action from July to September. While it's rare for other Northeast staples like weakfish and flounder to be caught this far north, Maine and New Hampshire both feature fair numbers of tautog around rocky structure, of which you'll find plenty in these states. But it is not until you hit the famed shores of Massachusetts that you enter the heart of Northeast surfcasting territory.

MASSACHUSETTS

Along the northern coast of Massachusetts from Salisbury to the southern end of Plum Island State Park, you'll find miles of sandy beaches that host bass and bluefish from late June through early October. But once you round Halibut Point State Park north of Gloucester, much of the Massachusetts coast becomes steep, rocky, and riddled with coves and bays that have smaller sandy stretches of beach interspersed. It is not until pushing south of Boston to the town of Hull that long stretches of sandy shore resume. While beaches like Nantasket and Humarock are excellent places to hunt for striped bass, they are not widely considered destination surf locations. Yet local crowds along this stretch of coast fish passionately and fare well. Perhaps the reason the northern Massachusetts shoreline never receives as much attention is that it is largely overshadowed by Cape Cod.

The beaches from Race Point in Provincetown at the tip of Cape Cod to the southern end of Cape Cod National Seashore on the Cape's east coast once offered some of the most spectacular surf

fishing in the world, particularly for striped bass. During the 1960s and '70s, it was on the Outer Cape beaches that surf legends like *Eastern Tides* author Frank Daignault hauled in incredible numbers of 40-plus-pound fish. It was here Cape surf guru Tony Stetzko landed a 73-pound striper from the waves in 1981 that for a time stood as the world record. Today the outer beaches of Cape Cod still produce striped bass spring through fall for dedicated anglers, though they are not the fast-action spots of yesteryear.

According to Rick Bach, formerly of Cape-based *On the Water* magazine, much of the decline stems from an increase in the seal population that ravages baitfish in the area. Another issue is what's locally referred to as "mung," a sticky algae that clings to lines and causes game-fish to shy away from the surf. In recent years, many anglers are noticing that the summering grounds of striped bass are getting pushed farther south, with fewer bass overall pushing north to Cape Cod and beyond. While Cape Cod will always be a summer tourist destination for

The Administration Building at Cape Cod's Nauset Beach. Though fishing is still productive here, it pales in comparison with previous decades.
Photo: Rick Bach

its beauty and culture, the surf bite during the warm months can leave a bit to be desired, as stripers and blues can be scarce, and species such as croakers, flounder, and kingfish are lacking.

While the outer beaches may prove slow, Bach cites the coast from Chatham to the West Falmouth area as providing the best surf fishing on the Cape, even though spots on the South Cape actually have you casting in Vineyard Sound and Buzzards Bay as opposed to the Atlantic. Places like South Cape Beach State Park near Popponesset are popular for their easy access and strong runs of fish. According to Bach, South Cape Beach is particularly noted for producing the first surf-caught bluefish on the Cape beginning in May. Other productive locations on this side of Cape Cod include Nobska Light near Woods Hole, which is a rocky point featuring jetties that see a good number of striped bass spring into early summer, then again in the fall. To the west, Old Silver Beach features flat sand and rocky points, making it perfect for anglers of any skill level. Here, too, May and June offer the best shots at bass and bluefish, with the fall also perking up the action as fish move south.

Bluefish are staples of the Northeast beaches prized for their strong fights and explosive strikes.

The islands of Martha's Vineyard and Nantucket, both of which can be accessed by ferry from Hyannis or Woods Hole on the main Cape, still offer outstanding surf fishing opportunities in Massachusetts. While here, too, fall striper catches are on the decline as of late, spring and early summer still provide great fishing for bass and bluefish. Though fishing slows a bit during the summer, you can still bring these species to the beach, and will increase your chances by using dead-sticked squid or bunker chunks as opposed to lures. During the fall, these islands are tops if you're itching to land pelagics from the beaches or jetties, with strong pushes of false albacore and bonito coming close to feed on migrating baitfish. While Nantucket and Martha's Vineyard may not be big, there is no shortage of public access to famous surf haunts, such as Wasque Beach and Great Point.

RHODE ISLAND

Moving south into Rhode Island, surf fishing takes on a more "hardcore" tone, as most of the prime fishing areas require a trusty set of cleats, no fear of navigating wave-pounded rocky shorelines, and the need to keep your wits about you. To quote Point Jude Lures owner and Rhode Island angler Joe Martins, "We are always listening for that 'green wall' of water that can roll in and smash us to bits on the rocks." Martins is referring primarily to the steep, jagged shores around Newport, generally set aside for advanced surfcasters, but this is certainly not the only area worth fishing in "Rhody."

The surf near the lighthouse at Watch Hill in Rhode Island. Notice the birds working a blitz in the distance.
Photo: Stan Kosinski

From Matunuck Beach down the coast to Watch Hill, you'll find plenty of sandy shore, though these stretches are not as favored by locals as rockier areas like Watch Hill, Napatree Point, Point Judith, and Weekapaug. The sand beaches in Rhode Island are relatively shallow, and though they can see good numbers of bass and bluefish, the coast is so structure-rich that most fish gravitate toward the rocks. Striped bass and bluefish begin to make a showing in May, with many fish lingering through the summer. From September to mid-October, both summering fish moving south and those migrating from farther north pass Rhode Island and feed heavily.

It is this time of year that bonito and false albacore can also make their way into the surfcaster's range in places like Point Judith. Don't overlook this jagged coast for tautog, either, as the fishing can be terrific spring though late fall, even into December. During the summer, if you're more interested in relaxing on the sand with a line in the water, flounder make occasional appearances, though Rhode Island, like the other New England states, is known primarily for stripers and bluefish.

While the mainland coast of Rhode Island is relatively short, offshore lies one of the most notorious surf destinations in the world. Block Island is rich in fishing history, having hosted many presidents and dignitaries since the early 1900s. But while big bass frequent the shoreline of this 10-square-mile hunk of land 13 miles off the coast, it can be a tricky place for beginners to fish. What makes this island so appealing to anglers is the steep, boulder-strewn beaches, plentiful rips, and swift currents. Many serious anglers fish the bluffs on the south and east side of the island, but there is opportunity for rookies here, too. Areas like Harbor Neck Cut, Grace Cove, and Crescent Beach offer easy access and sandy shores where bass, bluefish, false albacore and bonito show up from late spring through fall. Flounder can also be found in greater numbers here than the mainland. If you do plan to tackle the rugged side of Block, Mohegan Bluffs, Grove Point, Southeast Light, and Black Rock Point make up just a few of the hot spots. Fishing here needs to be done with extreme care, as trails to access the beach can be steep, wave action can be rough, and the rocks are slick. Another factor to keep in mind if you're planning to travel to Block Island is that ferry access is limited and will shut down in bad weather, especially during the fall. A visit to Block can also get rather expensive. Large groups of surfcasters often chip in together to rent a small house in season on this pricey island.

New York: The Atlantic Coast

Anglers brave the rocks below the lighthouse at Montauk Point, New York. Photo: Rick Bach

A typical Long Island South Shore "schoolie" striper taken in the fall on a teaser ahead of a metal lure.

Roughly 14 miles due west of Rhode Island's Block Island lies Montauk Point at the tip of New York's Long Island. When you pull into the state park at the lighthouse, blazoned on the entrance sign is the phrase SURF-CASTING CAPITAL OF THE WORLD. Perhaps no other place comes to mind faster than Montauk when anglers the world over think of northeastern US surf fishing. Aside from the fact that many trophy stripers fall at Montauk between May and November, it is also far more accessible to anglers than islands like Block or Martha's Vineyard. A long drive down Route 27—which starts at New York City, cuts through Long Island's bustling west end, and finishes in the quaint fishing village of Montauk—puts this legendary location within easy reach.

Though much of Montauk is rocky, requiring cleats and good balance, Long Island's South Shore from Shinnecock Inlet all the way to Breezy Point near Brooklyn begins the classic Northeast terrain of long sandy stretches of beach with many intermittent jetties. Between these two landmark surf spots you'll find Jones Beach, Fire Island National Seashore, and Smith Point, all of which provide easy access and stellar striped bass and bluefish action, primarily from May through early July, and again from late September through mid-November. What you'll also find along Long Island's South Shore is the beginning of prime range for surf-caught gamefish that don't make nearly as big a showing farther north.

Long Island jetties and inlets produce some very large weakfish, particularly in the spring, though they can be found here in summer and fall as well. Flounder are a popular surf target in the summer. Jetties here are loaded with tautog, and croakers and kingfish will readily strike small clam and squid pieces late summer into early fall. The Atlantic coast of Long Island as a whole is also excellent for hooking false albacore and bonito from August into November. While Montauk can see a ferocious pelagic bite this time of year, surprisingly, the jetties of the west end from Atlantic Beach to Breezy Point in the shadow of Manhattan are notorious for autumn action with drag-screaming "albies" and "bones."

Long Island Sound in New York and Connecticut

Long Island's North Shore, as well as the Connecticut coast, flank Long Island Sound. While these may not be ocean beaches, the Sound is big enough that it is worth mention as a surf destination. On the New York side, Wildwood State Park, McAllister County Park, Peconic Dunes State Park, and Orient Point County Park all provide access to the shoreline and excellent chances to hook stripers, blues, and weakfish. In Connecticut, Lynde Point Light, Hammonasset Nature Preserve, Seaside Park, Lighthouse Point Park, and Ocean Beach Park near the mouth of the Thames River are all good places to start a surf quest. But understand that because Long Island Sound is more of an enclosed body of water, gamefish movements will be more drastic and fluctuate heavily throughout the year. May and June see some of the most consistent striper action throughout the Sound, as does October. Because the Sound tends to heat up in the summer, many bass and bluefish push out to the ocean, though weakfish and flounder can still put a bend in a rod. Pieces of the Sound also see increased productivity at different times. As an example, the western Sound can experience a heavy push of fish in May and go stale by June, with those fish having moved east. Fall action tends to be better on the east end of the Sound, as many fish migrating south pass Long Island on the ocean side instead of working through the Sound and out the East River past New York City.

New Jersey

Surfcasters swarm the beach north of Seaside in New Jersey during the spring striper and bluefish run.
Photo: Stan Kosinski

Beginning with Sandy Hook at the mouth of Raritan Bay and running 130 miles south to Cape May, the New Jersey shore plays host to some spectacular surf fishing, even though the state has become somewhat of a pop-culture icon as the "Armpit of the Nation." In truth, while New Jersey does have its share of highways, refineries, and shopping malls crammed into a relatively small landmass, its beaches are pristine and fall right smack in the middle of the migration routes of striped bass and bluefish. In the northern part of the state, you'll find what is dubbed "jetty country," with these rocky structures nearly stacked on top of one another from Long Branch to Point Pleasant Beach.

South of Point Pleasant, jetties become more spread out as long sandy stretches of shore make up much of the coast all the way to Cape May. Some of the best fishing occurs from Sandy Hook to Brigantine Beach just north of Atlantic City. The uninhabited north end of Brigantine, south end of Long Beach Island, and Island Beach State Park are three places within this range that offer four-wheel-drive access and allow surfcasters to feel removed from the crowded suburbs and shore towns. Plus, these three areas account for some of the biggest stripers and weakfish from late April into June, then again in October and November, as mullet, bunker, and rain bait schools migrate close to shore. From Seaside Park in the center of the state south, anglers also have the opportunity to connect with black drum in the spring, some of which can top the 50-pound mark.

The author with a Jersey Shore weakfish that struck a black plug in the dark.

The southern end of New Jersey from Atlantic City to Cape May is in no way a poor area to target, though here the surf tends to be shallower, whereas the northern beaches feature abundant troughs and drop-offs within close range. Some of the most productive surfcasting in South Jersey occurs around inlets, such as Townsends, Corsons, and Hereford Inlets. Anglers fishing Cape May beaches can opt to cast in the ocean or along the mouth of Delaware Bay. The latter can be productive in late fall and early spring as bass migrate in and out of the bay.

Although striper and black drum productivity waxes and wanes along the New Jersey coast, croakers, kingfish, flounder, weakfish, and bluefish keep lines bent all summer, making this part of the Northeast shoreline excellent for wetting a line while relaxing with the family on vacation. Likewise, whereas New England and much of Long Island see their seasons wrap up by late November, action with striped bass and bluefish can continue to Christmas and beyond, provided baitfish like sand eels stick around.

Fishing "Delmarva"

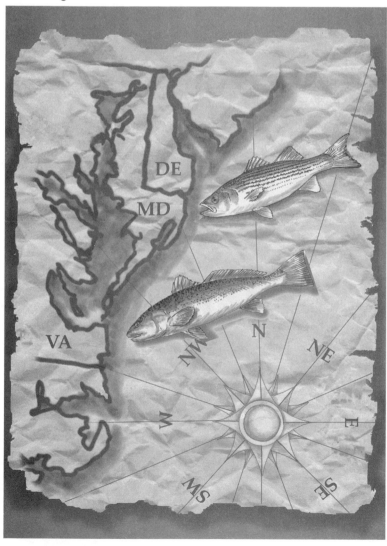

With a relatively short combined coastline of about 170 miles, Delaware, Maryland, and Virginia—often called "Delmarva"—may not make a big blip on the radar screen of surfcasters around the country, but the area gives up stellar fishing nonetheless. Perhaps what is most significant about this section of the East Coast is that it serves as a mixing ground of Northeast primary targets and southern Atlantic favorites. For fishermen with a love of striped bass and an equal itch for red drum, Delmarva is the best of both worlds. Likewise, as you move south through this region, spotted sea trout begin to mingle with weakfish, tautog remain plentiful, and cobia make elusive appearances.

DELAWARE

On the northern coast of Delaware, you'll find Cape

Henlopen where Delaware Bay meets the Atlantic. At this junction, currents collide, holding baitfish and attracting gamefish throughout the season. The tip of the point in Cape Henlopen State Park is accessible by four-wheel-drive vehicle, though there is plenty of walk-on access as well. While New Jersey's striper season lights up in May and June, veteran surf guide Floyd Morton says Delaware sees the peak of its bass and bluefish action in April and May. Cape Henlopen is just one piece of Delaware's tiny 28-mile coast where bunker schools migrating in the spring can produce stripers over 40 pounds and bluefish to 20 pounds. In the fall, Morton points to November as the month to find the same action as the bunker, bass, and bluefish migrations run in reverse down the coast. At this time of year, a heavy mullet migration out of the bays adds to the feeding frenzy. These time lines apply from the cape all the way south to Fenwick Island near the Maryland state line. Delaware's oceanfront is not chock-full of jetties and other structure like many Northeast beaches, and Morton notes that using lures during the striper run is not nearly as productive as fresh bunker chunks. Exceptions occur around Indian River Inlet, where pencil poppers and Heddon Super Spooks are area-favorite topwaters that can turn on a bite.

Surf fishing guide Floyd Morton proudly displays a heavy striped bass from the beach in Delaware.
Photo: Floyd Morton

Much of the reason Delaware relies so heavily on bunker coming close to shore in spring and fall is that it is one of the only incentives to get gamefish within reach of a surfcaster's line. As a whole, the surf is shallow, lacking deep troughs and drops that naturally attract large gamefish. However,

Morton says that the shore does have slightly more depth south of Dewey Beach. As you head even farther down the coast, jetties become a bit more abundant around Bethany Beach, and more cuts and troughs pop up between here and Fenwick Island.

Aside from blues and bass, May can bring a good weakfish bite to the Delaware surf, though the abundance of fish varies from year to year. Flounder, croakers, small bluefish, and kingfish roam the waves all summer, but during July and August the amount of rain Delaware receives plays heavily into surf productivity. "If we don't get enough rain, the salinity level can get very high in the summer," says Morton. "There will still be kingfish and croakers in the surf, but they won't necessarily be easy to catch. These conditions can make them picky." If it's Delaware panfish you're after, look for the strongest bites in September and October, as well as in the spring when black drum can also find their way onto your line.

MARYLAND AND VIRGINIA

Much like the Delaware beaches, the northern coast of Maryland, packed with the hotels, homes, amusement parks, and the boardwalk of Ocean City, features relatively shallow surf. But that's not to say April and May don't see stripers and bluefish roaming this stretch of coast. During the summer, kingfish, croakers, flounder, and occasional weakfish are found here, too, but Maryland doesn't really become a surfcaster's paradise until you hit Assateague Island.

With over 37 miles of uninhabited, undeveloped shoreline, Assateague stretches from just south of Ocean City, Maryland, all way across the Virginia state line, ending at Chincoteague Island. In this span of coast you'll find Assateague State Park and Assateague Island National Seashore on the Maryland side, and Chincoteague National Wildlife Refuge on the Virginia side. Assateague is a very popular tourist destination, especially in the summer, and both states do offer limited four-wheel-drive access to the beach. But during the spring and fall, anglers flock to Assateague for the fishing, as the surf here is deeper, with long troughs, wavy bottom contours, and an outer bar. The biggest draw to Assateague is that it is the northernmost point in the Atlantic Ocean that features a consistent beach bite with red drum.

Beginning in April and lasting into early June, drum moving inshore and

A nice spotted sea trout falls on a calm day along the southern end of Assateague Island. Photo: Ric Burnley

heading south to the Chesapeake Bay intercept bunker schools along Assateague, particularly from the lower Maryland portion south into Virginia. While the island doesn't have quite the same drum reputation as North Carolina, bull reds breaking the 30-pound mark are not uncommon on fresh bunker chunks or live spot. If the conditions are right and the fish are feeding close, topwater poppers, metal lures, and soft-plastic finesse baits can also draw strikes from these fish. During the fall, typically starting in mid-September, reds moving back offshore come through again, this time feeding on mullet, rain bait, and bunker. When the drum are running, you can also expect a mix of striped bass and bluefish, though the best action with these species generally occurs in April and early May, then again from November through mid-December.

Not only do red drum enter the picture at Assateague, but spotted sea trout and even cobia become viable targets. Sea trout fishing is best in the spring and early summer, then again in the fall during the mullet run, though it is quite possible to pull these fish from waves during the warmest months of the year. Because cobia are warm-water fish, your best chance with them will occur from June through mid-September, though Morton claims they are one of Maryland and Virginia's most elusive targets.

"I've been trying for years to catch a cobia from the surf at Assateague," says Morton. "I haven't yet. They're around for sure, but not in the numbers you'll find farther south. If you're lucky enough to be on the beach during a ray migration, you might see them finning above or behind the rays. Live spot are by far the best bait if you can get one in front of them."

South of Virginia's Chincoteague Island, sporadic barrier islands off the coast limit oceanfront surf access in a major way. Though these uninhabited islands are great for surf fishing, they are accessible only by kayak or boat, requiring you to anchor behind the island, wade across, and walk out to the surf. It is not until you reach Virginia Beach at the south side of the Chesapeake Bay mouth that prime fishing zones appear once again. Though the coast from Virginia Beach to the North Carolina state line at False Cape State Park isn't very long, it packs a punch with sea trout, red drum, stripers, and all the panfish you could ever hope to catch. In fact, Virginia surf expert Ric Burnley says he enjoys chasing spot, kingfish, and croakers with his daughter in this area as much as battling it out with bull reds. Though these panfish can be hooked all summer long, September and October are the best months for big croakers and spot near Virginia Beach.

"Bloodworms are a staple for these fish down here," says Burnley. "But sand fleas produce some of the bigger panfish. In the fall, kingfish will be right at your feet, but to get big croakers and spot, we wade out to the first sandbar and fish the other side."

Because the Chesapeake Bay dumps into the ocean at Virginia Beach, the area is treated to fall baitfish and gamefish migrations on a grand scale. This is not a little estuary draining into the sea, but a massive body of water that serves as the summering ground for red drum and sea trout. When trout and smaller "puppy" drum begin pushing out of the bay in fall, light-tackle reigns on these shores, according to Burnley, who opts for a 7-foot spinning rod and a tackle bag full of soft-plastic lures and small plugs. From Virginia Beach proper, south to False Cape, fall is the best time to hook into bull reds, which are locally nicknamed "old drum" if they measure more than 40 inches. Fresh bunker works well, though Burnley prefers a whole spot head or kingfish head. Many anglers keep a short rod handy for these panfish, saving the bodies for dinner when they catch them, and launching the heads back out on heavier 10- to 13-foot rods for drum. Stripers are an option on these same beaches begin-

Surf-pro-in-training Daria Burnley holds up a fat Virginia Beach spot. These fish are both a great panfish and a bait source for bull red drum.
Photo: Ric Burnley

ning in October, though Burnley points out that they don't often come in as close as they do farther north. However, persistent anglers will catch them all the way into February.

Should you find yourself in Virginia Beach and want to fish the surf, Burnley recommends making the effort to head south of town to Sandbridge Beach. Here, the condos and hotels give way to a shoreline that's more raw and "less groomed," as Burnley puts it. From Sandbridge you can work south to the Back Bay National Wildlife Refuge, though the road ends here. While Back Bay presses south until it meets False Cape State Park, there is no vehicular access. If you are up for a long hike and really want to avoid seeing other anglers, you can roam the beach for miles down into False Cape, though lugging all the tackle you'd need for species like bull red drum and striped bass will be a chore.

The Outer Banks and Beyond

In the town of Corolla in North Carolina, State Road 12 begins. One hundred fourteen miles south, it dead-ends in Ocracoke. If you travel State Road 12 between these two points, you have just traversed the Outer Banks, a stretch of coast that is one of the most revered in the world of surfcasting. The Outer Banks area may not feature the famed niche points, coves, and cliffs of the Northeast, but what it has that the bustling Northeast does not is breathing room. There really are no secret spots here that require knowledge of back roads and secluded paths. There are just miles and miles of sandy beach,

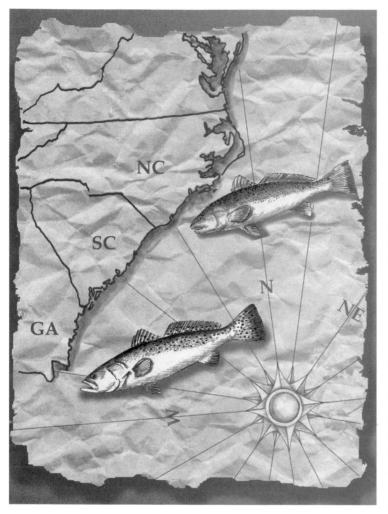

inlets with astounding fishing reputations, and the opportunity to hook loads of small fish that keep kids entertained for hours, or brute species that bite in rough conditions and test even the most seasoned anglers.

Seeing that the Outer Banks are already situated well offshore of the mainland, it's no surprise that they attract so many fish. In fact, Cape Hatteras—the easternmost point in the center of the Banks—is actually the closest piece of dry land to the Gulf Stream, which is the warm offshore current that runs along the East Coast. That makes Hatteras a hot spot for anglers interested in shorter runs for bigger fish like marlin and tuna. But Hatteras is equally special for the shorebound fisherman. Cape Point just south of the Cape Hatteras Lighthouse has actually been credited as the birthplace of

modern surfcasting, and it is here that 40-plus-pound red drum fall more commonly than on any other beach in the country.

While all of the Outer Banks offer good surf fishing, the epic red drum runs that occur in the spring and fall are going to be the heaviest around inlets. These fish are moving into Pamlico Sound from offshore starting in April, and moving back out again beginning in late September. Because the Banks are so vast, the farther you are from an inlet, the lighter and sparser the drum become. Starting at the northern end of the coast, Oregon Inlet is the first access to Pamlico Sound just south of the town of Nags Head. You won't find another for 62 miles, where you come to Hatteras Inlet. From there, Ocracoke Inlet it is yet another 21 miles south. While State Rd 12, the artery of the Outer Banks, provides ample access to the beach, most of the best fishing at the inlets is found on the sandy points that flanks their sides. Reaching them, however, requires a four-wheel-drive vehicle. It should be noted that as of this writing (2010), there are many access problems revolving around nesting shorebirds and sea turtles at some of the most famous fishing points near Banks' inlets, including Cape Point.

An angler works the ripping waves at Cape Point on North Carolina's Outer Banks. Despite the roughness of the water, these conditions can be prime for monster red drum. Photo: Rob Alderman

Therefore, no matter what time you year to plan to visit, check ahead for four-wheel-drive access closures, and be prepared for closures to occur at the drop of a hat. While walking the beach to reach these spots is not restricted, getting there would require a hike that most anglers are not willing to make.

The drum fishing that has made the Outer Banks famous revolves largely around the presence of bunker and spot in the surf during the spring, then again in the fall when mullet also join the party. Ten- to 13-foot conventional outfits, dubbed "Hatteras Heavers," are the norm for throwing the large bait chunks and heavy weights required to get the offering past the outer bar and hold in rough surf often found around the inlets. However, proficient casters can fare just as well with 10½- to 11-foot spinning outfits. According to Outer Banks veteran surfcaster Rob Alderman, there

Ric Burnley admires a bull red drum beaten in the North Carolina surf. Photo: Ric Burnley

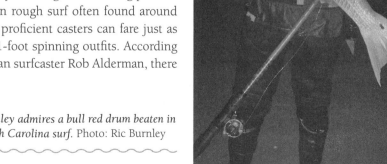

are also opportunities to hook drum on lures, and the most popular models are those that can cut through the wind and perform well in heavy wave action. Sting Silvers, a local-favorite metal lure, and pencil poppers are two of Alderman's must-haves.

Most of the drum are out of the surf during the summer, but kingfish and croakers are still available, though extremely warm water temperatures can make fishing slow. In the spring and fall, spotted sea trout are a viable surf target, as are pompano. Smaller pompano can actually be caught as far north as Delaware, but it is the Outer Banks that first see good action with fish to 5 pounds. As the water temperature warms in May and June, Spanish mackerel pop up frequently along the entire length of the Banks, but fishing inlet points can increase your odds of running into them. While their population in the surf has its upswings and downswings year-to-year, the Outer Banks can also get a push of large bluefish and striped bass, especially farther north around Oregon Inlet. Both of these species winter off the northern Outer Banks and straggle as far south as Hatteras. But according to Alderman, they could remain 3 miles offshore all fall and winter, never making it close enough to be in a surfcasting range.

What the Outer Banks do have in the summer are cobia within sight-casting range from the beach. These dark, shark-like gamefish start to show with frequency in late May and into June, though Alderman (who has led a client to a 92-pounder from the beach) says that cobia can be caught into early September. However, their abundance tapers off as summer draws on. Hardcore cobia chasers get a thrill out of spotting them when the water is clear and they can cast bucktail jigs, soft-plastic baitfish imitations, and live spot to moving fish. But you could just as easily hook a monster cobia on a chunk of bunker or spot dead-sticked in the surf.

The South End of North Carolina

To the south of the Outer Banks, Cape Lookout National Seashore provides 56 miles of unspoiled beach accessible by ferry only from the cities of Atlantic Beach and Davis. With proper permits, four-wheel-drive vehicle access gives you run of most of the park, all the way to Drum Inlet to the north, which, as its name suggests, offers red drum fishing spring and fall as the fish move in and out of Core Sound. Though Cape Lookout is somewhat overshadowed by the Outer Banks, the fishing here is outstanding, seeing equally strong runs of all the species found between Hatteras and Ocracoke.

Cobia make frequent appearances from the Outer Banks down to North Carolina's Cape Lookout National Seashore from late spring through summer's end. Photo: Ric Burnley

Once you travel south of Cape Lookout, much of North Carolina's accessible beachfront is home to well-developed vacation communities starting with Atlantic Beach and ending with Ocean Isle Beach near the South Carolina border. Though this stretch of coast is not wildly popular as a surf destination, red drum, pompano, sea trout, and panfish are abundant. However, if you are seeking the best action along the southern coast of North Carolina, you'd be wise to focus your efforts around inlets where gamefish can move in and out of the backwater bays and estuaries. Within this span of shoreline, Beaufort Inlet, New River Inlet, New Topsail Inlet, and Masonboro Inlet are all accessible and see strong runs of sea trout and drum.

South Carolina

Just across the border with North Carolina, South Carolina's Cherry Grove Inlet above North Myrtle Beach provides plenty of fishing access for drum, pompano, sea trout, and panfish, though the northern shore of this state is lacking overall for surf anglers. One problem is that the inlets only connect the ocean with small bays and winding river-like waterways as opposed to major systems like Pamlico Sound in North Carolina or the Chesapeake Bay in Maryland. Fish certainly still use them, but by and large these smaller backwaters don't act as summering grounds for thousands of migratory bull red drum. Therefore, while spring and fall are still some of the best times to fish, you won't find mass movements of large gamefish congregating around these inlets. Drum around Cherry Grove Inlet are likely to be "puppies," measuring no more than 25 inches, though unlike the Outer Banks, you have a much better chance of hooking them all through the summer.

South of Cherry Grove Inlet, bay access is nonexistent until you reach Murrells Inlet 32 miles away. With the exception of occasional Spanish mackerel, small bluefish, pompano, and panfish, the long span of coast between these inlets is relatively quiet, especially during the summer. Bull reds and pompano can be found more frequently around Murrells Inlet to the south of Myrtle Beach, though access here can be difficult. Access to the north side of the inlet is hindered by private property, but the south side point and jetty at Murrells can be reached via a 2-mile hike from Huntington Beach State Park near the city of Oak Hill.

As you continue down the South Carolina coast, surf fishing access becomes more and more limited, as a vast system of barrier islands puts oceanfront beaches out of reach of those without a small boat, but exceptions do occur on the developed islands near Charleston, such as Isle of Palms, Sullivan's Island, Folly Beach, Edisto Beach, Hunting Island State Park, and Hilton Head Island. Once again, fishing beaches in close proximity to inlet mouths will increase shots at red drum and sea trout spring through fall. During the late summer and early fall months, it's also not out of the realm of possibility to run into tarpon feeding on mullet on the lower South Carolina Island beaches.

Georgia

East of Savannah, Georgia, just across the state line, you'll find Tybee Island at the end out Route 80. Here, there is plenty of public beach access, where sea trout, pompano, drum, flounder, and panfish can be hooked with frequency spring through late fall, and even into the winter months depending on water temperatures. But Tybee Island marks the only easily accessible piece of oceanfront in Georgia until you hit St. Simons Island well to the south, as many uninhabited barrier islands are found in between. Georgia is arguably the least recognized as a surf fishing destination of all the East Coast states, largely because the expansive backwater systems are much more popular and productive for anglers than the beach. Past St. Simons, Jekyll Island is another popular tourist destination with ample beachfront access. While I don't think I'd recommend heading to Georgia specifically to fish the surf, one perk is that in the summer and early fall, these beaches are the first on the eastern seaboard where you can potentially find a big snook on the end of your line.

Florida: The Land of Surf Opportunity

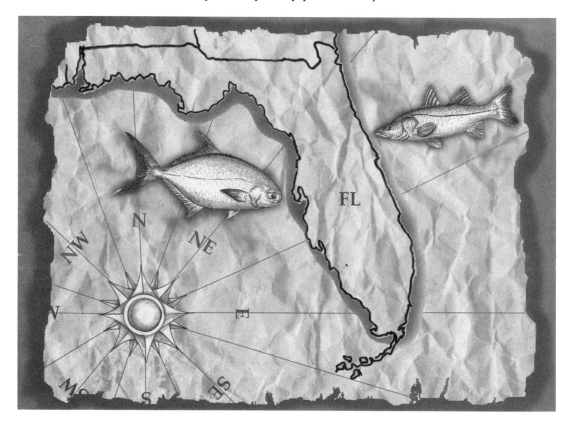

With nearly 1,200 miles of coastline touching both the Atlantic Ocean and Gulf of Mexico, it should come as no surprise that Florida is visited annually by more tourists looking for saltwater fishing action than any other state. Most of them come to fulfill dreams of tarpon on the flats of the Florida Keys, marlin and sailfish offshore, red drum in backcountry lagoons, and monster grouper and snapper on the inshore reefs. It is reasonable to say that not many of those visitors show up specifically to fish the surf, but perhaps more should, because Florida offers excellent shots at a variety of species on the beach, and it's mostly the local anglers taking advantage.

There is no shortage of smaller species that will bend a rod practically all year. These include croakers, various grunts, and kingfish. But if you had to peg the gamefish most sought after on Florida beaches, they would be pompano, snook, Spanish mackerel, red drum, and tarpon. Remember that the habitat and climate changes significantly as you move from north to south in this large state, and if you are willing to cover some miles, you will find one of the above feeding in the waves almost any month. Seasonal water temperatures may cause areas to be productive one year and slower the next, especially in the winter, but the Florida surf does not shut down like it does in the Northeast or mid-Atlantic.

FLORIDA'S ATLANTIC COAST

Starting on the Atlantic coast just over the state line, Fort Clinch State Park in Fernandina Beach is the northernmost point in Florida where you can cast from the sand. The park is actually situated on the north end of Amelia Island, and it abuts the ocean and the mouth of the Amelia River. It is just one of the beachfronts moving south to Jacksonville that produce red drum, pompano, sea trout, and even some snook and tarpon during the summer and early fall. Areas like Fort Clinch, where a sandy point touches both an inlet and the ocean, are frequent between Fernandina and Jacksonville, and two of the most popular include Little Talbot Island State Park and Fort George Island, where four-wheel-drive vehicles can be used on the beach.

Though places like Fort Drum in the north can offer excellent fishing, it is fair to say that on Florida's Atlantic coast, the stretch from St. Augustine south to Jupiter is most favored for surf fishing. Granted, this piece of the coastline is about 235 miles long, but for the most part it experiences the same prime fishing seasons, has similar surf structure, and there is plenty of public access at some of the best beaches.

Florida surf guide Mike Conner keeps a sharp eye on his rods, ready for pompano to strike.
Photo: Mike Conner

According to Florida surf expert Terry Gibson, when the water temperature reaches 80 along this stretch of coast, snook begin moving out of inlets and passes to feed along the beaches. This typically occurs in June, and snook remain viable surf targets right into the fall. However, these fish have a long breeding season that runs from May to September. Night fishing for snook is very popular among dedicated Florida surfcasters, though Gibson notes that new and full moon phases trigger snook to breed. Therefore, you shouldn't fish the beaches on these nights, as the snook will move into inlets and passes to get romantic.

In case you haven't picked up on the trend of fishing around inlets for the best action, it continues in Florida for snook, as they rely heavily on having bay access to spawn; in addition, should water temperatures suddenly not be to their liking, they can quickly move back to the sheltered shallows. From St. Augustine working south, Anastasia State Park, Summer Haven, and Daytona Beach are all fine places to plan a snook quest, but Ponce de Leon Inlet—better known as "Ponce Inlet"—at New Smyrna is perhaps the jumping-off point for prime snook territory.

What Ponce Inlet has that those at Anastasia and Summer Haven lack is a long north jetty. Snook are very structure-oriented fish and gravitate to jetties to spawn and feed. They will hold in jetty pockets, right along the rocks on the inlet side, or in the surf on beaches adjacent to the jetty. What makes snook such a great target is that they are receptive to a wide variety of live baits, lures, and even dead baits. Gibson says that a live croaker is by far they best bait, and these little fish can be easily caught almost everywhere along the Florida coast with sand fleas and small clam, shrimp, or squid

Snook account for some heart-stopping strikes along Florida beaches. Though they can be found throughout most of the state, beaches near inlets on the central Atlantic coast provide some of the best action. Photo: Courtesy of Riop.com

pieces. When it comes to lures, Gibson likes soft-plastic baitfish imitations, white bucktail jigs, and metal spoons for all surf conditions. When the water is calmer, diving plugs work well, as do topwaters early and late in the day, especially those with loud rattles. On bright, sunny days when the surf is flat and the water clear, sight fishing for snook is an incredibly addicting way to target these wily gamefish.

South of Ponce Inlet, the rocks and beaches at Jetty Maritime Park near Cape Canaveral, Cocoa Beach, Sebastian Inlet State Park, Fort Pierce Inlet, St. Lucie Inlet, and Jupiter Inlet make up the rest of snook fishing's ground zero. But in all these miles of shoreline, Gibson points to one niche area that shouldn't be overlooked.

"The beaches just south of Sebastian Inlet have a massive reef system that has been protected from dredging projects," Gibson says. "There is a huge gulley between the reef and the beach and thousands of snook spawn in Sebastian Inlet. It's the perfect habitat."

Gibson particularly enjoys this piece of the coast in fall, which can provide outstanding action for snook. When the mullet migration kicks off in September, snook pour out of all the inlets and put on the feedbag. Likewise, September into early November is a peak time to find red drum, Spanish mackerel, bluefish, and tarpon attacking the mullet schools. Gibson points out that large snook often let other species do the dirty work in the fall. Bluefish will cut and slash through the mullet near the surface, while the snook, redfish, and tarpon sit on the bottom waiting for dead and injured baits to sink down. Because these species can adopt this lazy approach, Gibson says getting whatever you're throwing—be it a lure, chunk of bluefish, or live bait—down below the mullet schools is vital. Unless you clearly see that it is snook or tarpon attacking the bait near the surface, casts placed directly into the fray will most likely be attacked by the species you're not targeting.

Though snook and tarpon are popular targets among the Florida surf crowd, not nearly as many anglers are dedicated to chasing them from the beach as they are pompano. These round, silver fish have a cult following, partially because they are abundant in winter when most species have moved out of the surf, and also because they make a fine meal. As fall gives way to winter, cooling the water in Georgia and the Carolinas, pompano make their way south. Captain Mike Conner is one of thousands of surfcasters that eagerly await their arrival. Even though a 6-pound pompano could be considered a trophy, these fish put up an excellent fight, and when the run is on, action can be furious.

Pompano are one of the most popular Florida surf species, praised for their hard fights, winter abundance, and excellent flavor. Photo: Mike Conner.

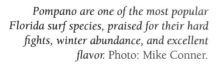

"If I had to pick a peak time for pompano, it would be February 1 through late April on the Atlantic coast," says Conner. "We'll start to catch 1- to 5-inch fish in our sand flea rakes as early as September, then they'll be a little bigger when we start fishing for them in October and November. By Christmas, we're catching a good amount of legal fish, but the nicest fish show up after the New Year."

Pompano are most abundant in season from Jacksonville to Jupiter, though winter water temperatures in northeastern Florida can make or break cold-season runs. Pompano anglers look for cloudy, roiled surf for the best results. Clear water can either push this wary species farther offshore or give them a case of lockjaw. When the surf is churning, it not only kicks sand to provide camouflage, but also exposes the sand fleas and tiny crabs pompano love. Sometimes the fish will feed a short cast away, but on the Atlantic coast, these silver bullets most often forage in troughs a little farther out or beyond the offshore bar. Even though they are not huge fish, serious pompano chasers use 11- to 13-foot spinning and conventional outfits simply to reach the feeding zone. But these rods have another advantage in that their height keeps more line out of the waves, thereby reducing drag and helping the bait stay in one place. According to Conner, while the rods might be heavy, they won't squander the fight. When pompano strike and run away from the beach, their tough, rubbery mouths hold the hook well, so you'll likely see your rod thumping hard in the sand spike. But Conner notes that sometimes these fish hit and run toward the beach. This makes keeping a tight line critical, as a sudden pop and slack line is an indicator that a hooked pompano is headed your way.

From Riviera Beach to Miami Beach on the Atlantic coast, Florida's beaches lose some of their luster for surf fishing. This is mostly because of condo, resort, and high-rise development along the ocean, as well as more limited access due to private oceanfront property. But a lack of major bay systems like those found to the north also contributes to slightly slower action. This doesn't mean snook, tarpon, and pompano won't show up in these areas, but finding a quiet section of beach with no swimmers, surfers, or sunbathers can be a chore. A few areas worth checking out if you do happen to be visiting Florida's southeast coast and don't mind fishing in the bustling setting are Boyton Inlet Park, Ocean Ridge Hammock Park, South Inlet Park, John Lloyd Beach State Park, the inlet at Bal Harbor, and South Pointe Park.

South of Miami, you begin to make your way into the Florida Keys. Although land-based fishing from Key Largo to Key West can be phenomenal, not much in the thin island chain really qualifies as surf fishing. "Surf" is defined by wave action, and in the minds of most anglers these waves occur on beaches with troughs, drops, and bars. But both the Gulf and Atlantic side of the Keys feature two main styles of water, those being shallow flats and deep channels. Fishing the flats is a game far different from true surfcasting, where wading in calf-deep water for great distances comes into play, and where you're essentially stalking fish that you can see. The majority of shore-bound Keys anglers fish off or below the many bridges that connect the islands for nontypical surf species, such as grouper and snapper, or they work cuts between islands for snook, tarpon, and sharks. It is an incredible place to wet a line, but the many tactics, locations, and intricacies involved in fishing here don't fall under the surf fishing blanket, and are therefore not covered on these pages.

FLORIDA'S GULF COAST

Moving northwest around Florida's mainland tip into the Gulf of Mexico, Everglades National Park takes up the first 140 miles of coastline. There is no surf to speak of, and little access anyway, as the thick, gnarly brush and mangroves keep this area untamed. It is not until you come to Marco Island that you can stand on sand again. Starting here, snook, sea trout, and tarpon reenter the picture, though Marco offers a relatively short piece of Gulf-front shore. Naples marks the true end of the Everglades, where vacation homes and groomed beaches stretch north to Tampa some 170 miles away.

All of the species targeted on the Florida's East Coast are found on the Gulf beaches, though there are some slight seasonal variations. According to Terry Gibson, summertime snook bites can be a bit stronger along the Gulf, but fish tend to be a little smaller than their Atlantic counterparts. Gulf surfcasters can enjoy a steady pompano fishery with keeper-size specimens most of the year. Pompano runs tend to be strongest in spring and winter. Many of the west side passes are notorious for tarpon, and Spanish mackerel cruise this coast practically year-round.

If there is one major difference between the Gulf and Atlantic coasts of Florida, it is shoreline access. Many west coast beaches are blocked off by private Gulf-front property, making it tough to find a way to get on the sand without taking very long hikes from public access points. Unfortunately this is a particular problem in some places with outstanding fishing, such as Sanibel, Captiva, and Gasparilla Islands, which Gibson points to as offering some of the finest snook sight-casting opportunities in the Gulf. Certainly there are public beaches here, but sometimes success comes from the ability to cover lots of ground, which is easier if you can take a quick ride up the street and walk back onto the sand. If you don't want to worry about access, places like Lower Key State Park, Stump Pass Beach State Park, and Boca Grande Lighthouse can give up tremendous fishing without the hassle. As a matter of fact, Boca Grande Pass at Boca Grande Lighthouse is arguably one the premier tarpon destinations in Florida. While most of the big tarpon are found in the central pass, the adjacent surf and inlet beach can produce epic "'poons," as well as some monster snook.

According to Gibson, the city of Tampa really marks the end of snook territory, and if you look at a map you'll see that it also stands as the end of the line for sandy beaches until you reach St. George Island nearly 300 miles away on the Florida Panhandle. Between Tampa and St. George, the coastline becomes a marshy, creek-filled and is largely uninhabited. Moving west from St. George, the coast from Panama City Beach all the way to Perdido Key near the Alabama state line offers ample access and plenty of opportunity to find pompano, sea trout, red drum, and Spanish mackerel, though in this part of Florida, tarpon on the beach become slightly less frequent and snook are about nonexistent. Much of this coastline section is loaded with well-developed resort communities. Fishing will continue to be stronger around inlets like those at St. Andrews State Park, Destin, and Fort Pickens National Park. The mullet run in this part of the Gulf is very strong during the fall months, producing some of the best fishing along the Florida Panhandle.

Low-Country Surf Fishing on the Gulf Coast

The Gulf coast from Alabama to Texas encompasses hundreds of miles, and within that span can be found some of the most outstanding fishing in the country. But in terms of surfcasting, those hundreds of miles don't offer as many productive spots as you might think. The sport falls within a gray area along this portion of the coast, where boundaries between what is truly considered surf fishing and what is considered wade fishing become hazy. Even on main Gulf-front beaches, the water tends to be calm and shallow. This makes it ideal for traditional wade fishing, where anglers use light tackle and

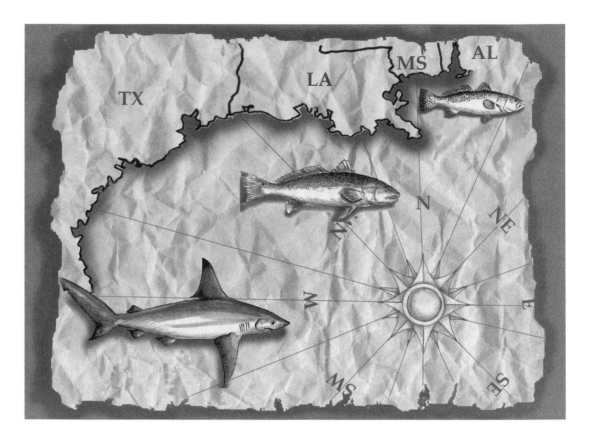

other gear not tied to traditional surf fishing to walk long distances in the water, hunting for spotted sea trout and red drum. On top of the frequent calm conditions, much of the northern Gulf shoreline is eaten up by miles and miles of marshes, creeks, and small islands that block the mainland from the Gulf and provide little in the way of sand on which to stand. This is particularly true of Louisiana, as its coast consists mainly of the lower Mississippi Delta's twisting and turning bayou. Coastal access is another concern in this region, because large pieces of the Gulf shores are uninhabited and have no roads leading to the water. The most noteworthy area in the Gulf where surfcasting is taken very seriously is along the South Texas coast at Padre Island National Seashore. But before touching on Padre, there are some other areas where surf action can be found between Alabama and the national seashore entrance in Corpus Christi, Texas.

ALABAMA, MISSISSIPPI, AND LOUISIANA

Alabama has a very short coast, but compared with Mississippi and Louisiana, it actually posses better surf opportunities. Orange Beach just across the border from Florida is a popular vacation destination with sandy beaches bumping up against Perdido Pass, which gives gamefish access to Perdido Bay. All year long, the shoreline from Orange Beach west to Fort Morgan sees roaming schools of Spanish mackerel, pompano, sea trout, and red drum that can achieve "bull" status. Summertime is good, but the fall months can kick action into high gear during the mullet run.

West of Fort Morgan across Pelican Bay, Dauphin Island is another place where Gulf surfcasting can potentially lead to bull reds, sea trout, and even the occasional cobia from late spring to early fall. Panfish, such as kingfish and croakers, thrive along these shores and are great for entertaining kids or stocking up for a fish fry. Pompano and flounder are two more viable targets from spring into fall, and Fort Gaines at the east end of Dauphin is particularly prized for drum and trout. Fort Gaines also features some jetties that give surf fishermen the chance to get a bit farther off the beach. These rocks also hold plenty of sheepshead throughout the year. The sparsely inhabited west end of Dauphin should not be overlooked for bull red drum, especially during the autumn months.

A nice Alabama redfish that crushed a topwater Spook poses for the camera prior to release in the shallow water's edge in Orange Beach.

Mississippi's coast is also not very lengthy, though some opportunities do exist around the well-developed Biloxi beachfront. As there are some pretty large barrier islands off the coast, the shore from Biloxi west to Buccaneer State Park generally has minimal wave action and not many troughs or sandbars. It lends itself perfectly to wade fishing, but if you are going to cast from the sand, panfish, sea trout, and redfish are all possibilities. To maximize action in this region, it's wise to focus around passes, such as those at Pass Christian and Lake Shore. Overall, though, you'll find surfcasting fairly unproductive in the Magnolia State.

Once you cross the border into Louisiana, there is really no place to fish the surf until the long drive is taken around New Orleans down Route 1 through the lonely Delta to Grand Isle and Port Fourchon. These locations offer the only sandy Gulf beaches with decent depth and moderate wave action until you hit Holly Beach and Peveto Beach near the Texas border, neither of which is noted for great fishing. In Port Fourchon, you can access the beach with a four-wheel-drive vehicle, and fishing is good year-round. Sea trout, Spanish mackerel, and red drum make up the bulk of the bounty, though panfish are also available. Local anglers find these beaches productive for shark fishing as well. Thanks to Grand Isle and Port Fourchon's proximity to marshy backcountry waters, the chance to catch bull red drum is actually quite good. You can expect to hook them here anytime, but fall through spring is actually peak for the heaviest fish. Shrimp are very popular baits, though panfish heads can be deadly.

Texas

After crossing the Texas border, there is little Gulf access until you reach the town of High Island. From here south through Galveston to Surfside Beach, panfish, small red drum, and some sea trout can all be taken, especially around the jetties abundant from Galveston south, and around San Luis Pass, Galveston Pass, and the pass at Bryan Beach. One point of note about the entire North Texas coast is that the surf is frequently off-colored, which can limit your chances of finding species like Spanish mackerel or cobia in this area. While panfish fare well in off-color water, depending on just how poor the visibility happens to be, it can hurt your chances with drum and sea trout.

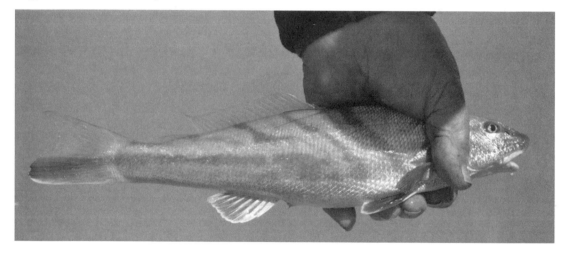

Southern kingfish—known locally as "whiting"—are a popular panfish targeted around Galveston, Texas.

Pressing down the coast, with the exception of the pass on the south side of East Matagorda Bay, the north beach at Port Aransas, and Mustang Island State Park, the surf is largely off limits thanks to intermittent spans of uninhabited coast or uninhabited barrier islands. But if you're going to travel as far as Mustang Island east of Corpus Christi, just keep driving, because you're not far from Padre Island National Seashore.

This untouched piece of coastline spans about 70 miles, and the only way to reach the south end at the Port Mansfield jetty is to ride over the sand with a four-wheel-drive vehicle. With this much space, it is the perfect place to find solitude, which is a lot harder in most other popular surf fishing areas around the country. What you'll also find at Padre is a reemergence of species like snook and tarpon that are more difficult to find elsewhere along Gulf shores, as well as favorable bottom contours, sandbars, and deep troughs within casting range. Padre is also a very popular destination for surf anglers who like to take the sport to the edge and target a vast array of shark species from the sand.

A tarpon lolls on the sand at the water's edge in Padre Island National Seashore. This stretch of beach in South Texas is one of the best for hooking "silver kings" from the surf.

According to Padre Island guide and Texas legend Captain Billy Sandifer, September is a superb month to visit, as the mullet run is just getting under way, bringing red drum, tarpon, and Spanish mackerel close to the beach. Sandifer is also the man to see for sharking. During the summer, sea trout and puppy drum action can be fierce, with topwater lures and soft-plastic baitfish imitations. There is also no shortage of panfish species to keep rods tapping all year long. You can read more about planning a visit to Padre in chapter 13.

California

The Golden State may have 840 miles of coastline, but when it comes to surf fishing, the sport's popularity is relegated to a few specific areas. California is a very diverse state in terms of coastal makeup. Likewise, because it is such a large state, climate changes greatly from one end to the other. On the Mexican border, San Diego rarely sees temperatures dipping below 50 degrees, even in the winter. With mild weather and little rainfall, the gamefish most commonly sought from the beach are available year-round, though there are certainly peak times when action is more consistent. Seven hours north in San Francisco—the second key California surf fishing area—winters see more rain, and temperatures are slightly cooler. While not a specific surf destination, but worth noting for reference, Crescent City just below the Oregon border gets up to 11 inches of rain each month from November through March; air temperatures drop well into the low 40s. While it's fair to say the coast around San Diego and San Francisco offers the best shots at larger gamefish like California halibut and striped bass, there is something to catch anywhere you can gain access to the beach from the Oregon state line to Mexico.

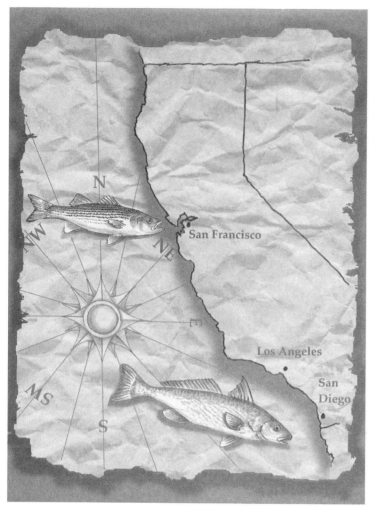

But what you'll often find between known surfcasting haunts is a lot of "maybe" water, where the most prized gamefish species make appearances, though consistency is lacking.

Part of the reason much of California experiences lulls in surf productivity is that the range of many species varies significantly. This can be related to water temperatures; in addition, fish congregate around certain shoreline features and only deviate so far up and down the coast. Such is the case with California's striped bass population, which was imported from the East Coast by train in the late 1800s. Bass were introduced to the San Francisco Delta and bay system, where they adapted well and continue to thrive. But they are so content in the inland waterways that only a small percentage migrate under the Golden Gate Bridge and out into the Pacific. Some fish do live permanently in the ocean, but many will feed along the surf in late spring through summer, then retreat into the delta during the rest of the year. With that in mind, it stands to reason that the farther north or south you move along the coast from San Francisco, the less your chances of running into solid bass action, even though it is technically possible to hook them all the way to Oregon, and as far south as Santa Barbara.

As much of the Central and Northern California Coast is cliff-lined, it's not easy to drive around until you find a likely spot. Access can be a big challenge. But if you are in the San Francisco area in the spring or during the summer, Thornton Beach State Park, Mussel Rock Park, Half Moon Bay Station Beach, Rodeo Cove in the Golden Gate National Recreation Area, Muir Beach, Stinson Beach, and the western beach at Point Reyes National Seashore are some of the more notable striper fishing locations. These fish feed heavily on sardines and anchovies, and if schools are pushing close to the beach, metal lures are favored for making long casts in often windy conditions. However, it is not unheard of for bass to come within topwater range, and just as on the East Coast, diving birds are telltale signs that stripers are on the feed.

A lucky angler on the beach near San Francisco drags a heavy striper out of the waves. Photo: Courtesy of Arka02 Photography

While striped bass are not a viable target in the San Diego surf, this area provides the most consistent fishing, with species larger than the various small members of the perch family that can be found all throughout California. Here, corbina are king, and though they are not huge, they are crafty. Getting good at catching them requires a bit of dedication, but once you get the hang of it, hunting corbina can be very addicting.

"Corbina can be found all year around San Diego, but they are predominantly a summer species," says area surfcasting expert Paul Sharman. "This is when they migrate into the beaches most heavily to feed on mole crabs. Corbina provide excellent sight-fishing opportunity as they surf up and down the beach with the breakers."

When anglers spot corbina, they will go to great lengths to keep a low profile so as to not spook the fish with their shadow. Light-tackle spinning outfits are preferred for this style of fishing, as short casts with small crabs and lightly weighted rigs are frequently required. Plus, corbina are scrappy fighters for fish their size, and light-action rods enhance their hard runs. Since these fish are so wary, thin fluorocarbon leaders are the norm, and freshly dug mole crabs produce better than frozen crabs.

Corbina can be found as far north as Ventura, though in these upper reaches, they are not as abundant. Places closer to San Diego—like Mission Beach, La Jolla Shores Park, and Moonlight State Beach north of Encinitas—are terrific locations to look for corbina. However, Sharman recommends Torrey Pines State Park for some of the best sight-fishing opportunities.

"Spring and fall are the best times to hit the state beach at Torrey Pines, as the summer hordes can make fishing impossible," says Sharman. "But even in the summer, it's still quiet at dawn and that's the best time for corbina anyway. Arrive at low tide if possible to spot all the close holes and fish them

Corbina may not be huge, but they are wily surf adversaries and a favorite among the SoCal surf crowd.
Photo: Paul Sharman

as the tide floods in. A small creek runs out to the ocean here under the Pacific Highway Bridge, which you can stand on at certain times and watch corbina commuting out of the small lagoon into the shallow surf. Once you know where they are, you can creep down and target them with a well-placed cast." All of the popular beaches for corbina also provide action with barred surf perch. These fish are most abundant from San Diego to Monterey Bay, even though by the book their range straggles across the Oregon state line. Near San Diego, perch can be found throughout the year, but Sharman notes that in the spring, the larger females come close to the beach to spawn. Like corbina, perch love fresh mole crabs, but sandworms are also productive. Many anglers have turned to Berkley Gulp! artificial worms and crabs and find that they can be just as effective as natural baits. Likewise, small curly-tail grubs ticked along the bottom can be deadly on perch.

California halibut fall frequently to soft-plastic paddle-tail baitfish imitations worked through near-shore troughs and depressions.
Photo: Paul Sharman

Wading-boot prints on the sand north of San Diego in Torrey Pines State Park.
Photo: Paul Sharman

California halibut are another extremely popular target around San Diego, though they can be caught from the beach as far north as the Oregon border. While these flatfish can reach the 50-pound mark, 8- to 20-pound specimens are most common in the shallow surf. Halibut will hold in troughs and depressions, remaining stationary and waiting for a meal to come to them. That means casting bait out and sticking the rod in a sand spike is not going to be as productive as actively hunting. Most anglers opt for bucktail jigs or soft-plastic paddle-tail swimbaits, hopping them across the bottom and hoping they land within striking range of a 'but. Halibut are available all year, but Sharman finds that the biggest fish come into surfcasting range during the winter.

The Northwest

Of all the coastal regions in the United States, the shorelines of Washington and Oregon are least synonymous with surf fishing. This certainly doesn't mean that there aren't passionate surfcasters living in these states, but much as in Florida, there are so many other popular fishing options offshore and inland that anglers largely overlook the beaches. Oregon historically had fair striped bass fishing

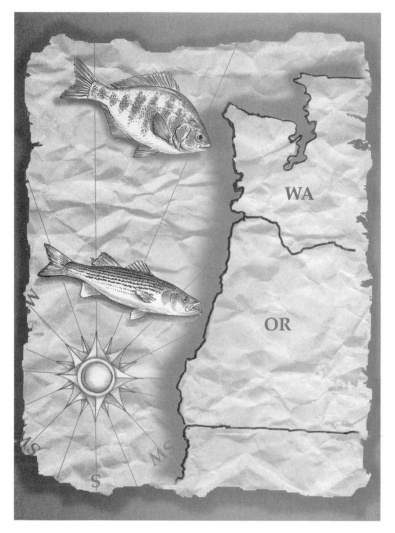

from the surf, as rivers like the Columbia, Umpqua, and Siuslaw spill into the Pacific along the coast and provide sheltered water and bass breeding grounds. However, *Field & Stream* contributor and Oregon resident Ted Leeson notes that these days, the small population of bass that remain in Oregon are pretty much relegated to the Umpqua River. That said, if you want to attempt a hunt for Oregon surf stripers, Ziolkouski Beach Park on the south side of the Umpqua River mouth and Oregon Dunes National Recreation Area on the north side are good places to start. In fact, the Oregon state-record striper, which weighed more than 60 pounds, fell at the mouth of the Umpqua River. Metal lures are a popular choice for artificials enthusiasts, while eels, anchovies, and local baits called candlefish can all put bass on the beach. You can target stripers in the Oregon surf year-round, though spring and summer are the most likely times to find them among the breakers.

In truth, the most popular surf species in Washington and Oregon is actually one that some stripers could easily eat for dinner. Redtail surf perch are the target of many local fishing derbies along the coast, require simple tackle, are great for anglers of all ages, and are available year-round. Perch expert Kelly Corcoran points to the beach at Grayland, Washington, as a prime location to find redtails, with the spring months being a particularly good time to hook larger fish as females move in to breed. At Grayland, anglers have over 10 miles of drive-on access, and according to Corcoran, the sand is hard enough that a two-wheel-drive vehicle can safely travel on the beach.

Technically, the range of the redtail surf perch stretches into Northern California, but they are targeted most heavily from Central Oregon all the way to Neah Bay at the northwestern tip of Washington, across from Vancouver Island. Accessing the sand along some of Washington's northern coast

A stringer of redtail surf perch awaits the grill on Washington surf pro Kelly Corcoran's deck. Photo: Kelly Corcoran

can be tricky when the shore becomes steep, but there are tons of public beaches on the central and southern coast that are easy to reach and prime for perch. Some of the best include Cohasset Beach, Ocean City, Pacific Beach State Park, Moclips, and Cape Disappointment State Park. In Oregon, Fort Stevens State Park, Seaside, Cannon Beach, and Arch Cape give anglers the chance to connect with whopper redtails.

Ghost shrimp and sand shrimp are two of the most common baits for this fish, and Corcoran prefers to use high–low rigs on stiff leader to keep the droppers from tangling. Iridescent floats sit in front of his hooks, as he feels these increase his rig's visibility in the often cloudy water found through the Northwest. When it comes to selecting a good spot to set up shop, Corcoran says he looks for sandy spits and bars with deep water on one side. Unlike striped bass that will cruise the beach, if redtails are being well fed, they'll hold in a trough behind a bar until their food source dries up. In fact, they can sometimes congregate so tightly that Corcoran switches to a slide rig so his bait rolls across the bottom with the waves in a sweeping arc. When he gets a strike, he'll note exactly where it occurred and try to achieve the same swing again. Usually the next bite will come in the same spot.

Regardless of the season, there is no better time to fish for perch anywhere in the Northwest than after a razor clam dig. On set days throughout the year, clammers hit the beaches in droves at low tide to collect a bag of clams for dinner. In the process, they break shells, exposing clam bits and releasing clam juice into the water. According to Corcoran, the next high tide after a dig will draw perch in like a magnet to pick up the pieces. It is during this time that a razor clam neck is becomes the go-to bait choice.

The next high tide after a razor clam dig can produce epic numbers of redtail surf perch. Photo: Kelly Corcoran

Redtails also fall to artificial lures like tiny grubs and pieces of Gulp! worm worked on a jighead, but Corcoran says bait will generally out-produce all other offerings. However, on occasion, you might spot some small baitfish getting pushed to the surface by perch. When this happens, small artificials can be the ticket, as you are dealing with a school that's rather aggressive, and you can sight cast based on the movement of the bait.

Chapter 13

Surf Meccas Made Easy

Casting from Legendary Shores

Anyplace where the Gulf or ocean meets land, you can catch fish. No matter how shallow or deep, calm or rough that beach may be, at some point in the tide or season, there will be gamefish in that surf. There is no such thing as a stretch of beach, no matter how long or short, that is 100 percent void of life all the time. This is why surfcasting is a sport that can be enjoyed by everyone. If you're on a beachfront vacation or live within close range of the shore, you can fish and be successful without paying too much attention to how that area is viewed as a prime fishing location. What does change from beach to beach is what you'll catch, how much you'll catch, and how big those fish will be. Part of the fun is learning your home turf and figuring out familiar coastlines. At the same time, there are places in the world of surf fishing hailed as meccas. It is a combination of history, geography, and, of course, fishing productivity that makes them revered. Most anglers who fish in these locations don't end up there by accident. What the Bahamas are to flats fishermen and Hawaii is to billfishermen, places like Cape Hatteras in North Carolina and Montauk in New York are to the surf angler.

But there is one big problem with many such locales, and I know because I've lived it: If you've never been there, intimidation can get the better of you. You worry about looking like an amateur. You worry that you'll get in the way of the locals. You worry that you'll face unknown circumstances you've never encountered on your home beaches. I grew up surf fishing, but I'll still never forget the first time I visited Montauk. Having no real sense of where to go once I got there, or even what to tie on my line, I fished like a bumbling fool for two days. At the tackle shop, reports were great, and locals weighed in striped bass all day. I caught two small bass during that trip. It was a humbling experience, but as I befriended a few Montauk regulars over time who helped me figure out the ways of this hallowed place, I came to learn that catching fish there was not all that difficult. More important, despite what you read or see in books, being successful didn't require you to have secret spots, be in with the local crowd, or know passwords to get the right lures at the tackle shop. But remember, there is a difference between being able to visit a place like Montauk and hook a 50-plus-pound striper and simply putting some fish on the beach.

The reason some of the most renowned surfcasters come from places like Hatteras and Martha's Vineyard in Massachusetts is because local knowledge and time put in always breeds the top anglers. No doubt, places like the Vineyard and Montauk produce striped bass of epic proportions, but when it comes to finding them, now you *do* have to have intricate knowledge of local tides, detailed information on specific locations, and a sense earned over years of fishing, how the stripers are moving, when the moon will produce the biggest fish, and the exact conditions that will make them bite. However, you do not need to have this inside track to get the full experience of famous surf fishing locations. My aim with this chapter is to break down and simplify a few of the best-known "destination" surf fishing beaches. I hope it will help take away any trepidation and encourage you to plan a trip if you've been holding off. Most important, while I can't say this information provides everything you need to know to catch the next world-record red drum or tarpon in these spots, I do promise that it is everything you need to know to simply catch fish during your stay. Naturally, the more you visit surf meccas, the more familiar you'll become with their details, which can ultimately lead you to becoming an elite hunter of trophy gamefish on their legendary shores.

Martha's Vineyard, Massachusetts

PRIMARY TARGETS: STRIPED BASS, BLUEFISH

Located 6 miles off the southern coast of Cape Cod in Massachusetts, Martha's Vineyard is accessible by ferry from the town of Woods Hole. Though the Vineyard is only about 88 square miles in size, its location and diverse beach types suited to anglers of any skill level or time limit make it one of the most famous surf fishing destinations in the Northeast. In fact, the annual Martha's Vineyard Striped Bass and Bluefish Derby held every fall is arguably one of the most notable fishing tournaments in the country, having begun in 1946 just after World War II. During the event, anglers from all over the country flock to the island trying to win in the boat and surf divisions. In the rich history of this tournament, anglers have weighed in striped bass that hit the 60-pound mark.

When to Go: During the fall months, Martha's Vineyard offers better-than-average shots at both bonito and false albacore, if you're after pelagics, but sadly, according to island resident and greatly respected surfcaster Cooper Gilkes, the fall season has shown a decline in overall striped bass numbers in recent years. If anyone has the credibility to attest to this, it's Gilkes, who is a longtime active member of the annual derby committee and owner of Coop's Bait & Tackle in Edgartown where fish are weighed and catch records kept. Though (hopefully) the fall will become a legendary season for big fish once again, at this writing, Gilkes says those looking for action with bass should visit the island from mid-May through June. During this period, the Vineyard has been seeing greater numbers of bass in its surf, as well as larger fish. At this time, you can also expect to catch plenty of big bluefish.

What to Bring: For starters, Gilkes recommends that all anglers visiting the Vineyard bring two rods. A 10-foot spinning rod will allow you to cast heavily weighted bait rigs and larger lures to distant troughs. An 8-foot spinning rod is better suited to lighter lures favored by smaller bass frequently caught close to shore on some of the island's calmer beaches. Because being mobile can help your success around the island, keeping your lures to a minimum—whatever will fit in an over-the-shoulder lure bag—will allow you to cover more water, although there are opportunities to put a rod in a sand spike and wait it out with bait. Even though air temperatures can be pleasant, colder water means you'll want to bring chest waders. Most beaches are sandy, though a few, such as Squibnocket Beach and the Gay Head (Aquinnah) Cliffs, are rocky and would require cleats.

Needlefish—an eel-imitating lure—can be considered a "must-have" in your tackle bag during a June visit to Martha's Vineyard.

Hot Lures: When it comes to lure selection, Gilkes recommends five patterns you should not be without on Vineyard beaches. Needlefish are eel-imitating lures often made of wood that are cast out and slowly dragged across the bottom. Though they could qualify as a plug, needlefish sort of stand alone in their own category. They don't have much action, but a needle slowly moving along the bottom is hard for a bass to resist. Gilkes also suggests carrying a darter, which is a lipless form of diving plug often favored for mimicking large baits, such as bunker.

Darters have a sloping head that lets them dig, while their erratic side-to-side action parallels no other plug. Most anglers prefer to make their darters bump the bottom during the retrieve. Because stripers can frequently pop up on the surface, a large pencil popper and Danny-style swimmer are also atop Gilkes's list. Finally, he's always sure to have a small Bomber Long A diving plug in yellow on hand when targeting bass with his lighter 8-foot rod. "There's just something about that lure that makes it deadly in the spring," says Gilkes.

Choice Baits: Serious surfcasters looking to connect with the biggest bass favor live eels on Martha's Vineyard, but—as mentioned in chapter 3—eels present their own set of challenges, from keeping them alive while covering lots of beach to stunning them prior to use. Though it's rare to find this in any other location, whole fresh squid is actually a big producer of bass on the island. During the late spring and early summer, a squid migration can bring massive schools close to the beach and the stripers follow. Some anglers jig their own squid from boats or around lighted docks, but this bait is not usually fished live. Therefore, you need not worry about catching squid, as Coop's Bait & Tackle usually has fresh or freshly frozen squid in season. Though bunker chunks can put bass on the beach this time of year, they are more likely to catch bluefish, and are generally favored for bass later in the summer when action on lures has tapered off.

The beach below the cliffs at Gay Head on Martha's Vineyard is well known as a striped bass hot spot throughout the Northeast. Photo: Steve Newfield

Where to Fish: Whether you're visiting Martha's Vineyard with your family and have limited time to fish, or are planning a serious striper hunt, the island offers beaches with varying levels of difficulty. On the milder side, Gilkes points to Lobsterville Beach on the west end of the island. Here you are actually casting into Vineyard Sound; access is easy via Lobsterville Road. "This is a quick hit. It's the perfect place to go when you've got a few hours at night after the wife and kids go to bed," says Gilkes. Though Gilkes cites Lobsterville as being better for light tackle, that doesn't mean the opportunity to catch larger bass doesn't exist in this spot. On the southeast side of the island you'll find the beach at Wasque an excellent area to hook bass, especially in the rips around the mouth of Katama Bay. You can park in the lots off Wasque Avenue to access the beach, though you're in for a long walk if you're headed for the point at Katama Bay. However, you can purchase a four-wheel-drive permit in Gilkes's shop, though they are year-round passes, and no weekend or day permits are sold.

If you want to try your luck at some of the island's most revered beaches, head to Squibnocket or the Gay Head (Aquinnah) Cliffs. Both of these shorelines, located in the southwest corner of the Vineyard, are rocky and require a bit more care when wading. Most anglers here stick to artificial lures or live eels, as dead-bait rigs tend to hang in the rocks. The beach at Gay Head can be accessed from parking lots along Moshup Trail, while Squibnocket is accessed via driving trails off Squibnocket Farm Road. There is a parking lot at the beach here, though there is only enough room for about 15 cars. If the bite is going off, finding a place to leave your car can be a challenge.

Where to Stay: There is positively no shortage of hotels and bed-and-breakfasts on Martha's Vineyard, though given that it's a major tourist destination and not that big an island, rooms can get pricey. If you're looking to book a fishing trip with the guys, Gilkes recommends the Surfside Motel in Oak Bluffs (mvsurfside.com) or the Clarion in Edgartown (clarionmv.com). Both lodgings are reasonably priced in comparison with other island accommodations, and you won't look funny dragging waders or rods into your room at either place.

Tackle Shop Contact:
Coop's Bait & Tackle
147 West Tisbury Road
Edgartown, MA 02539
(508) 627-3909
www.coopsbaitandtackle.com

Montauk, New York

PRIMARY TARGETS: STRIPED BASS, BLUEFISH, FALSE ALBACORE

Hailed as the "Surfcasting Capital of the World," Montauk is located on the very tip of the South Fork at the far east end of the New York's Long Island. One thing that makes it so productive is the strong tidal current that draws any bait and gamefish holding in the east end of Long Island Sound out to sea on the falling tide, right around Montauk Point where surfcasters' line are waiting. The fact that Montauk is already located well offshore also adds to its abundance of fish, as migrating species can't help but make a long pit stop to feed here when moving up or down the Atlantic coast. Not only do the Point and lighthouse stand as symbols recognized by surfcasters the world over, the town itself exudes fishing atmosphere, with local pubs and shops being the hangouts of some of the best surf anglers in the country. Montauk, I believe, is also one of the most intimidating locations, as fishing space is limited, the terrain can be rough, and the Point is easy to access, so it gets crowded. Still, some of the heaviest striped bass ever weighed from the surf have fallen from this famous stretch of coastline.

Anglers scan the rocky beach at Montauk Point in New York looking for a spot to squeeze in and hook some stripers.
Photo: Rick Bach

When to Go: Barring the winter months, there really is no bad time to fish Montauk. Starting in mid-May, stripers migrate en masse to the point and feed heavily through June before pushing farther up the coast. However, Montauk's geography and currents cause many fish to stay all summer long, so you have plenty of opportunity in July and August if you end up here for summer vacation. But if there is one time to visit that will show you Montauk in all its glory, it is the fall months when the leaves are changing and a plethora of species pile onto the point to feed before migrating south. Respected surfcaster and Montauk regular Alberto Knie says that every fall, the action tends to be at its height around October 15, though you can expect good fishing from late September through mid-November. While striped bass remain the focus of most Montauk anglers this time of year, big bluefish make an appearance, as well as line-ripping false albacore. On a good day when baitfish are trapped in great numbers against the Point, it can be a surfcaster's dream come true with near nonstop action.

What to Bring: In Montauk, casting distance makes all the difference in getting into fish. Although there are times when bass feed practically at your feet, more often than not fishing here requires a decent wade into the surf and a long bomb past the inshore boulders. To that end, you'll want at least a 10-foot spinning rod spooled with 15- to 20-pound monofilament or 30- to 50-pound braided line. Stiffer rods get the nod for throwing relatively light lures a good way. Cleats are an absolute must, as Montauk features some of the slickest rocks in the Northeast. Most anglers take the time to run duct tape around their cleats to ensure they stay put. A dry top is also not a bad thing to bring, because even on calm days, if you're going to fish Montauk correctly, you will have to wade far enough that waves will hit you. A dry top can also keep you safe if you got knocked over, as it will help stop your waders from filling with water. Montauk is not the kind of place where you park yourself on the sand and fish with bait, so be sure to have your tackle stowed in a bag that slings on your shoulder for easy maneuverability.

Hot Lures: Believe it or not, lure selection for Montauk is pretty simple. In truth, a ¾-ounce to 1½-ounce bucktail jig tipped with a red pork rind is one of the most productive lures at the Point. White bucktails are the local favorite, with chartreuse a close second and yellow a third. These lures mimic a wide variety of local baitfish, and should be worked with quick pops of the rod tip during the retrieve to keep them off the bottom and out of the rocks as much as possible. Likewise, 4- to 6-inch soft-plastic paddle-tail shads are also a must that account for lots of fish. But you'll want to carry plenty of bucktails and shads with you because it's a guarantee you'll lose some.

Though many anglers think Montauk strategies are complex, a simple white bucktail jig tipped with a red pork rind will rarely go untouched on the beaches at the world-famous surf haunt.

While I've literally spent days on end fishing Montauk without ever using anything other than a bucktail–pork rind combo, you will want to vary your lure selection just a bit. Alberto Knie recommends always carrying a metal lure, such as a Hopkins or Point Jude Po-Jee, in 1- to 2-ounce weights in case you need to reach bass blowing up on bait farther off the beach. These same lures will also catch bluefish and false albacore. Surface action at times can be fierce in Montauk, so Knie never shows up without a pencil popper, which make plenty of ruckus on top and will fly a mile, even into the wind. Danny-style surface swimmers can also come in handy here, but at the Point, diving plugs can be tricky to work around the rocks. However, on the sandy town beaches west of the Point, lures like Bomber Long A's and Rebel Redfins take plenty of bass and blues.

Choice Baits: Rarely will you see anglers fishing with bait at Montauk Point, with the exception of those who cast live eels on weightless rigs. This is simply because the bottom is too rocky, and sinkers attached to bait rigs will just get hung up in the rubble. On the town beaches that are sandy and rock-free, you can spike a rod or two and fire out some bait. Bunker chunks or mackerel chunks both work, but even on these beaches, bait fishing is not all that popular in the fall.

Where to Fish: With the exception of the north side beaches between Shagwong Reef and False Bar, access is very open in Montauk. The aforementioned spots are accessible, too, though they would require a serious hike and are reached mostly by anglers with four-wheel-drive permits. Non-residents can purchase a driving permit, though they are year-round only, so if you don't plan to frequent Montauk, you have easy access to many productive non-four-wheel-drive locations. The most famous is the area around the lighthouse in Montauk Point State Park. Here you can fish on the rocks directly below the lighthouse, north of the light at Jones Reef, or south of the light at Turtle Cove.

A view of Montauk Lighthouse from renowned Turtle Cove. Hundreds of thousands of striped bass have been taken from this beach over the decades. Photo: Darren Dorris

Farther west along the south shore back toward town, you can access a very productive stretch of beach called Ditch Plains, off DeForest Road. Here, the beach is still rocky, though sandy patches mixed in make walking a little easier. Cleats are still a requirement. Although they are not the beaches Montauk is most famous for, never overlook the sandy stretch of coast right downtown along

South Emerson Avenue. This is an especially good place to fish if you just don't want to deal with the rocks and hikes associated with the Point. I usually fish the town beaches when I need a break from the crowds and waves near the lighthouse. And for the record, a few of my most memorable catches came from these less popular beaches.

Where to Stay: There are plenty of motels in Montauk that are reasonably priced in the off season following Labor Day, which luckily coincides with the best time to fish. The East Deck Motel (www.eastdeckmotel.com) is located right on the beach at Ditch Plains, allowing you to walk out of your room right onto the surf. Back in town, the Snug Harbor Motel (www.montauksnugharbor.com) and Blue Haven Motel (www.bluehavenmotel.com) are clean and not too expensive. However, a quick Internet search will turn up loads of other options.

Tackle Shop Contact:
Paulie's Tackle of Montauk
131 South Edgemere Street
Montauk, NY 11954
(631) 668-5520
www.pauliestackle.com

Island Beach State Park, New Jersey

PRIMARY TARGETS: STRIPED BASS, BLUEFISH, BLACK DRUM

New Jersey's Island Beach State Park, located south of the town of Seaside Park, may not have the same legendary air as places like Montauk or Martha's Vineyard, though it is still a major destination for surfcasters that is steeped in sporting history. Perhaps what makes the park so unique is that it offers 10 miles of natural, unspoiled beach in a region where almost every inch of shoreline has been developed with houses or boardwalks. Not to mention, Island Beach sits right in the center of the state, putting it in the heart of route migrating stripers use when moving north from both Delaware and Chesapeake Bays. This stretch of beach also offers excellent shots at brute black drum during the spring, as well as large bluefish spring through fall. Though there isn't much structure in the way of rocks here, the surf is loaded with bars, troughs, and holes not found on as many beaches farther south. Every year, many 40-plus-pound bass fall at Island Beach State Park, and it is probably the easiest place for novice anglers to hook fish this size.

When to Go: Island Beach State Park has two prime seasons. The first typically begins around mid-May and lasts through June, though depending on how cool the water stays, striped bass can continue to provide action through July. The second prime time to visit would be mid-October through mid-December. The spring months see some of the heaviest striped bass taken from the beach, as bunker migrations coincide with northward bass movements. It's not uncommon to find large schools of bunker getting walloped by stripers within range of your casts. Aside from the bass, breeding black drum that can top the 40-pound mark feed heavily along the beachfront as they move into the back bays to spawn. In the last few years, the fall months have provided very solid action with bass and bluefish, though overall, fish sizes are smaller this time of year. You might catch 20 fish a day, but finding one over 25 pounds becomes more of a challenge. Unlike Montauk and Martha's

Trucks line the surf at Island Beach State Park during the annual Governor's Cup Tournament. Photo: Rick Bach

Vineyard, fall action at Island Beach can last almost to Christmas, as the last push of southbound bass and bluefish gorge on sand eels right in the wash.

What to Bring: Seeing that there isn't much hard structure to contend with and fish feed in near-shore troughs quite frequently, anglers throwing artificial lures generally opt for shorter 8- to 9-foot spinning rods at Island Beach. But if you plan to fish bait, a 10-footer is better suited to delivering the heavy chunks and sinkers required to keep your offering in the right spot. Chest waders are helpful here, though wading is not always necessary, so you can get away with hip waders or high rubber boots. Other than when fishing the North Jetty at Barnegat Inlet on the park's south end, you can skip the cleats.

Hot Lures: Because there are no rocks to snag and gamefish feed very close to the surf line, Island Beach is classically considered an excellent "plugging beach," making lures like Bomber Long A's, Rebel Redfins, and Mambo Minnows staples of the area. Of all the colors to choose, yellow has always been a personal top producer that I'll never be without on this beach. Black plugs are definitely an addition to the tackle bag that will catch lots of fish in the dark. Metal lures, such as Hopkins or AVA Diamond Jigs, are essential, especially in the fall when sand eels are in the surf. During the spring and fall, topwater action can be superb, so I always carry a pencil popper and standard popper, such as a larger Rapala Skitter Pop. But perhaps no other lure is a deadly at Island Beach day or night, spring or fall, as a soft-plastic paddle-tail shad measuring 4 to 6 inches.

Choice Baits: Unlike other Northeast meccas, the biggest fish caught at Island Beach usually fall to bait instead of lures. This fact greatly increases the chances for a rookie angler to beach a genuine trophy cow striper, as baitfishing success is largely based on luck. I've landed many a 10- to

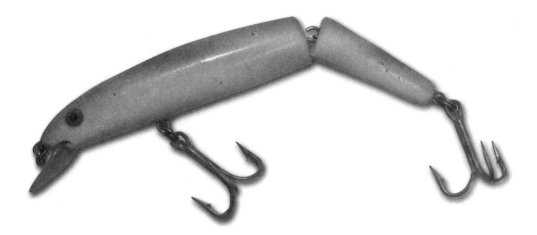

With little structure to snag and fish that feed close, Island Beach is considered a great "plugging beach." Yellow Bomber Long A's are the author's favorite.

15-pound striper on bait here, only to watch an angler on my right or left less than 50 yards away beach a 35-pounder. Was he in a better spot? Perhaps, though more than likely, that fish was simply cruising the surf and found his clam instead of mine. All kinds of bait will catch fish in the park, though without question fresh clams and fresh bunker chunks reign supreme for bass and black drum any time of year. When fishing bunker, don't be afraid to use the entire head, as bigger chunks often equal bigger fish. If you're lucky enough to find a bunker school tight to the beach, snagging one and letting it run free with the school can produce monster blues and stripers.

Where to Fish: All 10 miles of beach are prime for action, and "favorite spots" are designated more by local anglers who have found better success over long periods of time in one area than another. But the truth is that solid action can be had anywhere you find a good trough or cut in the offshore sandbar. Fish here are moving, so it's not likely one hole will be loaded with fish while the next is void of life. Many anglers flock to Gilikins, which is an area at the north end of the park.

Some believe the deep troughs and cuts here produce more fish, though I've had success everywhere in the park. The south end of the beach abuts Barnegat Inlet, and the adjacent jetty can offer fantastic fishing. Along the main road that runs down the park, you'll find plenty of parking lots and trails that go right over the dunes onto the beach. You can also purchase year-round and three-day four-wheel-drive permits at the park office. Just remember that to drive on the beach, you must have a tire gauge, trash bag, shovel, fire extinguisher, first-aid kit, jack board, and tow strap in your vehicle.

Where to Stay: You can actually spend the night on the sand at Island Beach State Park, though rules state that a line must be in the water at all times. If you don't want to pull all-nighters on the surf, the Island Beach Motor Lodge (www.islandbeachmotorlodgenj.com) and Windjammer Motor Inn (www.windjammermotorinn.com) have less expensive rates pre–Memorial Day and post–Labor Day. Both are located right near the park entrance. I personally like the Island Beach Motor Lodge, as it's somewhat of a fisherman's headquarters where waders hang outside of rooms and the beach right out front produces solid bass action.

Shown here is a typical fall striper at Island Beach State Park. Though this fish may not be a monster, it's not uncommon to catch a dozen or more this size in a day. Photo: Melissa Pulicare

Tackle Shop Contact:
Betty & Nick's Bait and Tackle
807 Southwest Central Avenue
Seaside Park, NJ 08752
(732) 793-2708
www.bettyandnicks.com

Cape Hatteras, North Carolina

PRIMARY TARGET: RED DRUM

When anglers think of red drum fishing in the surf, perhaps no other location comes to mind faster than Cape Hatteras on North Carolina's Outer Banks. Many people actually credit Hatteras as the birthplace of traditional surfcasting. Considering how far Hatteras juts out into the Atlantic, it is no wonder that fishing here is prime, and bull red drum are the main feature. But one thing that also makes Cape Point south of the Hatteras Lighthouse so notorious is the rough surf that red drum love. It is on this spit of land with Hatteras Bight on one side and the Atlantic on the other that drum heading toward Pamlico Sound in spring and out in the fall meet surfcasters' lines with force. Heavy tackle and a strong back are both requirements for beating these fish, as well as a four-wheel-drive vehicle to reach top-producing stretches. According to Hatteras surf pro Rob Alderman, Hatteras is easily the best and most consistent place on the East Coast to hook into 40-plus-pound drum with your feet on the sand.

An angler works the rough surf at Cape Hatteras for redfish. Notice the long, heavy rod, often referred to as a "Hatteras Heaver." Photo: Ric Burnley

When to Go: Traditionally, the first peak run of red drum occurs in April and May, but in the last few season, anglers here have been faced with a huge challenge. Sudden beach closures due to turtle and migratory shorebird nesting have greatly limited four-wheel-drive access along much of the Outer Banks. As of this writing Cape Point has not been closed, though Alderman says he's unsure what future seasons will bring as far as access is concerned. Without the ability to drive on the beach, Cape Point is incredibly difficult to reach, requiring a very long walk over soft sand. With that said, Alderman notes that the fewest temporary closures occur during the fall months, and luckily, late September through mid-November sees drum action just as hot and heavy as the spring. During this time, drum move down the coast and out of Pamlico Sound along with the bunker, spot, and mullet that make them fat prior to heading offshore for the winter.

What to Bring: Plan to get wet when fishing Hatteras in the fall. A good pair of bootfoot chest waders is standard gear, and a light dry top is not a bad idea. Because fall temperatures aren't normally frigid, try not to overdress, opting for light breathable waders and dry tops as opposed to heavier neoprene. Almost everything you read in magazines points to the "Hatteras Heaver" as a necessity. These rods are 11- and 12-foot conventional casting sticks used to launch heavy sinkers and bait a long way. If you're comfortable using a casting outfit, "heavers" are the preferred setup of the local surf crew. But according to Alderman, you will fare well with a 10- to 11-foot spinning outfit provided you are a proficient caster. "New anglers show up here all the time and think they need to fish conventional gear," says Alderman. "But it takes some skill to use a Heaver. They'll spend more time untangling bird's nests than fishing. A long, heavy spinning rod will perform just as well if you're comfortable casting it. I even know many locals that actually prefer spinning gear." Alderman also suggests keeping a shorter 9-foot spinning outfit rigged and ready with a metal lure in case bluefish or false albacore move through in the fall.

Hot Lures: Most drum anglers stick to chunk baits, though Alderman claims there is plenty of opportunity to hook big bulls on artificial lures. On calmer days, drum will actually pound topwater offerings, with pencil poppers being Alderman's go-to choice. Metal lures, such as Hopkins and local-favorite Sting Silvers, work very well for enticing big drum. They also cast a mile through the wind, which is a hindrance to plastic plugs and many soft-plastic lures.

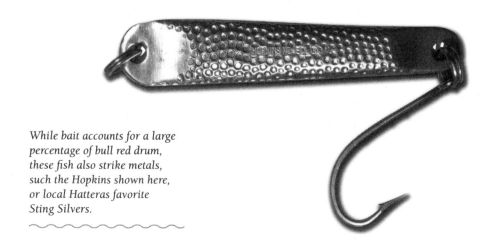

While bait accounts for a large percentage of bull red drum, these fish also strike metals, such the Hopkins shown here, or local Hatteras favorite Sting Silvers.

Choice Baits: In terms of the most productive baits for Hatteras drum, freshness is the key. Bunker, large mullet, and spot chunks are all staple baits of this surfcasting scene. Live spot also work well, though they can be more difficult to cast into the zone beyond the outer sandbar. Bunker and spot heads work particularly well, and most anglers fish them on specialized slide rigs with large circle hooks. There are two ways to tie this rig. The first is by using a 2- to 4-inch length of 50- to 80-pound monofilament or fluorocarbon leader with a barrel tied to one end and the hook to the other. The sinker slide rides on the main line and stops at the barrel swivel.

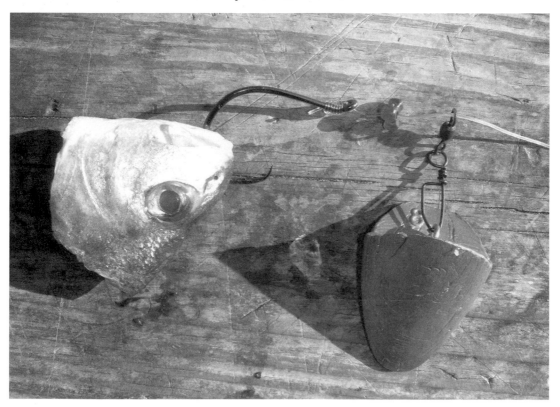

Whole spot heads fished on very short slide rigs are common for drum throughout North Carolina's Outer Banks. This rig style stops the offering from spinning during long casts. Photo: Ric Burnley

The second method uses a long leader of the same pound tests, with a simple bead placed between the hook and the sinker slide. In other words, there is nothing to stop the sinker from sliding all the way to the hook, and the leader is connected to the main via a line-to-line splice. Both of these rigs are designed to keep the overall offering compact and stop it from spinning during the cast. As wave action is rough and bait chunks are larger, 8- to 12-ounce sinkers are the norm for holding bottom in Hatteras.

Where to Fish: At the end of Lighthouse Road, you'll find four-wheel-drive access to the beach that leads to Cape Point. Note that in Hatteras, no permits are required to drive on the sand, but carrying a shovel, tow strap, and jack plate comes highly recommended. Though the Point itself is drum fishing's ground zero, solid action can also be found closer to the end of Lighthouse Road north of the Point, and west of the Point toward the town of Frisco. The west side of the Point can be accessed via Park Road. Both Park Road and Lighthouse Road intersect Route 12, the Outer Banks' main artery.

Surfcaster Ric Burnley shows off a nice Hatteras red drum. Photo: Rob Alderman

Where to Stay: A quick Internet search will pull up many hotels and motels within easy reach of Cape Point. A few of the closest include Outer Banks Motel (www.outerbanksmotel.com) and the Lighthouse View Motel (www.lighthouseview.com). If you'd prefer to stay in a chain motel, there is also a Comfort Inn (www.comfortinn.com) not far from the lighthouse on Route 12.

Tackle Shop Contact:
Red Drum Tackle
Highway 12
Buxton, NC 27920
(252) 995-5414
www.reddrumtackle.com

Padre Island National Seashore, Texas

PRIMARY TARGETS: RED DRUM, SHARKS, TARPON

With just about 70 miles of pure, unspoiled beach stretching from the city of Corpus Christi, Texas, to the jetty at Port Mansfield Pass, Padre Island National Seashore is a surfcaster's paradise. Though the other hot spots noted in this chapter offer amazing fishing opportunities, what they don't share with Padre Island is complete desolation, with zero sign of sprawl or development for miles and miles. If you are truly looking for a place to escape civilization and experience a piece of coast unchanged for thousands of years, Padre is for you. There is not even a road running down the shore. Once you leave the pavement at the Malaquite Visitors Center, the only way to reach the jetty some 60 miles to the south is to ride on the beach with a four-wheel-drive vehicle. Having that kind of room to roam is both liberating and a bit unnerving considering that getting stuck 60 miles from civilization is always a possibility. Unlike other parks, rangers are not frequently patrolling all pieces of the shoreline all the time. Care must be taken when fishing here, but the payout can be tremendous with many gamefish eager to strike.

  When to Go: There is action to be had in the Padre Island surf all year long. But ask local guide and fishing legend Billy Sandifer when to come down, and the answer would be fall. Starting in September, mullet pour out of the bay systems into the surf by the trillions, according to Sandifer. When this happens, red drum follow suit, sharks come in close, and tarpon make their most prolific

The entrance to Padre Island National Seashore in South Texas.

beachfront appearance of the year. Depending on water temperatures, action with drum can last into December, while the tarpon bite usually peters out by mid-October. Spotted sea trout, Spanish mackerel, and black drum are caught more often in spring and summer, though they are around in the fall.

What to Bring: Before talking tackle, if you do plan to traverse far down the length of Padre Island and spend the night on the beach, a spare tire, tow strap, shovel, jack board, good first-aid kit, fresh water, and food are all essential travel items. Should your truck break down or get stuck, you could be there for a while. As far as fishing goes, tackle selection gets a bit tricky for Padre, as approaches vary by species and water conditions. Sandifer recommends carrying a light 6- to 7-foot spinning or casting outfit for smaller red drum and sea trout. The surf here can also be very calm, which makes using light tackle much easier. At the same time, if drum are feeding a bit farther off the beach and you plan to primarily target them with bait, 9- to 11-foot spinning outfits will make reaching them much less of a challenge. Not too mention, the lighter rod wouldn't be suitable for casting heavier sinkers used with bait rigs.

A big tarpon rolls not far off the beach at Padre Island. During the fall, these fish move right into the waves to feed on migrating mullet. Photo: Brandon Shuler

These longer outfits can also come in handy for tarpon, which can easily top 100 pounds and require you to fire weightier lures. Shark fishing is a very popular attraction on Padre, but the tackle is not common in most surf pursuits. Anglers generally use kayaks to paddle whole dead fish out past the waves, and have heavy cable leaders with large hooks connected to custom rods with reels designed for offshore big-game fishing. Can you do this on your own? Sure. But if you really want sharks, I'd advise hiring a guide like Sandifer to show you the ropes. They'll have all the necessary tackle, plus the experience to beach, unhook, and release hammerhead, tiger, bull, blacktip, and sandbar sharks that can weigh in at a couple hundred pounds. This is very specialized surf fishing, but it's also a lot of fun, and catching one of these beasts can be a once-in-a-lifetime achievement.

Hot Lures: Many of the same lures that work well in the Texas bay systems produce on the beach, according to Sandifer. These include 5- to 7-inch Spook-style topwater lures, soft-plastic finesse-style baitfish imitations, and shrimp patterns, particularly those from Berkley's Gulp! line. Any plugs, bucktail jigs, or soft-plastic lures that imitate a mullet will catch fish in the fall. The only real specialty lure associated with Padre is the "Coon Pop," a local favorite for tarpon.

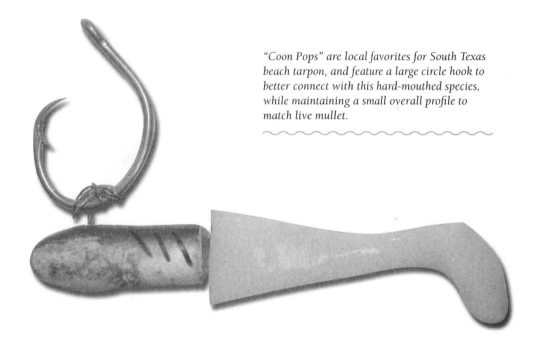

"Coon Pops" are local favorites for South Texas beach tarpon, and feature a large circle hook to better connect with this hard-mouthed species, while maintaining a small overall profile to match live mullet.

Coon Pops have a weighted, rattling, bullet-shaped head with a stiff rear wire on which is threaded a soft-plastic lure, usually a shad imitation. Your leader connects to a circle hooked that's wire-wrapped to the top of the lure's head, and this offering is worked with a popping rod tip, allowing it to flutter as it rises and falls. Because tarpon have such large mouths, the simple yet ingenious design of this lure allows you to use a hook big enough that a tarpon can't bend, while keeping the overall profile small to match mullet. Tarpon have rock-hard mouths, so circle hooks are actually more effective than J-hooks because they'll catch in the softer corner of the mouth.

Choice Baits: During the fall, mullet is going to be your best bet for connecting with tarpon and red drum in the Padre Island surf. It can be fished live on bottom rigs or below popping cork, or dead on float rigs and bottom rigs. If you're fishing whole dead mullet, make sure they are as fresh as possible. Many anglers use a cast net to gather their own mullet, so being able to throw one is a good skill to have when fishing this beach. Fresh dead shrimp will also take everything from reds to sea trout if mullet are in short supply.

A sandbar shark comes to the beach. Though it is possible to go DIY beach sharking on Padre Island, for tackle and safety reasons you may consider hiring a guide to help you battle these beasts. Photo: Rick Bach

Where to Fish: With 60 miles of beach to cover, you'll have no problem finding some solitude on Padre Island. As with any beach, keep an eye out for deeper troughs or bars by reading the waves, but even shallow stretches can hold feeding drum. If you make it all the way to the jetty at Port Mansfield Pass, you'll find some of the best fishing around the mouth, especially during times of heavy mullet movement when they flood out of the bay into the surf at this spot.

Where to Stay: If you don't plan to spend the night on the beach, there are a number of hotels near the park entrance, including a Hampton Inn (www.hamptoninn.com), Comfort Suites (www.comfortsuites.com), and the Passport Inn (www.hotelstravel.com).

Tackle Shop Contact:
Roy's Bait & Tackle
7613 Padre Island Drive
Corpus Christi, TX 78412
(361) 992-2960
www.roysbait-tackle.com

Chapter 14

Final Thoughts

As Waves Roll On

Right now as you're reading this, waves are lapping against every beach in the country. I know, I know, the idea of this perpetual motion happening all day, every day, while we're at work, painting the house, enjoying Christmas dinner, or lying in bed with the flu, is a bit cliché. But perhaps surfcasters have a tendency to dwell on the premise more than nonfishermen, or even those who prefer to spend their time on trout streams, bass ponds, or far offshore in luxury fishing boats. Waves might be breaking right now, but our breed is often more concerned with the red drum, striped bass, or corbina that are riding those tumbling walls of water while daily life presses on. Sometimes—hopefully more often than not—we're there when all the pieces of the surf fishing puzzle come together. Sometimes you can spend days on end pounding the surf in all the right places with all the right baits and lures and still come up empty. Though I hope the information on these pages gives you the confidence to take on the beach, Mother Nature can often make the surf a discouraging place to cast, even when everything feels just right. Don't be discouraged, because I can promise that when everything is clicking and rods are beautifully arced, it is a feeling that surpasses exhilaration. No matter how frequently you plan to fish, or how seriously you intend to take the sport, it may take a few tries to get it just right.

I've caught a lot of memorable fish from the beach, and visited some gorgeous shores, but there are two catches that will forever stick out in my mind. They are not fish of epic proportion, state records, or exotic species, yet they are cherished because one brought an end to a personal quest, and the other sparked a simple smile that will stay with me always.

That first memory is from October 2000, which was my junior year of high school. While I'd grown up fishing with my dad and grandfather, we embarked on different adventures that might be to

In this old Polaroid photo taken at Betty & Nick's Bait and Tackle in Seaside Park, New Jersey, the author (left) holds up his first surf-caught striper weighing more than 20 pounds.

the surf or perhaps to the catfish pond. Point being, there was no one kind of fishing to which we were entirely devoted. It wasn't until I got my driver's license (and subsequently a four-wheel-drive beach pass) that I really began attacking the surf with passion on my own, opting for a day on the beach over all other kinds of fishing. That first spring, fishing was slow, though I did manage to hook into a few bluefish and stripers. The problem was that while I caught 10-pound stripers, wiser anglers around me beached 20s and 30s. I vowed then that before the year was out, I would break the 20-pound mark.

By late June, I had gotten up to 15 pounds, then the season slowed down. In the fall, as some monster bass found their way to the tackle shop scales every day, I could not seem to find a striper bigger than that 15-pounder. It wasn't until late October when I was driving off the beach after yet another slow day that a very short trough caught my eye. I had never fished it before and deemed it worthy of a few casts with my favorite yellow Bomber Long A. Well, guess what? I walked into Betty & Nick's Bait and Tackle an hour later and put a 22-pounder on the scales. To any other surf fisherman, this was a small feat that really meant nothing. No jaws would drop. There was no tackle shop fanfare. I have caught many fish heavier than this since, but it will always be the bass I remember most.

Several years later, while dating my now-wife Christen, I suggested one pleasant May afternoon that instead of going out to dinner, we should get a couple of sandwiches and take a ride to the beach. Reports weren't great, but I was itching to get out and had just gotten her a custom pink surf rod I was dying to see her try. Wearing Jackie-O sunglasses and aqua rubber rain boots, she tromped to the water's edge with me and patiently listened as I gave a quick lesson on casting a metal lure. Once she got the hang of it, I walked back up the beach to rig my own rod when her scream caused me to swing around. She was tied into a fish, and that pink rod thumped and bucked while she tried her best to reel against a sizzling drag. It was only an 8-pound bluefish, but she had caught it on her own, and the smile on her face was worth more than any fish I had ever landed. Actually, she caught about a dozen more after that, getting so comfortable with casting and beaching the fish swarming the surf that she challenged me to a bluefishing competition. Naturally, I won. You didn't think I'd let her beat me, right?

Has Christen since become a hardcore surfcaster? Not in the least. But that's okay. Sometimes if you get too wrapped up in chasing tides, following baitfish migrations, and being in the right spot all the time, it's nice to step away, play it simple, and enjoy the beach with someone you love or someone new to the sport. And ironically, just like that epic night of catching bluefish, every once in a while it's when you don't plan for much to happen that the stars align and you just can't get the fish off your hooks fast enough. The biggest striper I ever caught in the surf hit at one in the afternoon. I slept in and wasn't even on the beach until eleven that morning. But when you know your home beach well, you'll come to find out that productivity doesn't always mean being there at sunup.

Perhaps one of the best pieces of advice I can give is to get to know a few beaches like the back of your hand. You will be far more successful if you learn the intricacies of a handful of spots rather than constantly jumping all over the place. Fish there on every tide, during every moon phase, and at different times of year, because if you can get to know your home waters well, you'll be better equipped to read an unfamiliar beach and relate it to your own turf.

The author's wife, Christen, proudly displays her first surf catch—a nice bluefish that slammed a metal lure.

With that said, I hope this book has helped to build confidence for fishing the beaches right down the street, as well as inspired you to visit some distant shores. Always remember that you define what is considered a trophy, and every fish you hook, no matter how big or small, should remind you that you've been successful in a place where success can be harder to come by than on many lakes, bays, or rivers. Whether it's been a good day or slow, if you struck out or bested a dream fish, those waves will continue to roll on and be right there where you left them the next time you walk out onto the sand and cast. And you just never know what that next set of breakers will bring.

Appendix: Go Fishing Online

The Internet is easily the most powerful tool for anglers these days, whether they are seasoned pros or just getting started. First and foremost, you can find out what's biting, what the conditions are like, tide phase, and weather for any beach you intend to visit. And I mean in real time for most of the above. While getting such information was once a matter of calling tackle shops or waiting for reports in newspapers and magazines (which would be dated by the time you read them), forums, online reports, and even surf cameras with 24-hour live footage feeds get you the lowdown fast. Most guide and tackle shop websites feature regular reports in season.

While I hope the regional information presented in this book serves you well as a jumping-off point, local surf fishing guides and web pages dedicated to fishing particular areas are invaluable for mastering your home beaches. Booking with a guide just once can teach you more about a species, location, or technique than you could possibly imagine. I've actually been guided by some pros in spots I've been fishing my whole life. I had a fine handle on them, no doubt, but it's shocking what you can learn about the seemingly familiar when you spend time with a guide who most likely fishes the area more often than you.

Finally, online communities and web forums are a great way to ask question and learn from veteran anglers without the awkwardness of approaching them on the beach. I'd highly recommend joining one that relates best to your area. It's free, and it's also a great way to keep up with current trends during the off season. While there is so much useful material online it seems impossible to find it all, I hope the websites presented here help further your love and knowledge of surfcasting.

Surf Fishing Guides

RHODE ISLAND

Jack Sprengal
(401) 338-1752
www.eastcoastchartersri.com

NEW YORK (LONG ISLAND/MONTAUK)

Steve Knapik
(516) 721-7595
www.tiderunner.com

Doug Larson
(631) 589-0065
www.ny-fishingguide.com

Bill Wetzel
(631) 987-6919
www.longislandsurffishing.com

NEW JERSEY

Shell E. Caris
(732) 528-1861
www.shorecatch.com

Eric Kerber
(484) 678-9083
www.omfishing.com

D. J. Muller
(732) 539-3629
www.djmullersurfcaster.com

DELAWARE TO ASSATEAGUE ISLAND, MARYLAND

Floyd Morton
(302) 822-3474
www.gosurffishing.com

NORTH CAROLINA (OUTER BANKS)

Rob Alderman
(252) 305-2017
www.fishmilitia.com

Joe Malat
www.joemalat.com

Outer Banks Fishing School
(252) 255-2004
www.obxfishingschool.com

SOUTH CAROLINA (CHARLESTON)

Ben Floyd
(843) 670-3123
www.charlestonfishfinder.com

FLORIDA (NORTH/CENTRAL EAST COAST)

Mike Conner
(772) 521-1882
www.captainmikeconnerfishing.com

Jim Hammond
(904) 757-7550
www.hammondfishing.com

MISSISSIPPI/LOUISIANA (CHANDELEUR ISLANDS)

Due South Charters
(228) 872-8422
www.duesouthcharters.com

TEXAS (PADRE ISLAND NATIONAL SEASHORE)

Billy Sandifer
(361) 937-8446
www.billysandifer.com

SOUTHERN CALIFORNIA

Jeff Solis
(858) 531-1436
www.solisonthesalt.com

Online Surf Fishing Communities

MULTI-REGIONAL

BigFishTackle.com
FinTalk.com
PierAndSurf.com
Sportfishermen.com

NEW ENGLAND TO NEW JERSEY

BassBarn.com
Stripers247.com
Striped-bass.com
StripersOnline.com
StriperSurf.com
SurfRats.com

DELAWARE TO VIRGINIA

Beach-net.com
MDangler.net
TidalFish.com
VBSF.net (Virginia Beach Sportfishing)

NORTH CAROLINA

FishMilitia.com
NCAngler.com

SOUTH CAROLINA TO FLORIDA

BoatlessFishing.com
FloridaSportsman.com
SouthernSurfFishing.com
SurfishingFlorida.com

ALABAMA TO LOUISIANA

LouisianaSportsman.com

TEXAS

ExtremeCoast.com
TexasFishingForum.com
Tx-SharkFishing.com

CALIFORNIA TO WASHINGTON

BloodyDecks.com
HookupSportfishing.com
OregonFishingForum.com
SCSurfFishing.com
SDFish.com (San Diego)
SurfFishingInsider.com

Tides

SaltwaterTides.com

Marine Weather Forecast

www.noaa.gov (National Oceanic and Atmospheric Administration)

Free Sea Surface Temperature Readings

www.marine.rutgers.edu/cool/sat_data/?product=sst&nothumbs=0

Live Surf Cameras

Surfline.com—Developed for surfers, this site has more than 80 live surf-cams around the country.

Index

About the Author

Joe Cermele is the Fishing Editor of *Field & Stream* magazine. His writing appears frequently both in the print version of *Field & Stream* and online in the magazine's "Honest Angler" fishing blog. He also serves as the host of *Field & Stream's* web-based fishing show, "Hook Shots." Cermele's articles have appeared in *Salt Water Sportsman, Men's Journal, The FlyFish Journal, Angling Trade, The Drake, New Jersey Angler,* and *On The Water.* This is his first book. Cermele currently resides in central New Jersey with his wife, Christen. When he's not traveling for *Field & Stream* (or whenever the striped bass are running) you can find him somewhere on the beach between Montauk, New York, and Ocean City, New Jersey.